BEST
SPORTS
STORIES
1985

Edited and Published by

The Sporting News

President and Chief Executive Officer
RICHARD WATERS

Editor
DICK KAEGEL

Director of Books and Periodicals
RON SMITH

Published in the United States by THE SPORTING NEWS Publishing Co., 1212 North Lindbergh Boulevard, St. Louis, Missouri 63132.

Library of Congress Catalog Card Number: 45-35124

ISSN: 0067-6292
ISBN: 0-89204-199-4
10 9 8 7 6 5 4 3 2 1

First Edition

Table of Contents

The Prize-Winning Stories

The Prize-Winning Photographs

BEST ACTION PHOTOGRAPH

BEST FEATURE PHOTOGRAPH

Other Photographs

The Prize-Winning Color Photographs
The Big Fall

by Bob Langer of the Chicago Tribune. The winning color photos (two of which appear on the back cover) show the ill-fated collision between Mary Decker and Zola Budd during the 3,000-meter run in the Summer Olympics and the collision's emotional, painful aftermath. The photos, the first and fifth in a series of six, were captured by an enterprising photographer who was talented enough to take advantage of being in the right place at the right time. Copyright © 1984, Chicago Tribune.

PREFACE

The world was watching and Los Angeles didn't disappoint, staging its own version of The Greatest Show on Earth. With the Winter Olympics in Sarajevo, Yugoslavia, having served as a fitting warmup, athletes, writers, broadcasters, cameramen and sports enthusiasts from all over the world descended upon Los Angeles for the big bash. And, despite the absence of the Russians and East Germans, the show drew rave reviews. Millions and millions of television viewers got a heavy dose of Olympic spirit and the U.S. athletes made the Summer Games their personal showcase.

It was the type of event that usually brings out the best in the journalistic community. And those writers and photographers who journeyed to Los Angeles for two weeks of flag-waving splendor didn't disappoint, either, producing the prose and pictures befitting their assignment. Rather than simply chronicle the proceedings of the athletic contests that surrounded them, they went behind the personalities and events for perspectives and insights that helped make 1984 a special year in sports.

The Olympics, however, were merely the window dressing. Other sports enjoyed their moments in the sun, too.

The renaissance of the Detroit Tigers, the resurrection of the Chicago Cubs, the selection of a new commissioner and the return of Pete Rose to his old stomping grounds in Cincinnati highlighted the baseball scene. Georgetown overcame Hoya Paranoia to capture NCAA basketball honors, the Boston Celtics rekindled memories of past glories, Wayne Gretzky and the Edmonton Oilers brought new life to the Stanley Cup and Walter Payton, Dan Marino, Eric Dickerson and Joe Montana captured the fancy of pro football fans everywhere. It was an exciting year, brought to life by those men and women whose quest for supremacy equals in intensity that of the athletes they immortalize in words and pictures.

The Sporting News is proud to present a small sprinkling of that life in the 41st edition of Best Sports Stories. This is the third edition published and edited by TSN, which assumed responsibility for the anthology that was created in 1944 by Irving Marsh and Edward Ehre. The contest, which attracted more than 800 newspaper and magazine entries, was open to all writers and photographers throughout the country and accepted only stories that were published in 1984. Serving as judges for the third straight year were five teachers from the University of Missouri, home of one of the world's top-rated journalism education programs. They are:

Brian Brooks, the *St. Louis Post-Dispatch* Distinguished Professor of Journalism at the University of Missouri and managing editor of the *Columbia Missourian,* a student and faculty-run newspaper that serves the city of Columbia, Mo.

George Kennedy, associate professor and city editor of the *Columbia Missourian.*

Ken Kobre, associate professor and director of the school's photojournalism sequence.

Daryl Moen, professor and chairman of the School of Journalism's editorial department.

George Pica, assistant professor and director of the J.C. Penney-Missouri Awards Program.

It can be agonizing to sift through more than 800 well-written and creative stories and then single out four. Likewise, the selection process for three pictures. But, after weighing the merits of each entry, the judges chose the following winners, each of whom receives $500:

WRITING

Reporting	Richard Hoffer	Los Angeles Times
Feature	William Gildea	Washington Post
Commentary	Steve Jacobson	Newsday
Magazine	David Halberstam	Parade

PHOTOGRAPHY

Color	Bob Langer	Chicago Tribune
B & W Action	Adrian Keating	Bristol (Conn.) Press
B & W Feature	Jayne Kamin	Los Angeles Times

Almost as agonizing for the judges was the process by which they weeded down the different categories to the choice few that would appear in this volume. By no means are they losers. In the truest sense, they are a tribute to the sports journalism profession. They bestow upon *Best Sports Stories 1985* the honor of giving its readers an entertaining year in sports as seen through the eyes and lenses of some of the country's top journalists.

Best Action Photo
We've Got It

by Adrian Keating of the Bristol Press. In sports photography, it is often the moment gone awry that makes for a dramatic picture. Such was the case here, when two youngsters playing baseball in the Bristol, Conn., Instructional League crossed signals and gloves and came up empty. This photographer froze the perfect moment —crossed arms, loose ball, closed eyes—for a single classic picture that tells the entire story. Copyright © 1984, The Bristol Press Publishing Co.

Best Feature Photo
Victory Hug

by Jayne Kamin of the Los Angeles Times. Evelyn Ashford and
United States teammate Jeanette Bolden combine in an evocative
picture that literally pulls emotion from the viewer and allows him
to feel the tension and excitement of the moment. This photo,
taken after Ashford had won the 100-meter dash in record fashion during the 1984 Summer Olympics in Los Angeles, does not
tell a complete story by itself. Rather, it draws in the viewer, with
the intensity and the tears piquing his curiosity and pulling him to
the caption. Copyright © 1984, Los Angeles Times.

Best Magazine Story

The Man Who Said No

HIGH SCHOOL FOOTBALL

By *DAVID HALBERSTAM*

From Parade Magazine
Copyright © 1984, Parade Publications, Inc.

It is not a very famous football team, nor is the school one of the modern high school football factories, its big muscular kids scouted by Notre Dame, Nebraska or UCLA. The coach does not know the college coaches of America by their first names. The name of the school is George Washington, but the team is not called, as one would suspect, the Generals, but rather the Trojans. The kids were born in a foreign land where no one ever played football, and they call their plays in Spanish. In a modern world of muscular athletes who have been beefed up by weight rooms even while in high school, a big kid for this coach is 175 pounds, not 225.

George Washington High School is on 191st Street and Audubon in Spanish Harlem, a Hispanic island in New York City, a world within a world. It is a hard and often crushing place. The young people who go here exist, by normal American standards, in a world largely without victories. Defeat is their norm. George Washington, for most of this century, has been a portal through which immigrant children have passed on their way to sharing in the American dream. Sen. Jacob Javits, Henry Kissinger and Kenneth Clark went here.

These kids are from the Dominican Republic. Most of them are rural: they arrive usually without a father, without the language and without citizenship. They are strangers in the land. It is in the most overcrowded school district in the city, with the lowest reading and math scores (in part because the kids cannot read English and therefore can barely be tested). It has the highest teenage pregnancy rate. The social forces that pull down a student, even the most ambitious and hopeful, are almost overwhelming. Often parents do not know that a child has dropped out. The students simply disappear, says Alex Levy, an English teacher. "Because they're Hispanic, we are not as sensitive to the pressures on them as they get pulled down and the stress on them mounts," he says. "We just don't see it or feel it. Then one day they're no longer in class. They've disappeared without our even knowing it." As many as 800 start in the ninth grade. At best, 300 graduate. But those who do are strong. They have beaten the harshest kinds of odds, and a surprising percentage of them go on to college.

In such an environment, football is almost completely alien, yet it is the vital link holding a certain number of kids together. These are not youngsters who eventually intend to return to the old country. Many want to be in the fullest sense Americans, and football can be the first step in the process of Americanization. That there is a football team at all defies the imagination. But it exists—small, undermanned and surprisingly good. The names of the players are Trinidad, Suarez, Castillo, Guzman, Tavarez, Gonzalez and Jefferson. Jefferson is black. The coach speaks Spanish. The players often weigh 40 pounds less than their opponents. Soccer and baseball are their native sports. They rarely go out for football as freshmen and sophomores; only by their junior year, as their courage in sampling something so American increases, do they go out for it. They become, gradually, almost unconsciously passionate about the game. They become, small or not, quick and tough football players.

★   ★   ★

The coach's name is Jim Walsh, and he is Irish. He is not just their coach and friend, but their teacher and foster parent as well. He is deeply emotional, sometimes breaking into tears during conversations about his players or about his boyhood. He is a man consumed with his own truth and passion. His own background as the son of new and less than affluent Irish-Americans remains real with him, and he finds it easy to project the alienation of his own boyhood into the greater pain and dislocation of their immigrant experience. He knows that their world is much harder than his. His sensitivity is heightened by the fact his wife is of Puerto Rican ancestry. His own family, more than most, reflects the tumultuous and pluralistic culture of New York City; one of his three children, Kevin Sanchez Walsh, plays football for Yale.

He is, in his own words, the American connection for the kids on his team. He is the only "Anglo" they have ever met who is at once a figure of authority and a friend. He not only gives them rules—hard and unbending rules—but he also delivers for them when they respond to those rules. They spend more time with him than with their parents.

He yells at them, chides them, disciplines them, forces them to behave in class and get good marks. He promises them that if they play football and graduate, he will get them into college, and he keeps his word. He holds the keys to the only future they may have beyond the streets.

Jim Walsh is a football junkie. He looks like a football coach. There is a certain pugnacity to both his manner and appearance. It is as if God, having made him, took him aside, gave him a sweatsuit and a whistle and said: "Walsh, with looks like that, there's only one thing you can do—coach football." ("Bulldog Walsh," the players call him, with a mixture of affection and fear). He talks a kind of coach-speak: short, sloganistic sentences which alternately inspire, implore and threaten. He feels certitude, as Alex Levy points out, "where most of the rest of us feel doubt. He is marvelous in a way— he has no interest in social issues, he scorns them, and yet his life is a walking exhibit on how to give to those who need it most. No one else could do what he does."

Walsh was an All-City player in the Bronx 30 years ago, played at a small college and then coached at his alma mater, Evander Childs High School. His coach, Sy Kalman, a former small college All-America at City College of New York, thought him the classic hard-nosed kid: a good player, not wildly talented, who by dint of absolute commitment and love of the game forces himself to become a great player. Walsh made All-City in his last year. He went off to college and the service, and in the '60s he came back and taught and helped coach at Evander.

"We had dropped football," Kalman says. "There had been a riot, and for six years we didn't play. Jimmy forced us to bring it back. He brought in the parents and bothered the administration, and in the end—as much as anything else to get rid of him—they brought it back." He was brought over to start a football program at George Washington in 1969 after the school was torn apart by conflicts between black and Hispanic students. Against all odds, he created a remarkably successful program.

Few programs have as many rules for their players as his. Rule No. 1 is that no one can miss a practice. The others are all about discipline. Since it is a fad in Spanish Harlem to wear a hat at all times, even indoors—this is considered cool—Walsh has a rule that no one can wear a hat indoors. Another fad is coming to school with shoelaces untied. Walsh hates it. He is strong on shoelace discipline. If a teacher sends over a note saying that a particular kid has sassed her in class, the other players sit in judgment on the offender. They always find him guilty. "My kids," says Walsh, semi-proudly, "are the greatest con men in the world. No one can con them, least of all their own."

Walsh sees himself as the shepherd of these kids. He is always aware of how perilous their parents' world is. At best, it is a world of tiny victories, each new one precariously balanced upon the last. "Getting here from Santo Domingo is a victory," says Walsh. "Finding a place to stay is a victory. Finding a job—and the job is usually off the books—is a victory. Getting the kids into a school is a victory. Knowing that the kids are beginning to learn some English is a victory. Maybe the kid will do better than they did."

"For the kids," he adds, "getting out of the bilingual class is a big victory. It means they can speak English, they can talk to other

Americans, the black kids on the team, and they can understand American sports. They are no longer completely outside. It's like being enfranchised. Before, they were Dominicans in America. Now, for the first time, they begin to feel like Americans in America. They have the same dreams as my grandfather. They want a piece of the rock, too."

★   ★   ★

If the setting is unusual (the handful of black kids on the team have to learn Spanish to understand the plays), Walsh is nonetheless the prototypical coach. His passion is victory in its many forms. That is why it came as something of a surprise to those who knew him and his program that Jim Walsh, on September 15, before the start of a game against Herbert H. Lehman High School, did a most uncoach-like thing. He asked one of his players to bring him the football just before the kickoff, and he personally handed it to the referee. He had prepared a small statement, and he read it. "Excuse me, Mr. Referee," he said, "but by the authority invested in me by the City and State of New York, I declare this game a mismatch and a forfeit and I do so to dramatize the plight of students who cannot speak for themselves and who are forced, against their will, to compete against numerical, physical and financial resources overwhelmingly greater than their own to the detriment of their physical safety and morale. This condition was created by an indifferent and incompetent Public School Athletic League."

With that, he had done the unthinkable: He had become The Coach Who Said No. He did this, he said, because the team was not physically able to play the larger, deeper teams that its schedule mandated. The authorities in Manhattan had placed it in the A League of the PSAL, and it had been playing against schools with two or three times the number of male students, students who were physically bigger and had been playing football since they were little kids. Some of these schools had substantial budgets and five or six assistant coaches; they dressed 75 kids for a game and played 45 of them. Walsh had a marginal budget, no assistant coaches, and he dressed and played every kid who came out, usually between 25 and 30. The result in the last few years has been dramatic mismatches between schools like George Washington and those like DeWitt Clinton and John F. Kennedy, the city's football powers. "They weren't games," Walsh says. "They were turkey shoots."

It was not so much the imbalance of the scores that bothered Walsh. More and more, he was bothered by the fear that one of his players would sustain a serious injury. His kids were much smaller; they usually played both offense and defense against bigger, well-rested players. A serious injury nearly occurred a year ago. One of his players, Sexto Benitez, broke his neck in a game against Kennedy. Fortunately, no permanent spinal damage took place. That injury terrified Walsh. To him, Benitez was a lovely kid who had almost become a quadriplegic.

For more than a year and a half before the Benitez incident, Walsh and his principal had been pleading desperately to have the school transferred to the B league, where it could be more competitive against schools with comparable programs. In an endless series of passionate letters, the principal, Samuel Kostman, and Walsh had pleaded with the officialdom to take action before something terrible happened on the field. The city's school system had only two responses: It either failed to answer or answered with quintessential bureaucratic blather, defending an indefensible position. That meant that before Walsh took his team off the field against Lehman, the struggle had been going on for two and a half years with no flexibility on the part of the bureaucracy. If what Walsh did offended many other coaches, he found a sympathetic hearing elsewhere. "He is my hero for the month," said Jerry Kretchmer, a former New York City commissioner and politician. "That is one of the worst, one of the ugliest bureaucracies in the city. It is supposed to do one thing —look out for the welfare of kids—and it does exactly the opposite."

"What he did was absolutely the right thing," says Sy Kalman, his old coach, who faces a comparable problem at Evander. "It's just like Jimmy, if he thinks it's right, to take on the world. He doesn't know fear. All he knows is right and wrong."

To an outsider, the PSAL's decisions seem incomprehensible. To Walsh, there is a rationale behind it all. The PSAL, he believes, tilts to the power within its jurisdiction, and the power belongs to the bigger schools. These schools like to fatten up on weaker opponents in the same league. Without a few easy games, they are forced to go out and play big schools in Staten Island or Queens, where they may not do as well and may not make the city's playoffs. That, he believes, is the explanation for the early intransigence. The latter intransigence may have something to do with Benitez's injury. Lawyers for Benitez already have filed a $20 million suit against the school system, and if the officials now moved George Washington to the B league, it might be an admission that they were negligent and should have done so much earlier.

By forfeiting on that day, Jim Walsh did the only thing he felt he could do honorably to protect his kids. The bureaucracy suspended him from his coaching job for insubordination. That cost him the $4,200 coach's supplementary salary that went with his $26,000 salary. It also ended the team's season. For Walsh, the only question in his mind was why he had waited so long. "My father," he says, "was not a coach, but he was a man of honor, and he would have done the same thing I did two years earlier."

★   ★   ★

ET is waiting outside the George Washington field for a practice that has been suspended. ET is Eliseo Trinidad, the Trojans quarterback. The team, wearing its football jackets, gathers each day after school as if waiting for some miracle. ET is slim and weighs 170 pounds. He did not want to be the quarterback. He much preferred playing wide receiver or defensive back, using his speed to come up quickly and hit offensive players. But Walsh had no other quarterback. They argued about it. Trinidad dissented. Walsh insisted. Trinidad pretended he could not throw the ball. Walsh insisted he could. Trinidad pretended he could not learn the plays. He deliberately busted the plays. Walsh insisted he could learn them. After three months, Walsh won.

"You think he's crazy," Trinidad says of Walsh. "Maybe he is. But it's my life, and he's changed it. I was a truant. Always on the streets, always in trouble. The first time Coach Walsh talks to you, he doesn't say, 'I'm going to make a football player out of you.' He says, 'I'm going to make a man out of you.' You laugh, and then he does it." Walsh is, says Trinidad, "the first Anglo I have given my trust to." He adds, "My future is in his hands. If I get a college scholarship, it is because of him. For a long time, I was unsure about him. Then, last year, kids I knew got college scholarships. Kids no smarter than me. I thought: This crazy redneck is making sense. Then he comes to me and says, 'ET, you can get 80s and 90s.' I was getting 60s and 70s. He says if I get 80s and 90s, I have a chance at Taylor University."

Trinidad already has the odds against him. He is 18 years old in a difficult land; he is married, and his wife is pregnant. If he does not go to college, he knows that he can disappear into the streets overnight.

"I have a dream," ET says. "First Taylor University. That's in Indiana. I have a friend there, Pedro Rosario, and he says it's a good place. Then a house. I own the house myself. I have a pipe, and I'm sitting in front of the fireplace, reading a newspaper. I want to go out of state to someplace where it's green, like it is on television."

★   ★   ★

For two and a half years, Jim Walsh has been an angry man. The injustice of the PSAL's decision is with him every moment. At one point during some of the interminable meetings that went on, he had to be physically restrained from going after one of his critics. On this day, he simply cannot bear the fact that his kids are hanging around the field, doing nothing. Everything with him is personal: Each kid that makes it is a personal victory, and each one that he loses is a personal defeat.

"The best thing about him," says his friend Alex Levy, "is that, in a very difficult world where it's very easy to give up and where most people give up, he has never given up." Talking about why he forfeited the game and did something that seemed so alien is difficult for him. He tells the story of a letter he tried to write to his mother just before the game he forfeited. Rules and codes and honor were very important to his people. His mother had told him, summoning the legend of the Trojans, never to come home without his shield. He could come home with it or on it. By that she meant he must never betray himself and act in a way unworthy of his home. He recalled this advice in his letter to her and tried to explain that he was coming home with his shield, that what he was doing was an act of honor. But as he tells the story, he becomes too emotional and cannot finish the explanation.

Walsh is bitter, above all, that the kids have lost their season. The PSAL, hoping to ambush him, has suggested sending another coach to George Washington, but the team has voted unanimously to honor Walsh's position and refuses to play for someone else.

Then, three weeks after his suspension, something happens. A special committee, convened by Mayor Edward Koch and headed by former Gov. Hugh Carey, ends Walsh's suspension and reinstates football. George Washington gets to play six games against schools of comparable size and wins its first, 14-6. The kids, so accustomed to defeat by authority, almost do not believe that they are playing again. Never has practice gone so well, never has it been so easy to coach them. "They were away from it three weeks," Walsh says, "and they realized how much they missed."

The kids are aware that it is a special kind of victory. "We won this time," says Raymond Ricketts, one of the black kids, in the locker room. "We did what we were supposed to and won. But it's not always going to happen that way. A lot of times you do that, the right thing or not, you lose."

It is a brief cautionary note for kids who need few cautionary notes, for they, more than most, know how hard it is to go against the system. But in this moment, there is no need to lessen the sense of victory; in this one rare moment, the whole world has come round to them, and to Jim Walsh.

Judge's Comments

David Halberstam is best known for his play in the literary leagues, but he is no stranger to sports.

This is good journalism. Fine story telling. Halberstam draws us in with the old underdog ploy, then lays out a dramatic chronology in which he carefully avoids any temptation to give away the bittersweet conclusion. Along the way, the author alternates between power and finesse to make his points; what's really nice, though, is that he doesn't poke the reader in the eye with them.

Jim Walsh, the hero of the piece, is not a household name. He probably wouldn't make it anywhere but at George Washington High. And he seems too naive to realize that sportsmanship is an ideal. But he's the kind of coach I wish I'd had, the kind I'd want my son and everyone else's son to have. I know because David Halberstam told me so by letting me draw some of the conclusions.

Best Reporting Story

She Throws Pair of 10s, Takes All-Around

OLYMPIC GYMNASTICS

By *RICHARD HOFFER*

From The Los Angeles Times
Copyright © 1984, The Los Angeles Times

She's a calculating coquette. You give her a chance, she'll take your heart. She's a shrewd, brown-eyed gold digger. Yeah, you give her a chance, she'll take your gold, too.

Mary Lou Retton, who has restored pixie to our vocabulary, stole both Friday night, winning, in order, U.S. hearts and Romanian gold. The little sneak. Who saw her coming, padding down the runway in those size-3 feet?

Ordinarily you'd want to hang her from your rear-view mirror. But Friday night, much of America, certainly most of the 9,023 in Pauley Pavilion, wanted to suspend this 4-foot-9 doll in the stratosphere of Olympic tradition, where the heroes belong.

This is what she did, relying on all the nerve and cunning normally available to 16-year-old girls with crushes on Matt Dillon. Battling back in her final two events, needing perfect scores and no less, she beat Romania's Ecaterina Szabo by 5/100ths of a point and Romania's Pauca Simona by 5/10ths to win the women's all-around title, literally vaulting into history.

Some quick perspective: This is the first individual Olympic medal ever won by a U.S. women's gymnast. Ever.

In the days and months and years that follow, this victory will no doubt be translated into a renewed boom in women's gymnastics, with new clubs opening and every pre-teen worth her pigtail paying money to learn how to somersault. Funny that the last big boom was in 1976, when another little pixie, Nadia Comaneci, transformed her sport. Try to picture 7-year-old Mary Lou, lying in her living room back in Fairmount, West Virginia, watching Nadia, suddenly inspired. "I thought, 'Oh, my gosh, she's so wonderful,' " she said. "Who would have thought?"

Yeah, who would have thought? Nadia, a guest of honor at Pauley Pavilion for these Olympics, offering her silent benediction to the Romanian girls? Romania's star gymnast, Ecaterina Szabo, who began the night with a 10 and a 9.95 to take a quick .15 lead?

Only Retton, as nerveless as plant life, could have thought it. And did. She knew that the order of events indicated Szabo taking the early lead. What's to worry. While Szabo was performing in her strongest events, Retton was performing in her weakest. Wait for the finish to announce this winner. "It was the luck of the draw," she admitted.

Szabo, a gymnast who is much like Retton in form and style, began the evening with a 10 on beam. Retton was struggling through an uneven bars set with a 9.85. Suddenly Retton's preliminary lead (from the team event) of .15 was gone, wiped out. Then while Szabo was scoring 9.95 on her floor exercises, dancing to a whacky medley that alternated "Rhapsody in Blue" with "Camptown Races," Retton was getting a 9.8 on her least favorite apparatus, the beam. Szabo, the 17-year-old heir to Nadia, a veteran international competitor who placed third in the most recent World Championships, was leading America's ingenue by 15/100ths.

U.S. Coach Don Peters was unmoved by this apparent momentum. "I knew that after the first two events, Mary Lou might be behind, just because they were Szabo's strongest and Mary Lou's weakest. It was just a matter of order."

Then Szabo got a surprising 9.9 on vault, her legs slightly splayed as she dismounted. Retton took the floor, where her tumbling power is most evident and best rewarded. She vamped through the old song "Johnny, My Friend," playing the crowd shamelessly, grinning out of each somersault. A double layout somersault on her first pass. Grin. A double tuck. Grin. Another. Then a smile that revealed what must have been hundreds of the whitest teeth you ever saw. On the side, Peters held up all the fingers he had. The judges didn't have it in them to argue. A 10. Szabo's lead was cut to 5/100ths.

On the last rotation, Szabo was up on uneven bars first, while Retton cooled her heels waiting to vault. "I watched her on bars," Retton admitted. "It was a nice set, a clean set, but she took a step on her dismount, and I knew it was a 9.9. I knew I had it."

Oh, and who does your arithmetic, Mary Lou? She only had it if she scored a 10, as in perfect. A 9.95 tied her for the gold. Anything less and she was trying to beat Simona going for silver.

"I knew the takeoff was good," she said, recreating her event, "and I knew the vault was good. And I knew I'd stick it." The way people talked afterward, everybody seemed to know as much.

"It was the biggest vault ever," proclaimed her private coach in Houston, former Romanian national coach Bela Karolyi, the Texan with the Transylvanian drawl. "When she hit the floor, there was no question."

Said Peters: "You have to give it a 10. It's the best vault I've ever seen."

Mary Lou didn't doubt as much. She pogoed halfway back to the runway for her second vault, arms in the air, arrested only by Karolyi himself, who had vaulted the railing. As far as Peters was concerned, that was the only moment of suspense. "I thought we'd get slapped with a deduction," he said, noting that Karolyi, not officially on the U.S. staff, was performing what might look like a terrorist act to the judges. "But I guess that only happens in movies."

It was a 10, all right. Her second, meaningless one, was a 10 as well. Mary Lou, her eyelashes reaching into the first row, saluted the crowd, and a lot of people, as Peters always notes, "wanted to reach out and hug her."

Szabo stood quietly behind the horizontal bar, staring. Wistfully? Sadly? Who could know what those silver-dusted eyes were seeing.

Later Retton rolled the gold medal between her fingers, looking up into the stands, spotting parents, friends and fans. And her coaches talked about this prodigy, the new wave in gymnastics, "this chunky leetle thing," as Karolyi describes, "not quite a butterfly."

What they talked about, even more than her effervescence, was her nerve. Karolyi, the man who developed Nadia and who started, for that matter, Szabo before defecting to this country, talked in his usual hyperventilating chatter.

"She shows this fantastic ability, an aggressiveness," he said. "Who could do it? Who could come back and do it? Nadia was a great champion, but I am telling you Mary Lou is bigger. I guarantee no gymnast in the world could have done what Mary Lou has. To have that strong a personality is fantastic, unbelievable."

Peters, somewhat more subdued, agreed that there are few athletes as mentally strong as Mary Lou. "She thrives on pressure. She never gets tight," he said. "The pressure is what did it, when she needed those 10s. That kid thrives on it. A great champion."

Retton, finally put atop a chair so she could stand eye-to-eye with reporters, shrugged. "Yeah, I work best under pressure." What more was there to say? One thing that is unavailable to this 16-year-old is perspective. When you're that small, it can be hard to understand how you suddenly get so big.

Judge's Comments

Richard Hoffer's account of Mary Lou Retton's victory in the women's all-around gymnastics competition at the Summer Olympics was the crowning touch to the Los Angeles Times' superb coverage of the event. Hoffer captured on paper what television had beamed to the world the night before. His story captures the excitement and thrill of the event as no other we have seen. Hoffer makes good use of quotations by choosing them selectively. The lead of this story is engaging; the reader is hooked immediately. Hoffer takes an approach that complements the television coverage that so many of his readers would have seen. Hoffer's effort is a standout among a host of entries from the memorable Summer Olympics, surely the major sports event of 1984. This article is one worth remembering.

Best Commentary Story

A Son's Death, A Father's Life

GENERAL

By *STEVE JACOBSON*

From Newsday
Copyright © 1984, Newsday, Inc.

I like telling about Tom DeLuca, the Long Beach coach. Except now I hate it.

We go back a long time together. We went to Long Beach High School when he was one of the great Long Island athletes. I call him Tommy as we always did and he calls me Stevie, which only my aunts still do. I admired what he was doing as a coach. He cared about his kids; he didn't intend to rise to fame on their hard work.

There's a universality in him, not pretense. His shirt comes out of his trousers almost the moment his basketball team goes on the floor, he paces the length of the field with his football team and his voice is worn raspy after each game. He's never been a mastermind of the X and O; his strength has been in throwing his arms in a hug around a player.

He began coaching in Long Beach 14 years ago, when Long Beach High was in a racial crisis, and he helped overcome that. He went often to the Martin Luther King Youth Center and made the black kids understand that he cared. He turned around the unsavory image of the football team, and he was even winning.

When his teams had success, he preferred to talk about the decent kids he was coaching, and to old friends he talked about family in the small office plastered with photos of his wife and children. "When Tom went home, he went home," athletic director Carmen Lombardo said. "When you went out with Tom, you went to his house."

Last basketball season, his undersized and undertalented team went to the state championship and lost at the buzzer. Today his football team plays Garden City in the first round of the conference championship and no Long Beach team had been in the playoffs since the system was instituted. Few men coach two major sports, fewer reach that level in both.

But now the circumstance is too universal. On Wednesday, Tom's son Tommy was killed making a solo flight in a T2-C Buckeye jet trainer out of Naval Air Station Chase Field in a place called Beeville, Texas. Nothing is more universal than a father's grief for a son, a parent's grief for a child.

The Long Beach assistant coaches recall riding to play Great Neck North eight days ago and Tom talking about Tommy being home and not about the game. That night Tommy was at the small party celebrating his father's team making the playoffs.

It was at a high point in the coach's professional and personal life. He had followed the basketball accomplishment with football. Tommy, an Annapolis graduate, was soon to earn his Navy wings of gold. Tommy and Ingrid Holgosh of West Islip were to be married in eight months.

On Wednesday, DeLuca was involved in a dual practice, getting the football team ready for Garden City and supervising basketball tryouts when the two Navy officers—a chaplain and a flier—arrived at the school. Tom knew his son was to have soloed at 7 a.m.

They never said a word; the sight of those two officers coming through the door was enough. "No!" Tom recoiled. "Don't tell me that!"

He ran for his keys to go home and be with his wife, Julie. It's a long drive from Long Beach to West Islip, but he refused the company of the Navy or the athletic director. "Please, please," he said, "I have to be alone."

On the way out the door, he pounded on the glass and said to whatever unseen force that causes bad things to happen to good people: "You don't understand; I love that kid."

And the assistant coaches and the athletic director sat in that office full of pictures and looked at each other for 45 minutes. The reaction of the players in today's game is their own. The assistants think perhaps the seniors feel something, but many of the players can feel little. "At that age they think they're immortal," assistant Harry Witkin said. "They don't understand death and 'never.'"

The assistants thought it would be unfair to burden the players with tears as motivation. "This puts the game in perspective, perhaps too much perspective," Kevin McElroy, another assistant, said. "Suddenly, winning and losing doesn't mean very much, but we owe it to the kids not to convey that to them." That kind of tragedy is not for youth to understand.

Tom and Tommy had a relationship. "He thinks just like me," Tom used to say to the assistants and the athletic director, "except he doesn't yell as much."

Tommy was a good athlete at West Islip High. He played two years of baseball at Navy and decided it was too difficult and moved on to intramurals. One line on him in "Lucky Bag," the yearbook, says: In 10 years "we expect to see him in the intramural Hall of Fame."

To him flying was the sport he wanted most. "If you feel a cool breeze in the future, look up," the yearbook says, "it will probably be The Duke in his F-18."

And Tom used to say about Tommy and the younger ones, Patti, Andy and Joey: "I'm blessed; I got smart kids."

Tom is devastated. "I could always bounce back," he told Lombardo, the athletic director. "I can't bounce back from this; he's my boy."

Lombardo and the football and basketball assistants worry about that. "Tom is the best thing that ever happened to this school," Lombardo said. "He understands the athlete; he understands competition; he had control of his teams. He wouldn't let his kids fight or curse. He said he could have good kids and they could win, too."

Wandy Williams, junior-varsity football and basketball coach and a proud black man, noted how DeLuca reached both black and white players. "They sensed he wasn't running a game on them," Williams said. "They believe he's fair and he shows it to them. He'd try to get kids eligible for their lives, not just for a winning team."

DeLuca made a place on the bus so Sol Bernstein, the 80-year-old father of basketball assistant Dick Bernstein, could go to basketball games in his wheelchair.

McElroy recalled how DeLuca could be "the only guy to bring you out of the dumps, no matter what your problem was."

And Witkin noted that what they were all doing was giving a eulogy for Tom DeLuca the coach. He's lived in the gym and loved the games and now he's saying he can never go back in the gym because all he'll ever see is those two Navy men coming in the door.

Ens. Thomas DeLuca, 23, Training Squadron 26, had completed one sequence of his solo flight and was heading for the base for touch-and-go landings. He was nine miles out, in sight of the field, when his plane went in. He never ejected. The Navy is investigating whether there was malfunction of the aircraft and whether Ens. DeLuca tried to eject and could not. The next man will benefit from what they learn.

"He was a very receptive, very alert student," said Lt. Alan Holmstrup, 26, an instructor who had been aloft near DeLuca. "The squadron hadn't lost a man in four years. We're close. It shakes you up. Then you go out and hop in the saddle again and continue doing the things you were doing correctly before."

Tom DeLuca has family and he has something outside that he loves. He has much to give. That's too philosophical for now. If he didn't come back, it would be more the tragedy.

Judge's Comments

Former Chief Justice Earl Warren once said that he read about man's tragedies on the front pages and his triumphs on the sports pages.

If he had been reading Newsday's sports pages on November 18, 1984, former Justice Warren would have read about a tragedy that is a triumph for the virtues of humanity.

Steve Jacobson wrote about that tragedy—the death of a friend's son—in such a way that the humanness of the father inspires all of us. Jacobson avoided purple prose; his restrained approach lets the story tell itself. Neither in the man Jacobson writes about, nor in the style he uses to tell us, is there pretense.

There is clarity. He describes his friend so well we know him immediately: *"His shirt comes out of his trousers almost the moment his basketball team goes on the floor . . . his strength has been in throwing his arms in a hug around a player."*

He first tells us why he cares, and why we should care about this man, before we learn about the tragedy. Rather than telling us, he shows us. We are in the gym, we see the two Navy officers come through the door, we hear Tom DeLuca denying what they are telling him, we see him running off to be with his wife.

The writer feels, but his tears are not washing over the scene. When you are done reading, you feel for DeLuca, but you are also happy that there are people such as him coaching your children. That's the triumph Justice Warren was looking for on the sports pages.

Best Feature Story

American Summer: A Baseball Odyssey

BASEBALL

By WILLIAM GILDEA

From the Washington Post
Copyright © 1984, Washington Post

Meeting DiMaggio: A Journey in Time
(First of three parts)

"Your father always wanted a son, to take to the baseball games," my mother told me once. He started me out almost before I realized it. We'd talk baseball as we rode in his black '46 Ford to the big wooden horseshoe stadium across the city. Friday night and Sunday afternoon doubleheaders were our specialty, our common joy.

He took me to New York, for the 1951 World Series. From a seat six rows behind home plate at the Polo Grounds, I saw Joe DiMaggio connect with one of his long, looping swings. I can still see the ball rising in the smoky haze of an autumn afternoon against the second tier in left. Many years later I realized . . . it had been DiMaggio's last home run.

Now my own sons are almost grown. They can't remember the Senators. Baseball connects fathers and sons, and we've been bereft of that generational glue. I realized this a July night two years ago as I drove my boys through the city streets to a baseball game, the first Cracker Jack Old Timers Baseball Classic. My sons had never seen DiMaggio, Aaron, Musial, Feller, Vander Meer, Blackwell, Kaline . . . Johnny Mize, he hit 51 home runs one year. But Johnny Mize is the "Big Cat" only in the mind; he has trouble walking.

We drove home replaying the game, talking baseball as I had done with my father, a memory dusted off as if from storage. Maybe, I suggested, we should take a trip ourselves, a baseball journey into the country. Baseball, because of its timelessness, can be shared in a special way. It exists as a game of memory and myth almost as much as an actual game. I wanted to show my sons old parks like

Wrigley Field and Tiger Stadium, life deep in the minor leagues, maybe meet some old-timers, maybe even meet DiMaggio. The boys knew him as Mr. Coffee.

SAN FRANCISCO—Of course he remembered the last home run. "It was a good hit," said Joe DiMaggio. "Left-center field. Line drive. Upper deck. One man on base, I believe. Off Maglie." He spoke with an economy of words, like the inning-by-inning scoring summaries in agate type in the papers. He paused, and when he resumed he spoke swiftly, his pictures of the past rolling forth as clear as scenes from a new film.

"My last opportunity at the plate came at Yankee Stadium." That was two days after the home run. "I hit a ball into left-center field off Jansen and wound up at second base. Gil McDougald was the next batter. He tried to advance me to third with a bunt. But it was tapped just a little too hard and they threw me out at third base. As I started to run from third across the field to our dugout, the fans seemed to sense that that was my last appearance—speculation was around, it seemed like it might be. And they gave me a standing ovation." He said this eating breakfast, and it was quiet. We were alone; he could talk.

A week later we would meet again, at the 1984 All-Star Game at Candlestick Park. ABC has set up a large red-and-white-striped hospitality tent next to the stadium. It is packed. But one section of the tent is curtained off. DiMaggio sits at a large round table with his two granddaughters and their two friends, whom he has brought to the game. My two sons, Billy and David, ages 17 and 16, sit next to him. All the other tables are empty. But the word gets around; Joe DiMaggio is here. The word spreads like a California brush fire.

The autograph-seekers come unrelentingly, two and three at a time, now a half dozen. Here comes some more. Small boys, old men, a woman, a state senator, a judge. DiMaggio signs: baseballs, a glove for a boy ("I want to sign this," he says in an aside), programs, pieces of paper. The line is gone. He puts his pen in the inside pocket of his sport coat. "It can get awfully tiring," he says wearily, but not loud enough for the approaching man to hear. The man says, "Mr. Di-Maggio, I know this can get tiring but . . ." "How'd you know?" says DiMaggio.

What sets him apart from other icons of American sport is that he continues to play the aftergame as elegantly as he played the game itself. A shy boy grown to an ever-private man, DiMaggio has faced the harder half of life since he retired from baseball. "I no longer have it," he said when he quit.

He has signed, perhaps, more autographs than any other human being, a record set while trying not to, while using side doors, back doors, no doors at all—just staying home. The game itself came naturally, the graceful ways he ran and fielded and threw and hit, to form the composite that elevated him. Fame always has its burdens, though, and the price today is the line in front of him. Willie Mays may be San Francisco's adopted son—he roamed center field here almost 15 years for the Giants—but DiMaggio is San Francisco's native son, an idol carved from truth.

He is 69, tall, his elegance enhanced by his perfect attire: dark jacket, gray slacks, blue shirt, maroon tie, yellow sweater. The body is still lean, the face softened now. The face of the 25-year-old DiMaggio could look taut and angular. He liked to wear wide-lapeled, double-breasted suits, with a triangle of handkerchief jutting from the coat pocket. Now at times the face seems faintly sad.

A short man approaches. "They find you, they search you out," DiMaggio says. The man arrives at the table. But DiMaggio pretends he doesn't see him. He looks toward my son, taps him on the knee. He looks to the ceiling, surveys it. He reminds me of my grandfather—he'd pretend he didn't hear my grandmother. DiMaggio looks around and greets the man, feigned surprise. "Oh . . . yes. Yes, sir."

DiMaggio asks the girls when they want to go to their seats before the game. He worries that maybe they won't find them easily. He is, after all, a grandfather. He wants the boys to get some plates and fill them. "C'mon, the best part is it's free," he tells them, laughing. He insists. But they'd rather eat hot dogs in the stands than steak. The grandfather shakes his head.

"Last one. Last one." He takes out his pen once more. Thinking he is finished, he puts it away.

But people keep coming.

"I think you'd better keep it out," my son says quietly. DiMaggio nods in agreement.

★　　　★　　　★

One thing about DiMaggio: Before he ever got to New York, in 1936, he was already a hero, at least on the opposite coast. Once, the mayor of San Francisco, no less, ran onto the field in the midst of a game to shake his hand. DiMaggio was 18 then. Before he left San Francisco he had saved, in the throes of the Depression, an almost bankrupt baseball franchise, perhaps an entire minor league. He hit .398 one season for the San Francisco Seals, drove in 169 runs in a single season, hit safely in 61 straight games, which is a nearly forgotten feat in the wake of his 56-game hitting streak with the Yankees in 1941. The world followed that one.

"Was he big like Winfield? Or Reggie?" my older son asked me. He was smiling, knowing the response.

We had stopped for sodas at a small corner grocery. San Francisco is full of little neighborhood grocery stores. DiMaggio once delivered groceries.

"Well, he *was* named the greatest living player at the baseball centennial celebration in Washington in 1969." But I agreed with them, the modern game is better—but no baseball player ever captured a nation's imagination the way DiMaggio did, or for as long.

One evening, I remembered, my father and I were driving home from a softball game he had played in. My uncle drove up in the car alongside, next to me.

"How'd he do?" my uncle asked.

"Two for four," I said.

"As good as DiMaggio," he shot back.

DiMaggio was in "The Old Man and the Sea," I reminded the boys.

"Hemingway. I forgot." They had both forgotten.

There was a song, too. When it came out in 1941, DiMaggio was on his hitting streak. It was played by Les Brown and his Band of Renown:

He'll live in baseball's Hall of Fame.
He's got there blow by blow.
Our kids will tell their kids his name,
Joltin' Joe DiMaggio.
Joe ... Joe ... DiMaggio ... we want you on our side.

There's no whole answer why DiMaggio became fixed in the culture of the 20th century, except to say America seems to prefer its heroes strong and silent, a person solitary, competing against large odds and maybe even pain. Consider Lindbergh. In DiMaggio's case, lasting fame was secured, like a lock, by two circumstances. The idol suffering the things that didn't work out in later life, especially his failed marriage to Marilyn Monroe. Of her life and death he will not speak. Finally, the grace with which he has, alone, borne his lasting grief.

He grew up in the first-floor apartment at 2047 Taylor Street. The three-story house is still there, immaculately kept, the stucco structure a freshly painted mocha. It sits in the middle of a block of similar houses on a steep hill rising above Fisherman's Wharf on the way to Nob Hill.

Not a block for playing ball in, my sons and I agreed as we drove down the hill, riding the brakes.

As a boy, DiMaggio had to go somewhere to play ball. Often it was down by the wharf to the "horse lot," so called because it was owned by a dairy and used for parking horses that pulled the wagons. Even when they came to get him, DiMaggio often had to be persuaded by his friends to join in their pickup games. In the beginning, he wasn't that interested. As a boy, he didn't know what he wanted.

He had been brought to San Francisco as an 11-month-old by his Italian-born parents from the California fishing village of Martinez, 25 miles across the bay. His father had heard that the fishermen were luckier off San Francisco. The house where DiMaggio was born has been destroyed by fire and only a vacant lot remains. He's been by there, he says.

His father thought he should be a fisherman. But you can stand on the wharf on this brilliant summer day, and look out in the bay, out toward Alcatraz and beyond, and understand why DiMaggio wanted no part of being a fisherman. Beneath the cloudless blue sky, the wind slams through the waterfront. It could be even colder, and competitive, out on the water.

The elder DiMaggio didn't know what was going to become of his quiet son. But this was certain—he wasn't a father who was going to lead his son to baseball. Already, an older son, Vince, was playing, and that was more than enough. Boccie was the father's game. "He thought baseball was football—he thought you could get hurt," DiMaggio says. And: "Baseball was tough on the shoes. We played on asphalt, and we didn't have rubber-soled shoes. When you'd come home with scuffed shoes and present yourself . . . and the shoes were new . . . and you made your entrance . . ." DiMaggio rolled his eyes.

In the irony of this instance, the son would lead the father to baseball. When DiMaggio made the Triple-A Seals of the Pacific Coast League, his father began to understand. "He'd take the street-car," says DiMaggio. "He'd get a transfer. Settle down in his seat at the park. Then he'd come home the same way." Only a few years before, DiMaggio could not have imagined the sight. With a convert's fervor, the father followed the game and his player-sons, Vince, Joe and then Dom. "When he'd hear the paper hit at 4 in the morning he'd go out and pick it up, and he'd take it back into the kitchen and scrutinize all the box scores. He learned what 'AB' and 'R' and so forth all meant."

DiMaggio played in some pickup games at Funston Field, now called Moscone Recreation Center, after the slain mayor. It's still a serious ball field, a large grass square in the quaintest of settings: one block from a marina, and beneath a panorama of tan and white houses on the hills. Hardball diamonds are set on two corners, softball on the other two. My boys and I went there a couple of evenings. They had brought their equipment. One evening, the field with the most serious business featured a spirited game between two softball teams, the Jazz Room, whose players wore San Diego Padre-like yellow and brown uniforms, and the red-and-black clad Protojays. The game went on into the night, under the lights, and spectators drifted down from the city.

On the opposite diamond, in front of small, concrete stands, my boys threw out imaginary runners at second base, called for me to inspect the curve balls they broke off from the high mound, shagged distant flies. In that outfield, perfectly level, with the grass clipped short, even some of the old boys can move fast enough to catch up with former glories.

A thought while standing there: DiMaggio, the teen-ager, on that field with the wind at his back.

I saw a plaque above the main entrance to the stands, and walked closer: "Dedicated to the memory of Edward (Spike) Hennessy, for years of service to semi-pro baseball . . ." Spike Hennessy, I suddenly remembered, was the San Francisco Seals' scout who found DiMaggio in 1932.

He didn't have to look far. Tapped the kid on the shoulder outside the fence at Seals Stadium. DiMaggio had been peeking through a knothole, watching his brother Vince play for the Seals. Hennessy invited the kid brother in. He had seen him play for the Sunset Produce sandlot team that summer. DiMaggio had hit .632. He was an erratic-armed shortstop, but Hennessy had never seen anyone who could hit like that. The scout introduced DiMaggio to the team's owner. "I want you to meet the greatest 'lamb' I have ever recommended," Spike Hennessy supposedly said.

"I was nervous," DiMaggio says, "nervous being around the clubhouse, around these fellows who were professionals. But on the field, it was a little different. The first time up I hit a triple to right-center off a good pitcher, Ted Pillette. I went two for nine in the series." But his future was not at shortstop. "As the series wore on, no one would sit in this particular box (behind first). I kept hitting the seats in that box. I threw six times over the first baseman's head. I must have broken two seats."

The next season was 1933. "To my utter amazement, Ike Caveney sent me up to pinch-hit. I walked on four pitches. After the inning, I went to the bench, picked up my glove and headed down the runway to the clubhouse like I was finished. Halfway down the runway I turned. Vince came running up and said, 'He wants you to play right field.' That's how it started." He pauses, looking for a few seconds into the far distance.

"I was never replaced since," he says.

★   ★   ★

At 16th and Bryant streets, where Seals Stadium stood, there is no marker to DiMaggio, no sign that a stadium was ever there except for the one over the Double Play bar on the corner. We stopped to take a look, the boys and I, thinking first that the stadium must have been where the little green park is, up on the hill. On the steps we met a man who pointed across the street . . . at the San Francisco Autocenter, a block-long auto parts complex. "It was over there," he said. "That's where Candlestick Park should be today. That was San Francisco's biggest mistake, putting that stadium where it is. They could have had a beautiful park here. You don't feel the wind too much here, either, not like Candlestick."

On the auto-parts site, and up and down the Coast, DiMaggio hammered out three of the most remarkable seasons in the game's history—.340, .341 and the .398. He could hit and he could field. An old San Francisco sportswriter's story: One day a writer was drowsing in the press box when he was partly roused by the crack of the bat. "Is the ball in the park?" he asked the gent next to him. When told it was, his head lolled back but not before he said, "DiMaggio will get it."

In 1934 he didn't play as much; he suffered an injury to his left knee—torn cartilage—and for part of the season the leg was encased

an ice bucket—it was there because it was so hot and we'd come in and towel off, you know. Well, the bucket was up against a post and I gave the thing a kick. Water leaped up and Joe McCarthy got wet and let out a yell. And I said something like, 'Go to hell,' and I went down to the end of the bench. God, my foot was sore. But I didn't rub it. McCarthy came down and said, 'I didn't want you to hurt your foot.' I had this black-and-blue spot on the foot, on the big toe. It stayed there for six weeks.

"I tell you, the park that would have helped me the most was Ebbets Field. It was longer than Fenway but not as high a fence. I hit line drives that would rise, not the towering kind that would carry. That's the way Foxx hit, and Ted. I guess Babe did that, too. I classify myself more as a line-drive power hitter. Somebody told me, as far as Ebbets Field was concerned, 'Upper deck or no count.' Toots Shor told me that. Meaning that if I hit one into the lower deck, it shouldn't count." He smiles.

Certainly no stadium stopped DiMaggio. Only a war—temporarily—and age stopped him.

★   ★   ★

My sons and I almost missed DiMaggio in San Francisco. It was our fourth day in the city on our baseball trip and we were preparing to move on. We had left a message for him at DiMaggio's Restaurant, which has been in the same family since 1937 and is now owned by Dom. I was at a laundromat when he called.

"Did he send the laundry out or is he doing it himself?" DiMaggio asked.

"He's doing it himself," said my son David.

I am not in DiMaggio's laundry league.

"Good for him," DiMaggio said, charitably.

At that critical juncture in the conversation there reportedly was a pause—two reputed non-talkers holding the line. DiMaggio said he was moving on, had to meet some friends. But in that fleeting moment David arranged our rendezvous, time and place—forevermore, I think, to be viewed in a new light by his older brother.

The boys came away from meeting DiMaggio knowing that fame has its costs. "I'd *never* ask him for his autograph," one said. They liked him, I think, because he seemed to care. He talked about college with the older one: "You're accepted, and everything? . . . You're going to need a lot of spending money . . ." And golf with the younger one: "Riviera—you've heard of Riviera? That's a course that only gives what you earn."

DiMaggio appears at, but doesn't play in, about three old-timers' baseball games a year. He isn't rich, but he's more than comfortable. He has a number of business involvements. He'll attend a few charity dinners, make a few other appearances. Otherwise, he keeps to himself or with close friends and often can be hard to find. He doesn't like saying complimentary things about himself, which is one reason he almost never wants to be interviewed. I had asked him about a

particular incident at Griffith Stadiu[m] 1951. Players used to leave their glove[s] and one ball DiMaggio hit, a ground ba[ll] a glove on the grass in short center. He

He didn't remember that play but large turn (at first). If that outfielder instant, I was on my way. That's the wa[y] played me so deep, I could hit the ball ou[t] ond; I'm not talking about a line drive, but took a little while to get out there. Of cour[se] and I would know if I could make it."

Then he interrupted himself. "OK," he s[aid] there." But immediately, as if to excuse it, hard. I really did. I loved it. I enjoyed it. I was another quality the boys noticed about h[im]

★   ★   ★

At the top of the seventh inning of the All[-] stick Park, I looked down from the second de[ck] hind the American League dugout where DiM[aggio] It was dark and cold. The wind was coming in was gone.

The next morning we drove out of the city. T[hey] about the place, and DiMaggio.

"It's one of the prettiest cities I've ever seen, [ ] don't you think?"

"He doesn't look 6-foot-2, or 6-foot-1."

"He definitely doesn't look 69."

"Why doesn't he play in those old-timers' game[s]"

He hasn't played in 10 years, he had said—"I sa[y] get hurt. I have the bad back. I couldn't swing." A[nd] don't want to get up and look like a fool."

"He wouldn't," one of the boys said.

At the Heart of the Game
(Second of three parts)

APPLETON, Wis.—We had wandered 1,000 miles journey. By now the cities and interstates were past occasional house or barn or lake checkered the landsc[ape] still carried with us, my sons and I, like unwanted bag[gage] city impatience. We wished a small town and its team t[o] charms, right away. We wondered, in our different ways, Could the images of baseball's farm life, deep in the min[d] have been a false psychic tug?

My passengers wondered: Was there a Holiday Inn? W[ould] there be to do in Appleton? It looked like rain. An easterly w[ind] the car hard to hold to the road.

We followed a sign with an arrow: Goodland Field. That it. Then, down tree-lined blocks, came the sight of a little b[all]

steel gir[ders] tions. T[ ] foul lin[e] green o[ ] humili[ ]

A [ ] champ[ ] be a 5[ ] before[ ] would[ ] as if [ ] down[ ]

seats[ ] Greg[ ] the [ ] blon[ ] Indi[ ] Gre[ ]

on[ ] Am[ ] Le[ ] fu[ ] dif[ ] A[ ] sa[ ] ba[ ]

d[ ] M[ ] l[ ] V[ ] [ ]

in an aluminum splint from ankle to thigh. He considered himself "damaged goods" from 1934 on. Big-league scouts shied away from him. Bill Essick was the Yankee scout who didn't. "A dapper man," says DiMaggio. "Tie with a stick pin, glasses with a chain like Roosevelt, a fedora. He looked more like a banker than a Coast League scout."

And so, in 1935, the Yankees paid the Seals $25,000 and gave them five players for DiMaggio—the Seals got the money and players immediately *and* got to keep DiMaggio for one more season. On the final day of that season, DiMaggio went eight for 10 in a doubleheader in San Francisco to finish up with his .398. Meanwhile, down in Los Angeles, a speedy spray hitter with the unlikely name of Ox, Ox Eckhardt—he was more apt to get on base by chopping balls into the ground and beating them out than by hitting home runs—was laying down three bunts for base hits in the first game of a doubleheader. That gave him a batting average of .399. He sat out the second game, figuring correctly that he had enough to win the batting title.

DiMaggio has a long memory. He muses: "Had he known what I was doing he might have played the second game . . . Or if he didn't bunt safely *three* times he might have played the second game . . ."

In 1936, DiMaggio's older brother Tom arranged for him to be driven to spring training in Florida by two of his new teammates, Tony Lazzeri and Frankie Crosetti, both from San Francisco. None of the three talked much. One story goes that after a couple of days on the road, somewhere around Kansas City, DiMaggio said from the back seat, "Where are we?" To which came the reply, "Shut up, kid, you're talking too much." Actually, it was kind of like that. "It took five days to get there," DiMaggio says. "They would change off driving every 200 miles or so. One time we stopped for gas, a bite to eat, and it was Tony's turn to drive. He said, 'I'm tired, Frankie, you drive.' Frankie said, 'I'm tired, you drive.' Then they said to me, 'Hey, you drive.' That was just their way of kidding me, they knew I didn't know how to drive.

"But Crosetti and Lazzeri made it easier for me. They took me to the park when we got there and introduced me. Red Ruffing, the pitcher, was there. He said, 'You're the hotshot from the Coast. I guess you'll hit .500 up here.' 'Why's that?' I asked. 'Well, down there, they play with scuffed-up baseballs, black baseballs. Up here, you get a shiny new one to hit each time.' " Everybody around laughed, but DiMaggio was ready. That year he hit .323, had 44 doubles, 15 triples and 29 home runs, drove in 125 runs and threw out 22 runners, to lead the league. For 13 seasons he didn't let up.

Not even Yankee Stadium, made for Ruth, for lefthanded hitters, a cavern for righthanded hitters, could stop DiMaggio. But it could frustrate him. "One day I hit four line drives. They carried 440 feet and I came up empty. It was a hot day, hot and miserable. I came back to the bench and the first thing I saw I kicked. It happened to be an ice bucket—it was there because it was so hot and we'd come in and towel off, you know. Well, the bucket was up against a post and I gave the thing a kick. Water leaped up and Joe McCarthy got wet and let out a yell. And I said something like, 'Go to hell,' and I went down to the end of the bench. God, my foot was sore. But I didn't rub it. McCarthy came down and said, 'I didn't want you to hurt your foot.' I had this black-and-blue spot on the foot, on the big toe. It stayed there for six weeks.

"I tell you, the park that would have helped me the most was Ebbets Field. It was longer than Fenway but not as high a fence. I hit line drives that would rise, not the towering kind that would carry. That's the way Foxx hit, and Ted. I guess Babe did that, too. I classify myself more as a line-drive power hitter. Somebody told me, as far as Ebbets Field was concerned, 'Upper deck or no count.' Toots Shor told me that. Meaning that if I hit one into the lower deck, it shouldn't count." He smiles.

Certainly no stadium stopped DiMaggio. Only a war—temporarily—and age stopped him.

★   ★   ★

My sons and I almost missed DiMaggio in San Francisco. It was our fourth day in the city on our baseball trip and we were preparing to move on. We had left a message for him at DiMaggio's Restaurant, which has been in the same family since 1937 and is now owned by Dom. I was at a laundromat when he called.

"Did he send the laundry out or is he doing it himself?" DiMaggio asked.

"He's doing it himself," said my son David.

I am not in DiMaggio's laundry league.

"Good for him," DiMaggio said, charitably.

At that critical juncture in the conversation there reportedly was a pause—two reputed non-talkers holding the line. DiMaggio said he was moving on, had to meet some friends. But in that fleeting moment David arranged our rendezvous, time and place—forevermore, I think, to be viewed in a new light by his older brother.

The boys came away from meeting DiMaggio knowing that fame has its costs. "I'd *never* ask him for his autograph," one said. They liked him, I think, because he seemed to care. He talked about college with the older one: "You're accepted, and everything? . . . You're going to need a lot of spending money . . ." And golf with the younger one: "Riviera—you've heard of Riviera? That's a course that only gives what you earn."

DiMaggio appears at, but doesn't play in, about three old-timers' baseball games a year. He isn't rich, but he's more than comfortable. He has a number of business involvements. He'll attend a few charity dinners, make a few other appearances. Otherwise, he keeps to himself or with close friends and often can be hard to find. He doesn't like saying complimentary things about himself, which is one reason he almost never wants to be interviewed. I had asked him about a particular incident at Griffith Stadium—it must have been 1950 or 1951. Players used to leave their gloves on the field between innings, and one ball DiMaggio hit, a ground ball up the middle, stuck under a glove on the grass in short center. He ran it into a double.

He didn't remember that play but he said, "I always made a large turn (at first). If that outfielder just bobbled the ball for an instant, I was on my way. That's the way I played. Sometimes they played me so deep, I could hit the ball out there and still make second; I'm not talking about a line drive, but a ball hit not too hard that took a little while to get out there. Of course, I knew the outfielders, and I would know if I could make it."

Then he interrupted himself. "OK," he said, "I gave myself a plus there." But immediately, as if to excuse it, he added, "But I played hard. I really did. I loved it. I enjoyed it. I really enjoyed it." That was another quality the boys noticed about him: his modesty.

★   ★   ★

At the top of the seventh inning of the All-Star Game at Candlestick Park, I looked down from the second deck to the box seat behind the American League dugout where DiMaggio had been sitting. It was dark and cold. The wind was coming in hard off the bay. He was gone.

The next morning we drove out of the city. The boys were talking about the place, and DiMaggio.

"It's one of the prettiest cities I've ever seen, maybe the prettiest, don't you think?"

"He doesn't look 6-foot-2, or 6-foot-1."

"He definitely doesn't look 69."

"Why doesn't he play in those old-timers' games?"

He hasn't played in 10 years, he had said—"I saw too many guys get hurt. I have the bad back. I couldn't swing." And, he added, "I don't want to get up and look like a fool."

"He wouldn't," one of the boys said.

At the Heart of the Game
(Second of three parts)

APPLETON, Wis.—We had wandered 1,000 miles on a baseball journey. By now the cities and interstates were past and only an occasional house or barn or lake checkered the landscape. Yet we still carried with us, my sons and I, like unwanted baggage, a big-city impatience. We wished a small town and its team to work their charms, right away. We wondered, in our different ways, if it would. Could the images of baseball's farm life, deep in the minor leagues, have been a false psychic tug?

My passengers wondered: Was there a Holiday Inn? What could there be to do in Appleton? It looked like rain. An easterly wind made the car hard to hold to the road.

We followed a sign with an arrow: Goodland Field. That has to be it. Then, down tree-lined blocks, came the sight of a little ball park, steel girders supporting a roof that slanted over its middle three sections. Two more sections of uncovered stands stretched down each foul line, embracing a trim infield of dirt and grass and a roomy green outfield with signboard fences—so distant as to impress instant humility on aspiring long-ball gods.

A gem of a place: the home of the Appleton Foxes, defending champions of the Class A Midwest League. This evening there would be a 5 o'clock game with the Wausau Timbers. Now, three hours before game time, things were just coming to life. In minutes we would be co-opted by the handful of people in the park, made to feel as if we were at long last coming home. You're in, you're sitting down, you're talking.

"They're grooming him to be a manager," says a lone man in the seats, nodding toward the first player dressed in his Appleton whites: Greg Tarnow, a catcher, heading for the field, his spikes clacking on the macadam. He looks like a catcher, about 5-feet-10 and muscular, blond and all curls. His father, up for the weekend from La Porte, Indiana, sits down next to me in the stands. "You know the story on Greg?" he asks.

"His mother died when he was 9 years old," says Gerald Tarnow, once a St. Louis Cardinal farmhand. "I have three kids, just a typical American baseball family. I played ball, coached a lot of Little League. We live on a farm. When his mother died we went to the funeral parlor and he picked out the casket—he crawled up on 19 different caskets to make sure he got the right one for his mother. And when they laid her in there he got a baseball, he signed it, he said, 'I love you mother. I promise you I'll play professional baseball.' He put the ball in her hand.

"A day or two later he saw this baseball school in Fort Lauderdale advertised in Baseball Digest. He said, 'Dad, I promised Mommy I'd go to play professional ball. Can I go down there to learn?' He went down there every year, three months at a time. When he was 17 years old, he got his professional contract. Course he's struggling yet."

"But he's going to be a manager."

"I think so. He's got a good future in baseball. He's worked hard. As a boy, he dedicated himself. Doesn't smoke, drink. Good churchgoer. I'm proud of him. He's a hell of an instructor. He knows the game. That's what baseball needs. People who teach."

★   ★   ★

My father taught me, though I scarcely knew how well. He taught me that the love of baseball does not demand perfection, that the game can exist on many levels and in many leagues. My first introduction to life deep in the minors came at his side, in the hot baking stands of the never-celebrated Susquehanna League: Aberdeen, Havre de Grace, Elkton, Rising Sun.

At Havre de Grace one Sunday, I stood with my father in the high grass that covered foul territory in left field and watched my slug-

ging idol, Howie Moss, just a few feet in front of us. "The Howitzer"
had launched 53 home runs one season with the International
League Orioles, but now I felt sorry it had come to a weekend league
for him. My father tried to explain that Howie Moss was simply
keeping connected to the game he loved, but the romance eluded me.
  At length I understood . . .

★   ★   ★

Up in the Appleton stands, an usher is pointing out to my older
son, Billy, the prospects he thinks will make the major leagues someday. It turns out Billy knows Greg Tarnow; last spring Billy's high
school team attended the Gulf Coast Baseball School in Sarasota,
Florida, which the Tarnows own. Before long, Tarnow gives my son
one of his bats, to keep. And Pedro Guzman, a Foxes pitcher, asks my
other son, David, to come out to the mound and snap his picture—it's
Guzman's 23rd birthday and he wants to send a shot home to the
Dominican Republic. That quickly we are wrapped into Appleton's
fabric.

Bill Smith offers to find the boys and me a place to stay. He gets
on the phone in his small office underneath the stands. Smith, 26, is
the Foxes' general manager. In the major leagues, general manager
is an exalted position. Here, his door is always open and slamming
shut.

A player stops in.

"Pepsi or orange?" Smith asks.

Smith takes the Pepsi from an ancient, peeling refrigerator in an
even smaller back room. The player slides 50 cents across the counter.

"Very few free ones go out of here," Smith says after the door
shuts.

His black hair parts in the middle. He majored in French and
seemed headed for a more esoteric calling when he heard about a
possibility in baseball. He got the job, in the commissioner's office in
New York. The next year he worked in the Chicago White Sox office.
In 1983 the White Sox appointed him general manager at Appleton,
their lowest farm club. "I may be the only guy in baseball working
his way down," he says.

The door opens again.

"Hey, Bill, got a mop?"

Smith cleans up spills, rakes the infield, helps out at the concession stands, makes speeches downtown, gets companies to stage pro-
motion nights at the ball park. This season he's had Wendy's Paint-
er's Cap Night. Tonight he has the Security Bank sponsoring a
breakdancing exhibition after the game by an out-of-town group.
"But this is the one I *really* want to do," he says, going into his back
room and pulling out a fisherman's hat from a big box. "Looks good,
huh? Maybe next year. Couldn't get a sponsor this year."

Smith is the only Appleton salaried employee, and he is paid by
the White Sox. A baseball rarity: The Foxes are a community-owned

team—$5 will buy one share in the team. The board of directors includes a janitor, plumber, machinist, shipping clerk, school principal, tavern owner, police chief and commercial artist who designed, without charge, the team logo.

It's almost game time when Patti McFarland arrives, scorebook and pencil in hand. She's wearing a blue Appleton Foxes pullover jersey and red, white and blue Chicago White Sox cap. McFarland has been to practically every Foxes game since 1958, and has been coming to the park since 1940, when the team was called the Papermakers. Even when she gets off late from work two nights a week, at the Prange Way discount department store out on the highway, she makes the last few innings. Always, she's loved to take pictures. "I have oodles of 'em. Some in albums, some in boxes. I'm trying to get 'em sorted," she says.

Two of her favorites are little black-and-white snapshots she got of Earl Weaver, former Oriole manager who managed the Foxes in 1962, and the Orioles' Cal Ripken Jr. as a 2-year-old. "His dad, Cal Sr., was the catcher here," she says. "Drove the team bus, too. Weaver had an argument with the bus driver. I forgot how it went, but I think the driver abandoned them. The Ripkens lived in an apartment over Kirby Cleaners."

★   ★   ★

The game begins. The covered stands are almost filled. Everyone is settled in like an extended family on a large back porch, watching the kids at play on the lawn. Like distant relatives, some visitors are introduced. The public address system acknowledges: the parents of Jim Hickey, a pitcher; a busload of White Sox boosters up from Chicago to see the farmhands ("Give 'em a hand"), and "a great group of people who drove all the way over here from Hastings, Minn., to see tonight's game—300 miles just to watch a minor-league game. How 'bout that?"

Patti McFarland sits on the left-field side with Ollie and Bob Fondow, from Oshkosh. The two women yell as loud as anyone.

"C'm-o-o-on, Mr. T."

An explanation by one: "Mr . T—that's Mike Taylor. Mr. T hits everything."

An addendum: "They play their hearts out."

"C'm-o-o-n, Mr. T. You can do it."

After every inning, there's a rush to the beer stand. Russ Luebben, the retired deputy chief of the Appleton Fire Department, slides cans of Bud and Miller across the counter. Luebben is the secretary of the Foxes; he keeps apprised of the action by peeking around the corner of his stand to the new Miller scoreboard in left-center field, and serves as major-domo to the boys who retrieve foul balls, which, scuffed or not, are re-used in the game. "Two bits a ball we give them," says Luebben.

In time, the umpire calls for the lights, but Bill Smith is missing —probably off averting some crisis. But he's got the key to throw the switch.

"Hey, Milt, have you paid the light bill?" a fan yells.

Milt Drier, the team's treasurer, assures him he has, and continues chatting with a big, dark-haired man who is blowing rings of blue cigar smoke directly upward. Little white NY letters are stitched on the heart of his dark blue polo shirt. Joe Begani, scout for the Yankees.

His sunglasses are pushed back on his head. He's got a yellow pencil behind one ear, and a stopwatch that seems small in his hand. He may look laconic—he yawns now and then—but he doesn't miss a thing. He's always timing—runners going from home to first, the catchers' throw to second. Begani says he once scouted the Foxes' young first-year manager, Sal Rende. Rende used to be an Indian farmhand. "He could handle the bat," says Begani, "but he had concrete feet." He laughs.

Drier moves over to say a few words to Lyle Weden, president and part-owner of the Timbers. They both hold cans of Miller. "We farm, that's our business," says Weden, a heavy-set man with glasses. He is speaking not of his farm team but his primary occupation—tomatoes, corn, things like that. "I guess the distinction of our county is that we have more cows than people," he says.

He drinks some beer. The Wausau third baseman is wearing No. 60—an old Seattle Mariners shirt probably used at spring training by a raw rookie. "It's a hand-me-down situation," says Weden. "But in minor league baseball you're right here, 50 feet behind the plate. You see all the little things that you don't see in the big leagues, sitting way up in the stands . . ."

Actually, the view is exquisite. In the bottom of the 10th inning, Russ Morman, the Foxes' first baseman, slides into home with the winning run as the Wausau catcher applies the tag an instant late. It's as if the whole place is on top of the play, leaning over for a perfect look, and just about everyone goes wild. The Foxes, en masse, charge from the bench and mob Morman before he can dust himself off or move more than a few feet. Meanwhile, the Wausau catcher and his manager, who has bolted from the wings, argue jaw to jaw with the umpire right on top of the plate.

5-4, Appleton.

A half-hour later, the Wausau players queue up at the door of their bus. Most of them are silent and have their heads bent. They had wanted that game. Their fans are getting on a second bus, right behind. They'll all head home, 85 miles to the northwest. One bus, with the players, not their fans, will be back first thing in the morning. It's a grind, but nothing compared to the ride from here to, say, Burlington, down in the southeast corner of Iowa. That one goes on forever; this weekend is merely a Midwest League "commuter series"—it saves on the motel and meals.

A soft rain, almost a mist, falls. Lyle Weden's satin baseball jacket glistens.

A Wausau fan, quietly and earnestly, to a departing player: "You'll get 'em tomorrow."

A small-town Saturday night is almost over.

But not quite, not for Bill Smith anyway. His biggest problem still remains: The breakdancers haven't shown up. The crowd is growing restless.

"The breakdancers just left Oshkosh," somebody says.

"Oh, God," says Smith, clapping his forehand.

Ten minutes later, a long 10 minutes in the life of Bill Smith, someone runs up: "They're here. They're here."

Smith takes the grandstand steps two at a time, up to the public address announcer, Bob Lloyd, 39 years behind the mike: "Could we call on your talents once again? Just thank everyone for their patience and everything. It'll only be a few more minutes."

Pausing, Smith brushes back his wet hair that has fallen across his forehead. He's been running around in the rain.

"Tomorrow," he says, "will be better."

★   ★   ★

Tomorrow comes up perfect: blue sky, bright sun, low humidity. A great baseball day.

My sons shag flies in the outfield during batting practice, one in left standing next to Russ Morman, the other in right alongside Tarnow. They're out there talking to the players between hits. They chase, they talk some more. They've fallen into the rhythm. Milt Drier, the Foxes' treasurer, has just sat down from taking some swings in the batting cage.

"The only way to make it go at this level is volunteer help," he says, taking a Salem from his shirt pocket. "You have to have a whole bunch of people giving a whole lot of time." Behind a counter in the clean yellow corridor beneath the grandstand, Drier's wife, Helen, and daughter, Becky, are turning over hot dogs on a grill.

In his office, Smith is handing out a Pepsi but gives the player his 50 cents back. "Thank you." A big smile from the player. "That's Charlie Moore," Smith explains shortly. "He got the winning hit last night."

"Hey, Bill," says a man sticking his head in the door, "the concession stand needs four rolls of nickels."

Patti McFarland is about to tack up newspaper clippings on three bulletin boards under the stands. They're from the local Post-Crescent ("Foxes Shade Kenosha on 11th Inning Balk"), and items from papers in Glens Falls, New York, and Denver, so that fans can keep up with ex-Foxes progressing in the White Sox organization. The people here never forget a Fox—names like Boog Powell, Bucky Dent, Rich Gossage, Dean Chance, Sparky Lyle, LaMarr Hoyt, scores of others who came through here.

The crowd is smaller today. A man has a radio on the seat next to him, listening to the Cubs' game. The radio voice is saying there are more than 39,000 squeezed into Wrigley Field, and then a few minutes later he's saying something about 40,000. Another man nearby wonders, "How many can they get in there?" My boys are up in back, eating hot dogs. Down close, Drier's 83-year-old mother, Lila, is licking an ice cream cone.

"I hate to see those $10 hits," says Smith, after a broken-bat single by an Appleton player.

Begani puffs on his cigar, and gets Tarnow's "release time," from when the ball leaves the catcher's hand until it smacks a glove out at second. Two seconds flat. "He's quick," says Begani.

A Wausau pitcher, who worked last night and is sitting in front of Begani timing pitches with a radar gun, turns and asks the scout, "Did you get our catcher's time?"

"Oh, he's 1.9," Begani replies instantly. "I got him last year at Quad Cities."

Once a player in the West Texas League and the Mountain States League and some other leagues he can't easily recall, Begani now roams the Midwest League. Every once in a while he'll see something that will make him sit up straight. It happened last summer in Waterloo. Begani grades speed from the batter's box to first base from two to eight. Last year he saw an eight.

"First eight I've ever seen," he says. "Pookie Bernstine."

★   ★   ★

Late in the afternoon, after the Foxes have lost, 7-4, in 12 innings, we say goodbye to Bill and Milt and Joe and Patti and Russ and Helen and Becky. The boys wait for Greg Tarnow, thank him for the bat, and they talk for a while next to the grandstand.

Every other Sunday when I was a boy I rode with my parents up stop-light-choked U.S. 40 to visit my grandparents. Now the tourist cabins and 20-unit motels of the '40s are replaced by globs of concrete—shopping malls and "clothing outlets." On the bend coming into town I look for the tiny park where my father took me Sunday afternoons, yet I don't even see the corn that ringed the outfield fence. But though their number has shrunk, there still are towns where minor league players bring their major league dreams. From the ghettos and the suburbs, from California and Caracas they come —to places like Appleton.

We drive out of town, heading south.

"So Bill is engaged to Becky?"

"Yeah. Did you meet her?"

"Yeah, she's nice."

"Where'd the scout say he was going next?"

"Beloit."

"Where's that?"

"Where's the Mississippi from here?"

The sun slants through the car's side windows.

"Wisconsin looks better today than it did yesterday."

"I think Tarnow fell under .200 today. If he could just hit a little more..."

And then: "You know, we didn't get to do *everything* in Apple-ton." I am tempted to remind them that yesterday they were worry-ing about not having *anything* to do in Appleton.

We liked the small-town virtues we had seen. But we knew, too, that $600 a month or so, even for the pleasure of playing baseball, was not great, and that another small-town principle was at work: up and out. The best often move on.

"Look at this. Al Jones pitched here last year and this year he got up to the White Sox. Amazing."

As we drive along, even the searing sounds of rock seem all right to me.

"Hey, did you see that, did you see that? Dad turned the radio *up*."

We look at each other and laugh. We don't say anything else for a while, nor do we have to.

The Diamond Palaces
(Third of three parts)

To really know the game of baseball, you must feel something for the parks. The old parks, vine-covered Wrigley and whitewashed Comiskey and history-laden Tiger Stadium, home of Cobb and Ka-line. Think of Fenway in Boston, which John Updike called "a lyric little bandbox of a ball park." You just take the green line.

The outfield fences at Ebbets Field were festooned with signs for Gem razor blades and Botany ties.

The Polo Grounds had short foul lines and a Grand Canyon for center field.

And then there was and is the Big House itself, Yankee Stadium, once three-tiered in all its glory but now wearing modern clothes. The subway still comes out of the hole and, bang, there the stadium is, right out the window.

We go to parks to see the game, of course, but also perhaps to remind ourselves in a tactile way how constant baseball is in a tur-moiled world, even if the turmoil itself has taken some of our best-loved fields.

DETROIT—Ernie Harwell's catbird seat hangs low and close behind home plate at Tiger Stadium. There's the Yankees' Ken Grif-fey, taking his pregame cuts in the batting cage. You can almost reach down and tap him on the shoulder. Ernie Harwell's been sit-ting here 25 years, broadcasting games.

To him, Tiger Stadium is the perfect place to celebrate baseball. The game's been played on the same city corner since 1900; Ty Cobb played here every day. Once green, now blue, either way the park's interior is distinctive, not like those new sterile *facilities.* "Cookie cutter stadiums," says Harwell, shaking his head. "They have no personality, like drug stores and shopping malls. You don't know whether you're in Des Moines, Kansas City or Providence, R.I."

The night before my sons and I began our baseball trip, we had watched the Tigers on Monday Night Baseball. We decided then to make Detroit our first stop. The Tigers were way out in front in the American League East. More than that, I had long wanted to show them Tiger Stadium. It's a shrine—Ruthian blasts left there and landed on streets; Gehrig took himself out of the starting lineup there after playing 2,130 straight games, 14 years' worth.

That night their mother packed a medicine bag of Bufferin, Amoxil chewables, erthromycin, Cortisporin, Neosporin, metaproterenol, Phenergan. Modern-day pilgrims we were. At 7 the next morning we kissed my wife and daughters goodbye, and pulled away. We made a beeline west, turned right at Toledo and headed north. Destination: Motown, and the ancient white cube at Michigan and Trumbull.

Now it is nearly game time, and the narrow concourses and ramps are jamming with humanity. Never have we seen such intensity. People are shouting, chanting, filling up at the concession stands: They have a pennant on their minds. Ernie Harwell is taping a car commercial as we squeeze into his booth. "Tell 'em Ernie Harwell sent you," he ends the spiel.

"Ernie Harwell is a professional," my father used to say. Together, we'd listen to him on radio, either the big brown floor model or the little white Philco box with the volume knob gone and the two wires hanging out the back. Harwell's reassuring voice was the best thing about the Orioles in the mid-'50s, when they first got into the majors and sank to the bottom of the American League, sticking there. He'd give us the game's skeleton, and he'd flesh it out in our minds. At the beach one night, we went out to the car and picked him up on the radio. "Here comes the ninth," he was saying, and I could see the teams changing sides.

Ernie Harwell, a slim man with a big voice, has gotten the car ad the way he wants it, and tells us of the time he broadcast the third and deciding game of the Dodgers-Giants playoff in 1951, a large piece of Polo Grounds history. In the bottom of the ninth, with two men on base, Bobby Thomson hit a ball into the lower left-field seats for a 5-4 Giants victory and the pennant. But it was Harwell's fate to be doing the game on TV. The narration that became instant lore belonged to Russ Hodges, on radio: *The Giants win the pennant!!! The Giants win the pennant!!! I don't believe it! I don't believe it! I do not believe it!!!*

"A fan in Brooklyn had turned on his tape machine and got it," says Harwell. "He sent it to Russ, and Russ sent him $10."

Harwell pauses for a wry glance at the past.

"Only Mrs. Harwell and I know I broadcast it, too."

Harwell loves coming to Tiger Stadium. It seats 52,687, but it's homey as a parlor. No matter where you sit you're *in* the game.

We're in the right-field stands. Right out in front of us, hands on knees, is Rusty Kuntz of the Tigers. Dave Winfield plays right for the Yankees. "He's huge," my older son, Billy, says. Six-feet-six, 220 pounds of huge.

The crowd does the "wave," one section after another jumping to its feet with arms upraised. "I see Ernie up there," says my other son, David. In the late innings, the Tigers cöme back to win, 7-6, and the crowd, 41,192, leaves as it came, in uproar.

In the Tigers' clubhouse, Alan Trammell, the shortstop, is saying, yes, he grew up in San Diego and used to go to the games there, but the experience was nothing like that here at Tiger Stadium. "We'd sit up in the top deck of the concrete stadium. Everybody looked like ants."

Behind the Tigers' third-base dugout, the players' wives are sitting in a cluster, waiting. There's no one else except the grounds crew watering the infield. The burning white lights still beat down. It's so quiet you can hear the water tapping the earth.

★   ★   ★

One weekday afternoon my father took me to the Polo Grounds. We rattled uptown on the subway, then walked to a gate in front. Suddenly, it began raining and we stood there awhile, just under cover, waiting. Maybe only a half hour had passed when they called the game off. Back to the subway. We rode a long time, long enough for it to stop raining. We were in Brooklyn now. Wash hung on lines. The Dodgers were playing that day, and we went in . . .

"Let's go to Wrigley Field now," one of my sons says.

Now? It's 10 o'clock at night. Nothing's going on there. Can't you wait until tomorrow?

"C'mon. We want to see it," says the other.

We drive north, then come to Clark—it sounds like the street. Could be we are the only three people in America, at least the only three on Clark Street, searching for an empty ball park in the dark.

"There." The neon in the Chicago night lights up the art deco sign: "Wrigley Field. Chicago Cubs."

"Bad."

One of the boys leans out the car window and takes a picture.

The next afternoon we come out on the El.

★   ★   ★

If Ernie Harwell has the alpha of baseball seats, Bill Veeck occupies the omega.

He sits in Wrigley Field's bleachers, dead center field.

He is shirtless, with *his* people. Even when he owned baseball teams—the Indians, Browns, White Sox twice—and could hobnob with whom he wished, he chose instead the company of wise men in cheap seats. His dictum then and now: a fan's knowledge increases in inverse proportion to the price of his ticket.

"What could be better than an afternoon out here?" he asks. "I'm a fan of escape. I happen to think escape is a very good thing."

On the public address system: "Get your pencils and scorecards ready and I'll give you the starting lineups for today's bal-l-l-l game."

Veeck has come home. He began as an office boy at Wrigley, $18 a week. In 1938, he hung the vines on the Wrigley wall. Veeck, whose father was a sportswriter-turned-Cubs' president, suggested ivy to Phil Wrigley, who wanted to beautify the park. Wrigley preferred trees, and had them put in. But the leaves all blew away. One day Wrigley called Veeck and said he'd be bringing by friends the next day to see the ivy. *Ivy!* Veeck worked fast.

He got ivy and bittersweet uptown and rounded up a couple of friends at the park and some lights and that night strung the lights. "It's the only time," Veeck laughs, "that Wrigley had lights." The bittersweet carried Phil Wrigley's day and the ivy eventually took over. Now, after all these years, Veeck has the time to look down and contemplate his work. Dust to dust.

"Did you see this?" He points to his artificial leg, poking out from his tan Bermudas. "I got a fresh paint job. Now it matches the tan on the other leg."

The appendage has become another part of the Wrigley charm.

Veeck also got the scoreboard put up years ago. The large artifact rises behind him from the top of the bleachers. One of my boys noticed later, "Don't you think there's a lot of wasted space on it." There is. On most weekdays, all other major league games are at night. And so, next to every other matchup goes the notation "Nite Game," nothing more. The big board mutely testifies to Wrigley's ultimate, and unique, charm: day ball.

What numbers do come up on the board are put there quaintly. The score by innings and the pitchers' numbers are still changed from inside the scoreboard, by hand. The numbers for batter, ball, strike and out look like bulbs, but they're actually little aluminum discs that come through slots in the scoreboard when a button is pushed in the press box. It takes eight discs to make a "1". You can hear the clicking of the discs if you're high enough in the bleachers.

Some people sitting out here have seen Grover Cleveland Alexander, maybe even Tinker, Evers and Chance.

Younger ones, as the Cubs growled a bit in the late '60s, gave off this chant:

Every time I go to town,
The boys all kick my dog around
Makes no difference if he is a hound
Ya better stop kicking my dog around.

It used to be when all ball parks were in cities, part of the ambiance was the sight of people craning from the windows of buildings or sitting on rooftops. From a window beyond Ebbets Field a person could flash a mirror in an enemy batter's eye. Behind right field at Wrigley today, many faithful have climbed atop the old brick and stone houses that line Sheffield Street like a Hopper painting.

PUHLAY BALLLLLL!

My kind of town, Chicago is . . .

When I get back to the boys—they had been off eating—I explain about Veeck. Most of all, they approve his having had the artificial turf infield torn out of Comiskey Park in the mid-'70s. If you look out there in center field, I say, you can see him. You can pick him out by his painted leg. It's glinting in the gloaming.

I tell them I also met Yosh Kawano, the Cubs' clubhouse boy. A Wrigley fixture, he has an agreement with the team that he can stick around as long as he wants. Hardly a boy, he showed up in Chicago in 1938. He had made himself useful at the White Sox spring training camp in California that year, and to the surprise of the Sox met them when they arrived home.

We start talking about Wrigley and he gets all excited. He takes me up in the stands to show me how wide the cross aisles are. Then he gets onto the subject of seats. Wrigley's seats are comfortable, he says, but "let me show you something." You have to move quickly even to keep close to Kawano, but he's distinctively dressed so you don't lose him in a crowd: He's got on a white tennis hat with the brim turned down all around and a white T-shirt, and he's got a cigar of extreme length mashed in his teeth.

"Come here. Come here." I follow him into what is the Cubs' old clubhouse, where a group of ushers are sitting, and then through a door, and then we're under the stands, crouched beneath a bare light bulb. He's rooting around in stuff. Finally: "Here." And he pulls out a chair. It's a great old Wrigley Field chair, nice and wide.

"Now come with me." So I follow him, past the ushers in the room, back outside, right past the ticket taker at the gate, *out of the park.* "Hey, Yosh. Hey, Yosh," people call as we pad down Waveland Avenue behind left field. At the corner he takes me into Murphy's Bleachers, a bar. I follow him upstairs, then downstairs. All the time he is looking around. "Here's one. Sit in this chair. Now that's a chair." An even older vintage Wrigley chair.

"So you were out on the street?" asks one of the boys. "And they let you back in?"

Walked right back in with Yosh.

"Did you meet Murphy?"

Sure. He was out on the sidewalk, rolling in a keg of beer.

"You see that guy up there? That's Harry Caray."

Sure enough. And in the middle of the seventh, of course, Caray interrupts his TV broadcast to lead the crowd in singing "Take Me Out to the Ball Game."

The only person I'm sorry we haven't met is Ernie Banks, because he's Mr. Cub. Five hundred and twelve career home runs. Yet, quite by accident a couple of weeks later, we almost bump into him. We're walking around the outside of San Francisco's Candlestick Park before the All-Star Game when there is Banks at my shoulder. "Do you know where the party is?" he asks. He is looking for one given by the Giants' owner, but the real party as he knows is going on every day at Wrigley.

"Wrigley Field. Beautiful Wrigley Field," he exclaims. Ernie Banks talks that way when it comes to Wrigley. "Hey, we're going to have a World Series at Wrigley Field this year. Are you guys coming to the Series? OK. OK. I'll see you at the Series."

It is strange to see Mr. Cub on the West Coast. He lives now in Los Angeles, but Wrigley Field, Chicago, was home to him for 19 years. It still is for him a spiritual haven.

His first look came in September 1953: "You know, it had no lights, brick walls, vines on the walls, close to the fans, daytime baseball. I just looked around . . .

"Then I got up to bat for the first time—this was batting practice. As I look back, I don't know why I didn't think about getting nervous. I heard them say a few things, like this guy is really little—I wasn't very big, 150 pounds. But I think the second pitch I hit into the seats. Boom, that ball just jumped out of there. And in my mind I said, 'This is easy. What's the big deal about this?' I just did what was natural."

★　　　★　　　★

To Comiskey Park, oldest in the majors. The gates opened July 1, 1910. It was billed as "the world's greatest baseball palace." We get off the Dan Ryan Expressway and we're there.

No game today. The Sox are in Minnesota. Inside, it's cold and green and haunting and huge-looking. It's double-decked almost all the way around. Actually, it holds fewer than Tiger Stadium but the more distant seats and the outfield acreage give the feeling of expanse. A premier pitcher of the old White Stockings, Ed Walsh, had something to do with all that space in front of the fences. "An empty ballpark is awesome," says Billy. This one has arches, and steel girders that sprout from between green wooden chairs, all with their seats upturned, all in order. Today, Joel Glass takes us around; a junior at the University of Iowa, he has a summer job here, the kind to which the boys immediately aspire. "Last year," he's saying, "Luzinski hit three on or over the roof . . ."

The dugouts are dug deep and the crown of the field is high, so we imagine while sitting in there during a game you might not see much of the shortstop or third baseman, maybe just their caps. The exploding scoreboard in center field—another Bill Veeck idea—has a control room behind home plate that looks like the cockpit of a 747, with more knobs and dials than can be learned without a formal course. But the image we savor most is the panorama from up here in the second deck in right, as far around and high up as we can climb. The green seats, row upon row, roll away in perfect straight lines to the yellow right-field foul pole, turn toward home and curve on around, wrapping our reverie.

"You can't get this feeling," says Billy, "even on color TV."

★　　　★　　　★

What lay ahead after a game was maybe the sweetest part,

coming home. I was younger then than my boys are now, but I re-member the rides in the car, replaying the victories, making sense of the defeats. The defeats wouldn't seem as bad by the time we had reached the vinegar works and slid the windows up, my father hav-ing by then spoken to my soul. It was like that all but once. He had brought me what seemed a long way to a major league game: De-troit at Washington. We sat in Griffith Stadium's upper deck, left field. I recall growing tired, then magically waking up in bed the next morning, my father having plucked me from my seat and put me there. That one game remains frozen and unfinished, like a dream.

A few weeks later, the boys and I are watching the Angels and Brewers at Anaheim Stadium. The Big A is a facility, not a park. Still, it's a good place to watch, and play, baseball. The seats are orange and red. The field is as fine as any we've seen on our trip. Like Dodger Stadium, where we've just been, the grass is Bermuda and the clay of the infield is mixed with brick dust. The grass is cut short, almost like a golf green. Our seats are down in the left-field corner. Across the outfield, a bright full moon hangs directly above the right-field foul pole. A cool breeze makes me happy I've brought along a windbreaker.

"You know, 30 years from now," says Billy, "maybe I'll bring my kids here. I'll say, 'Son, this is one of the fine old parks. See that green stuff out there—that's grass. And there's no dome. Look up, see the sky.' "

A few days later we head home.

Judge's Comments

In a strong field, one entry stood out this year. William Gildea's three-part story of his baseball odyssey succeeds, as all good writing does, in capturing the essence of its subject. It is a subject that is close to the heart of America, and Gildea also captures the heartbeat. He does it with writing that is detailed but concise, clear but compelling.

The foundation of every good story is, of course, a good idea. The idea to roam the nation in search of the national pastime is a natural. The result is a story that, like the game itself, is slow-paced, thought-provoking, rich and satisfying.

The thread that runs through this story and those of all the other finalists is the writers' attention to detail, the solid reporting and careful observation that are the foundation on which good writing rests. The lesson that these pros offer to the rest of us is that facility with the language is a complement to, and not a replacement for, old-fashioned legwork. First, they have gone out to look and listen. Then they have thought about their observations. Finally, they have found the precise words to convey observation and insight.

Only the Good Die Young

HIGH SCHOOL BASKETBALL

By *JOHN SCHULIAN*

From the Philadelphia Daily News
Copyright © 1984, Philadelphia Newspapers, Inc.

The news was like death itself. Someone ran up and said Ben Wilson had been shot, and the next thing Bob Hambric knew, he was racing out the door and down the street, not quite believing that any of this was happening.

Hambric was Ben's coach, the surrogate father who had overseen the growth of a skinny, clumsy freshman into the nation's foremost high school basketball player, and every step he took jumbled his emotions a little more. "I was in a fog," he says, "but then I saw the school policeman hustling out there, too, and I knew there was trouble. He's used to panic."

So Hambric moved even faster, increasing the distance between himself and the elementary school students he had been introducing to the wonders of Simeon Vocational, the students who were supposed to hear Ben Wilson speak next.

And Ben Wilson lay on the gritty sidewalk half a block north of Simeon, felled by two bullets from a .22-caliber Ruger revolver and numbed by shock.

He was propped against the wire fence next to the A&A Store, where he had come on his lunch hour with two girls to wander amid the video games and school jackets. Simeon's football coach was giving Ben first aid by the time Hambric reached his side, and inside the A&A a student was describing how it had happened, Ben bumping a stranger and saying, "Excuse me," and the stranger telling the kid with him to shoot Ben. It was the Tuesday before Thanksgiving and a dream had been shattered.

Now the school policeman was trying to hold back the crowd that was spilling out into Vincennes Avenue. A crowd—how ironic. Ben

Wilson always drew a crowd. He was 17 years old, and what he could do with a basketball meant that he was forever surrounded by teammates, admirers and recruiters. They filled his ears with the sound of adoration, but in these tortured minutes, he couldn't hear a thing.

Maybe it was just as well. The air was flooded with the wailing of sirens and grief. "The kids were crying," says John Everett, the pro football official who flexes his muscles as an assistant principal at Simeon. "I broke down, too." But Bob Hambric held his ground, refusing to let the tears inside him fall, waiting for his world to stop spinning out of control.

He looked for a pool of blood, saw none and took heart. The wound that was visible in Ben's side seemed almost harmless, just a puncture in his windbreaker. "I was thinking the kids he played with would have to learn to get along without him for a while," Hambric says. They could start that very afternoon, in fact, when a photographer from USA Today was scheduled to take their picture as the No. 1 high school team in the country. There were plenty of pictures of Ben that could be sent along later.

That was the only consolation Hambric could find as he watched Ben being placed in an ambulance. The attendants worked with the practiced haste of men steeled by the random cruelty on Chicago's South Side, and yet they still overlooked one thing, Ben's blue-and-white stocking cap.

Hambric picked it off the sidewalk, flicked the dirt off it and put it in his pocket. He figured Ben would need the cap when he came home from the hospital.

★   ★   ★

They say this city has never seen a funeral to equal it. More people turned out when Mayor Richard J. Daley died, and the same was true of the passing of Cardinal Cody, the archbishop of Chicago. But Ben Wilson was a kid.

He wasn't a politician who built an empire by trading jobs for votes, and he wasn't a religious leader who weathered controversy by showering his flock with blessings. Ben Wilson was a black basketball player with a golden future. He was someone for his people to rally around in a city where not being white can still get you chased from your home, chased into the bitter night.

So they came to say goodbye to Ben Wilson, both the family and friends who had known him as "Benji" and the strangers who had merely seen his name light up the sports page. There may have been as many as 8,000 of them at his wake in Simeon's 600-seat gym. "They were three deep for something like six hours," John Everett says. "At one time the line stretched for two blocks. It was unbelievable." And the funeral was even more so—perhaps 10,000 mourners crowding inside and outside the headquarters of Operation PUSH, the civil rights organization, before Ben Wilson was laid to rest.

The swell of emotion was as startling and heart-tugging as his mother's courage. Five hours after her son died at dawn on November 21, Mary Wilson stood before a student assembly at Simeon and said, "I know hatred can never return good. I'm just sad. I don't feel hate for anyone."

Whatever chance there was for hatred must have been eliminated by sorrow when Mary Wilson listened to the doctors tell her how badly her son was hurt. She is a nurse, which means she has listened to those droning, unemotional voices before, but now the wounds she was hearing about were in her son. One of them was in his groin—no problem. But the other had struck his aorta. "When they told Mrs. Wilson that," Bob Hambric says, "I'm sure she knew right away how serious it was."

It was serious and it was wrong, the way every senseless shooting is. But there was something that made the killing of Ben Wilson worse yet, because it violated one of the unwritten rules of inner-city life: Athletes are off limits to violence. They are the ones who have a ticket to better places, and they are not to be deterred by either gangs or free-lancing thugs.

Simple geography should have reinforced that premise at Simeon, for the school is surrounded by a steel mill, a 7-Up bottling plant and an assortment of warehouses. There is no neighborhood for a gang to call its turf, and when houses finally do come into view, they are clean and solid, a proud statement that the rules of decency are meant to be obeyed.

But every time Coach Hambric's friend, Mike Washington, thinks of the two 16-year-olds charged with Ben Wilson's murder, he knows how little all of that meant. "Those guys," says Washington, "broke the rules."

And they ended a story that shimmered with happiness.

★　　　★　　　★

In the beginning, Ben Wilson was a project. He came to Simeon on the coattails of a better player, a player who was stronger and faster but couldn't live up to the academic and athletic demands that Bob Hambric put on him. He flunked out, but Ben Wilson stayed.

He wasn't just skinny then, he was short, too. Somehow, though, Hambric saw beyond those 5 feet, 11 inches. "I'd always wanted a big guard," the coach says, "and I thought Ben could be it." Nobody else understood why when they saw Ben flopping around as the last man on the freshman-sophomore team.

"He didn't even start a game, and Coach Hambric was always talking about how great the kid was going to be," John Everett says. "I just shook my head and said, 'Good luck, Coach.' "

But luck didn't make Ben Wilson the player that Indiana, DePaul, Illinois, Georgetown, Iowa and Michigan were fighting over. Oh, maybe you could argue otherwise after learning that he grew to 6-3 by his sophomore season, and 6-7 as a junior, and 6-8 going on 6-9 this year. "You could almost see him growing when he was walking down the halls," Hambric says. The measuring tape didn't shoot 150 jump shots a day for Ben, though, nor did it jump rope for hours, run mile after mile, or soak up everything his coach told him.

"Ben was special," Hambric says, "and I felt I was special because I was chosen to guide and train him. There was a natural attraction between us. We did things together, went to shows, played basketball Sunday mornings with the old guys I usually run with. Ben did all his studying in my office at school, and if he wasn't studying, we'd talk about things. I'll probably never have another player like that."

The reasons are as obvious as the Illinois state championship that Simeon won last March, and as obscure as the day Ben Wilson discovered what he could be. Hambric had the varsity practicing at one end of the gym, and he wanted to make a point to a senior guard who was loafing. "So I looked down to the other end of the gym and hollered, 'Ben, come here,' " Hambric says. "Ben came down, got a couple baskets, did what I wanted him to do. I thought it would make the senior angry, but he just laid down right there. I asked Ben, 'You want to stay here?' and he said, 'Yeah, yeah.' " He didn't leave until he had no choice.

In between, he laid the foundation for Simeon's current 34-game winning streak and convinced the prestigious Athletes for a Better Education to name him this season's premier player. It was an honor that escaped Isiah Thomas and Mark Aguirre and Terry Cummings and all the other big names Chicago's high schools have produced in the last decade. Maybe Ben Wilson earned it because he covered more of the court than any of them did.

Whenever fouls hog-tied Simeon's center, Ben would move into the middle and throw his 185 pounds around as recklessly as he could. If there was trouble against the press, he would bring the ball upcourt, using his height to see over the defense. Sometimes, however, he made you forget about his size.

"He was always able to maintain the ability of a small person," Hambric says. "He could drive to the basket and fold his body up. There wasn't a crack he couldn't get through if he needed to."

And yet the way to remember him is standing tall. Think of the game he played against Corliss High School last season when Hambric had benched two starters for missing practice and Simeon trailed in the first half by as many as 10 points. "Ben just rose up over everybody else," Hambric says. In the process, the deficit shrank to three points, and then to one as Ben dunked an offensive rebound. A heartbeat later, he was blocking a shot at the other end of the floor and taking the ball back to where he could unleash the last-second jumper that won the game.

That was Ben Wilson as he seemed destined to be forever—unstoppable.

★   ★   ★

He was buried in his traveling uniform. His mother will hang the new home uniform he never wore in his closet. His coach gets the ski cap and the game films from last season that he didn't think he'd have the courage to watch.

"I thought at one point I would just erase them," Bob Hambric says. "I guess I'll have to buy a new case of tape instead."

That way, he can always have Ben Wilson.

It is something everybody in Chicago is trying to do now. They will retire Ben's number 25 at Simeon in the spring, and when the school builds a new gym, it will be named after him. Money is coming in from across the country for a memorial fund to aid Ben's family and the 2-month-old child he fathered out of wedlock. Scarcely a day passes when a newspaper story doesn't point out that Ben was just one of 90 young people Chicago has lost to gunfire this year, and in City Hall politicians of every persuasion are grinding their axes on the tragedy. So much tumult, so much shouting, but some things never change.

In front of Simeon Vocational, its doors locked by a city teachers strike, a kid dribbles a basketball. How old can he be, 11, 12? He feints and whirls, even flicks the ball between his legs as he works his way past the school and toward the spot where Ben Wilson was stopped by two bullets.

Surely the kid knew who Ben was. Maybe he is even imagining himself as Ben in full blossom. But you will never get anyone to believe that he can hear Ben's coach saying, "Tomorrow isn't promised to you," or that he understands he is traveling on a street of broken dreams. And that is as it should be.

Pincay: Monkey Off His Back

HORSE RACING

By *ART SPANDER*

From the San Francisco Examiner
Copyright © 1984, San Francisco Examiner

This time the frustration would end for Laffit Pincay. This time he would grab for roses while others grasped for answers. This time on a gray afternoon in the Blue Grass country he would have a horse under his saddle and a monkey off his back.

He had been called the finest jockey never to finish first in the Kentucky Derby. Bad mounts and bad breaks always left him back in the pack, picking up the dirt clods while somebody else, a Shoemaker, a Delahoussaye, picked up the accolades. He was Sam Snead in the U.S. Open, Ray Meyer in the NCAA basketball tournament. He couldn't win the big one. Until yesterday.

Then, in marvelous control of Swale, a beautiful colt with a pedigree as impressive as the House of Tudor, Pincay arrived at horse racing's most cherished locale, the winner's circle at historic Churchill Downs. A mountain had been climbed.

Pincay, with millions in winnings, with the respect of his peers, said persistent failures in the Derby did not concern him. It was just a horse race, he suggested. Indeed. And the Mona Lisa is just a painting.

★   ★   ★

Hemingway said it isn't wise to want something too much. And wisely, Laffit tap-danced around the disappointment when his horses couldn't run quickly enough around the oval.

"A lot of people say it is a monkey on my back," Pincay would reassure, grinning in defense. "But I don't think so. Maybe I'm destined to run this race all my life and never win. I am prepared to accept that."

Acceptance is no longer required. Ten times he had come up short. Ride No. 11 took him into history. The association of the best horse and best jockey made light work of the 110th Kentucky Derby and of the idea that a female horse could keep up with the boys.

Swale is an offspring of 1977 Derby and Triple Crown winner Seattle Slew. In the hyperbole and dreams of a normal pre-race week, the horse was surprisingly ignored.

We had been told about the ladies, the favored filly Althea and her stablemate, Life's Magic. About Silent King, starting in the 20th post position out there near Cincinnati. About Taylor's Special, trained by Bill Mott, who once slept in pig stalls in a barn. About Vanlandingham, ridden by local hero Pat Day. And, of course, about the horse that wasn't here, Devil's Bag, trained by the old man, Woody Stephens.

★   ★   ★

Stephens withdrew Devil's Bag on Tuesday. But he didn't weep. Instead he came out of a hospital bed, where he had been recuperating from pneumonia, and predicted his other horse, Swale, would capture the Derby and a nation's fancy.

This was a marriage of fable: Swale, owned by famous Claiborne Farm, which had never won a Derby, ridden by Pincay, who had never won a Derby, saddled by Stephens, whose hopes seemed to be disintegrating. Swale, in post position 15, where horses get jostled like shoppers at a bargain basement sale.

For Pincay, Swale might as well have been marked Fragile. Laffit brought the colt out quickly and smoothly into the first turn and the crowd of 126,453 thundered its approval, alongside Althea.

What was a nice girl like that doing in a place like that? Trying to escape being trapped against the rail, having been assigned the difficult first post position, Althea was flying. Swale was breezing.

★   ★   ★

Pincay had been Althea's rider in previous races. He sensed what the filly could do and couldn't do. On the backstretch, drawing even with Swale, Pincay was filled with excitement. His horse was still filled with fight.

"Coming into the stretch my horse pricked up his ears," said Pincay. "I showed him the whip, and he responded."

Althea, the betting choice, also responded. By giving up. Two fillies have won the Kentucky Derby. This year there would not be a third. As Pincay brought Swale into the lead that grew with each powerful stride, jockey Chris McCarron was reining in Althea.

She would finish 19th, and Pincay, her former rider, would sigh correctly: "I thought running a mile and a quarter with the boys would be tough for her, and especially from the No. 1 post."

The mile and a quarter on Swale was easy for Laffit. And rewarding.

Moment of Glory

by Mike Brown of the Plattsburgh Press-Republican. The Chazy High School girls soccer team from Plattsburgh, N.Y., rushes out to greet Carol Latremore (7) after she had connected for the winning goal in a shootout against Eastport High of Middleton, N.Y. Eastport goalie Raen Wolfe lies on the ground, stunned by the impact of sudden loss. The victory vaulted Chazy into the New York state championship game. Copyright © 1984, Plattsburgh Press-Republican.

Look Out Below

by Dale Young of the Detroit News. Rodeo rider Donnie Shattuck does a 2½-gainer, courtesy of bronc Lazy J. The action took place in the Pontiac Silverdome during a tryout for the Longhorn Rodeo. Ironically, the tryout was held for the horse, to see if he had major-league bucking ability. He did. Copyright © 1984, The Detroit News.

Emotional Pain Dooms Ex-Football Star

PRO FOOTBALL

By *IRA BERKOW*

From The New York Times
Copyright © 1984, The New York Times Company

A shout from below her window awakened Charlotte Smith. She had been sleeping in the bedroom of her second-floor apartment at 131 North 15th Street, a three-story red-brick building in Center City, here early Friday morning, October 26.

She heard, "Back against the wall! Back against the wall!"

It was still dark outside, around a quarter to three, and Charlotte Smith climbed out of bed. Her window was partly open because it was an unseasonably warm and humid night, and she pushed the window higher and leaned out.

On the sidewalk, she saw a large black man—she also is black—and the man was wearing a dark jacket or sweater and tan pants, she would recall. He was moving toward a policeman. The policeman, a white man and considerably smaller than the other, was hollering, "Back against the wall!" and slowly retreating from the advancing man.

She didn't notice a weapon or anything else in either one's hands. An empty police cruiser with a flashing blue light rotating on the roof was alongside the curb. The two men were now stepping into the yellow light on the sidewalk that spilled through the window from the night light in the closed luncheonette. Several yards away, at the corner of 15th and Cherry, two young black teenagers on mopeds watched. Otherwise, the street was deserted.

Charlotte Smith has on occasion been roused in the dead of night because, she told a reporter, "derelicts" come around that area—there are mostly office buildings, but the "derelicts" drift over from the bus terminal a few blocks away—and sometimes cause problems. Her immediate worry was that her boss, Murry Auspitz, might be in trouble. Murry Auspitz owns the luncheonette on the ground floor, where she works as a counter attendant. He arrives early to open the store.

When she saw it wasn't her boss, she said she "didn't pay it no attention," and got back into bed. A moment or so later, a loud crack rang out. "It was a gunshot," she recalled. "I've heard gunshots before."

She jumped up and looked out the window again and now saw the black man lying on the ground, bleeding. The policeman was at the squad car and, she recalled, "radioing in for help."

"I was hysterical in the window," she would say, "screamin' and crying."

She did not learn who the black man was until the following day, Saturday, when she saw the headline in the Philadelphia Daily News. It read:

"Cop's Bullet Kills '50s Grid Star."

★   ★   ★

The dead man was Charles Fletcher Janerette Jr., age 45, an English teacher at the Daniel Boone School in Philadelphia and a former All-America lineman at Penn State and one-time player in the early 1960s with both the New York Giants and the Jets. For the last 12 years, Janerette had suffered from what was described by his parents as manic depression.

His killing would raise numerous questions and inflame passions, particularly in the black community of Philadelphia. In the official police statement, the officer would say that Janerette had gotten into the marked squad car when the policeman stepped out to talk to the two youths on mopeds. Then, the policeman stated, he pulled Janerette from the car. He said that a scuffle ensued and his revolver went off. Janerette was shot in the back of the head. Janerette was taken to a hospital and died about 12 hours later.

Was Janerette, in fact, up against the wall? Was this a case of police brutality in extremis, or an accident, or did the policeman have no recourse in order to protect himself? How was it, if there was a scuffle, that he was shot in the back of the head? Had Janerette taken medication that helped control his mental problem? Toxicology reports, which should show whether he had been taking the medication, will not be available for several weeks.

The police officer, Kurt VonColin, age 33, who reportedly stands about 5-feet-7 inches tall and weighs about 160 pounds, bears a well-known last name in Philadelphia. In 1970, his father, Police Sgt. Frank VonColin, age 43, was shot to death while alone at his desk in the Cobbs Creek Park guardhouse by a group of black men, members of a radical organization known as the Revolutionaries. The killing was considered by the police to be part of a conspiracy by the group to kill whites.

That crime touched off the largest manhunt in Philadelphia history. All but one of the assailants were caught. The only one still free is the one who is said to have pulled the trigger.

There are other questions that the story of Janerette raised. Some deal with the adjustments of life after football, some with racism in American society, and others with the problems of the manic-depressive, a psychosis from which, according to his family, Janerette had been suffering for the last 12 years.

★   ★   ★

Charlie Janerette grew up in Philadelphia, first in the Richard Allen projects, and later in a better neighborhood in West Oak Lane, and became an all-city and all-state high school lineman. He went on to Penn State, where he was chosen a second-team All-America by The Sporting News in his senior year, and he played seven years in professional football. He was with the Los Angeles Rams in 1960, the Giants in 1961 and 1962, the Jets in 1963, the Denver Broncos for the next two years, and finished his career in 1966 with the Hamilton Tiger-Cats in Ontario.

In 1956, Charlie Janerette became the first black president of Germantown High School. He was popular, gregarious and exceedingly bright. By the time he was a senior, he had reached his full height, 6-3, though, at about 240 pounds, not quite his full weight, which would go as high as 270 pounds with the Broncos. "Charlie," said a longtime friend, Garrett Bagley, "was a gentle bear."

Two of his boyhood friends were Harold Brown, now a North Carolina businessman, and the comedian Bill Cosby. Brown is believed to be the model for Cosby's comic invention, Weird Harold, and another Cosby character, Fat Albert, is believed to have been loosely based on Charlie Janerette.

Brown smiled when he recalled Janerette. "He was funny and he could take a joke," he said. "We said his shoe size kept up to his age."

Brown was asked if Janerette was in fact the inspiration for Fat Albert. "The guys have always thought he had a lot to do with it," said Brown. "He was rotund, robust, as a kid. Not fat sloppy, but robust sloppy."

The boyhood friends kept in touch through the years. Last year, said Charlie's sister, Hope Janerette, when Bill Cosby opened a show in Lake Tahoe, he sent Charlie Janerette a round-trip first-class ticket to Nevada. Cosby told Charlie he'd have a Rolls-Royce waiting for him to use there.

Charlie told Hope, "I can't drive that thing. What if I had an accident. I could never pay for the repairs."

One of the many bouquets of flowers sent to the Janerette home bore this note to the family: "I'll see you later." It was signed, "Bill Cosby." Several attempts to reach Cosby were unavailing.

Charlie Janerette was the oldest of five children, and the only male, born to Charles Janerette Sr., now a retired postal office supervisor, and his wife, Lillian Ernestine. The five children—the other four are named Carol, Faith, Hope and Charity—would all earn doctorates. Charlie had dreamed of becoming a physician, and he enrolled as a pre-med student at Penn State.

But, he would say, the requirements of football didn't give him enough time to pursue the rigorous discipline of medicine, and he instead earned a bachelor's degree in science, and later a master's in educational counseling.

When he first went to Penn State, Joe Paterno, now the head coach but then an assistant coach, recalls that they thought there might be a problem. "He was a sensitive, shy kid and we wondered whether he was aggressive enough to be a good football player," Paterno said. "But he was very committed, and he wanted to make something of himself. He was very quick and had a lot of explosiveness, and he got tougher and tougher."

Janerette was thrilled to receive a scholarship from Penn State, but, he said in a newspaper interview a few years ago: "They didn't tell me I'd be the only black on the team. I didn't worry about that, though. I saw all the huge freshmen, and I just wanted to survive."

In the mid-1950's, blacks were just beginning to be recruited on a large scale for college athletic teams at major state universities around the country. It was no different at Penn State, the school tucked away in an area known as "Happy Valley." Janerette, though, seemed to make adjustments.

Janerette was drafted in 1960 on the fifth round by the Los Angeles Rams. His contract called for $7,500, and he received a $500 signing bonus.

It was enough for Janerette to put a $3,000 down payment on a house for his parents and sisters, a brick, semi-detached four-bedroom house on a street lined with spruce and cedar trees in the quiet, East Mount Airy section of north Philadelphia.

He started some games for the Rams, but at the end of the season, was picked by the Minnesota Vikings in an expansion draft, and then traded to the Giants.

In two years with the Giants, he would recall to The Philadelphia Tribune, a black newspaper, he played "a lot of defensive tackle when Rosey Grier was hurt, and I played on all the special teams. I even played with a broken hand. I had to."

Andy Robustelli, a defensive end on the team, remembers him as a "happy, jovial, always upbeat guy. But the Giant teams were so strong then and it was tough for anybody to break in."

In 1963, Janerette was cut by the Giants and picked up by the Jets. Weeb Ewbank, then the Jets coach, remembers him as a "nice person, never caused any problems, but we let him go because he was on the downside of his career, and we were building."

Janerette went to the Broncos as part of a nine-player deal with the Jets. "I remember Charlie getting up at a club we used to go to, called 23rd Street East, and doing great, funny imitations of James Brown," said Cookie Gilchrist, a teammate of Janerette in Denver. But there was another side. "He didn't play enough, and he and I both thought he should have," said Gilchrist.

Denver, where Janerette earned his highest salary, $17,000, cut him and he played for a year in the Canadian Football League. He was 27 years old and finished as a professional football player.

He had married in 1965, and he and his wife, Joan, soon had a daughter, Dariel. There seemed no evidence of problems. He spent five years in the marketing department for General Electric in Syracuse, and it was in August of 1972, said Joan Janerette, when difficulties developed.

"He began acting strangely," she recalls. "Very hyper. His movements were very quick at times, and he began to say strange things. Like he was going to solve all the problems of the world."

He began to leave without telling her where he was going, and wouldn't return for days. She urged him to go to a psychiatrist, and he was eventually admitted to a Syracuse hospital and stayed there 10 days, she said.

She wondered about the source of his problems.

His wife believed he was suffering from manic-depression, in which there are sudden mood changes, surging from euphoria to deep depression.

The problems intensified. She went to a therapist, and she was told that he could be dangerous. "He was a big man, and I found it hard to restrain him," she said. In October of 1972, she left him, taking their daughter to Pennsylvania.

On October 18, 1972, he was charged with driving while intoxicated when he was involved in a car accident in which a pedestrian was killed. He pleaded guilty to a reduced charge and as a result his driver's license was suspended for three months.

"Charlie was so broken up by that accident," said Hope Janerette, "that every October 18 he would not go out of the house."

Following the accident, there were days of unexplained absence from work, and he lost his job.

Paterno, who stayed close with Janerette and knew of his problems, hired him as a graduate assistant. Janerette stayed at Penn State for two years and earned his master's degree.

But Paterno saw times in which Janerette would not be "acting right." And when Janerette next went to Cheyney State in Pennsylvania as an assistant coach under Billy Joe, there were more problems. "He was a good assistant," said Billy Joe, "and then on occasion he would do something completely out of character." At a football dinner, Janerette, the guest speaker, rose and soon, "began yelling out and cursing," said Joe. Janerette had to be led away.

He moved to Washington, where he sold computer software to federal agencies. He told a friend that one day he had been picked up off the streets by the police for no reason and jailed for four days.

He returned home to Philadelphia, where he got teaching jobs.

After his death, a student whom he had taught, named Angela Hurts, wrote a letter to Janerette's parents: ". . . I really do miss Mr. Janerette. He could joke with us, but he was also serious about his students getting to work, because he wanted us to learn. Even when I said, 'Mr. Janerette, I can't do this,' he would say, 'yes, you can. Try it.' "

Although he took several jobs teaching in the Philadelphia public schools, he would continue to talk to friends about his dreams. "He wanted some kind of entrepreneurship," said Garrett Bagley, a friend, "or he wanted to get back into football. He missed football a lot, and he missed being a star. There were no more locker rooms, no planes to catch, no more autographs to sign."

Janerette was aware, of course, of his mental problem. "He always thought that the last episode—he called them episodes—would be his last," said his sister, Charity. "He didn't really want to admit that he had a problem. And when he took his medication—lithium carbonate—he was fine. But when he didn't take it, and sometimes he didn't want to, he would be out of control. He was never violent, that we saw, but he'd be blinking his eyes and moving the furniture and talking fantasies."

He lived for the last three years in the house he had bought at the corner of Boyer and Horttler. But Charity said he considered it "only temporary."

"We knew he was in pain because of the illness, and he suffered with it and we suffered to see him that way," his sister Carol said. "But it was pretty well hidden. Almost no one outside the family knew about it."

His parents worried, too. "I hoped he wouldn't be a street person," said Mrs. Janerette, "and when he was out late, we waited for him, and when I finally heard the key in the lock, I could go to sleep."

He was working then at Boone, a remedial disciplinary school for boys. "He really related well to the boys," said the principal, Willie J. Toles, "and we had absolutely no problem with his performance or his attendance. And he always looked nice—suit and tie."

On Thursday October 25 he did not report to school. The school called his house. He had not been home the previous night.

That afternoon, a student had seen Janerette in Center City, and the teacher gave him a few dollars, even though the boy hadn't even asked for it. Later, Janerette was reported to have asked a storekeeper he knew to lend him some money, and the storekeeper said Janerette berated him vulgarly for giving him so little.

At around midnight, Paul Jones, an old friend of Janerette's, and now a cab driver, saw him near the bus terminal.

"He didn't seem right," said Jones, who said he did not know of Janerette's mental problems. "He talked okay. We spoke about guys from 30 years back, but his movements seemed too quick, and his jacket and pants were disheveled.

"I said, 'Charlie, can I drive you home?'

"He said, 'No, but can you let me have a few bucks?' "

Jones did, and told him he had to get a fare and would come back in a little while.

He never saw him again.

It was a couple of hours later that police officer VonColin was in his cruiser near 15th and Cherry.

He stopped two teenagers on mopeds for a possible traffic violation. During the ongoing investigation of the death, VonColin is not speaking publicly. According to the formal police statement, one of the teenagers told him that someone was trying to steal his squad car.

According to the statement, VonColin moved toward Charles Janerette.

"Charlie once told me," said Hope Janerette, "that he had heard that if you ever have trouble, or don't have money, and need help, then you should get into a police car. He said, 'They have to take you home.'

"When Charlie was in a bad state, he always had some presence of mind. He was never totally out of control. And I wonder if his getting into that police car wasn't a kind of plea for help." It was just about this time that Charlotte Smith heard shouts, and, soon after, the gunshot that killed Charlie Janerette.

★   ★   ★

Hundreds of people milled outside the gray-stone Beran Presbyterian Church on Broad and Diamond streets last Wednesday at noon, before the services for Charlie Janerette.

People were angry about the way he died.

Willie J. Toles thought that it was a "classic case of misunderstanding."

Inside, in a gray steel casket strewn with flowers, lay Charles Fletcher Janerette Jr.

"I'm glad for one thing," said Hope Janerette. "I'm glad that now Charlie is out of that little private hell he was living in."

Charlie Janerette was eulogized by the Rev. J. Jerome Cooper, and then Cookie Gilchrist read a poem he had written for the funeral. Next, Faith Janerette, a dramatic soprano, shook the church with a moving gospel, "Right On, King Jesus." Some of the congregants moaned and sobbed.

The mourners then filed out, and some of them sang along with the church choir accompanied by an organist to the "Hallelujah Chorus."

As the funeral procession was about to leave for Northwest Cemetery, Harold Brown spoke to someone beside him. "When Charlie and I used to sit in church, and they played the 'Hallelujah Chorus,'" he said, "and on the last 'Hallelujah,' Charlie, under his breath, would add a '50s rock group ending, a little doo-wop. And today it was there. Damned if I didn't hear it. He was speaking. And it made me think, 'Charlie's okay now. Even with all the tears here, he can still play jokes.' "

Sweating and Starving For a Pound of Flesh

COLLEGE WRESTLING

By *VIC ZIEGEL*

From Rolling Stone
Copyright © 1984 Straight Arrow Publishers, Inc.

Darren Abel was up on his toes, pushing, getting nowhere. His opponent was employing a strategy known to serious students of college wrestling as pushing back. The toes on Abel's left foot crunched.

"Something's broke," he told his father, Stan Abel, the wrestling coach at the University of Oklahoma. This is the difference between cartoon characters and amateur wrestlers. Yosemite Sam would have had the good sense to grab his foot and begin screaming, "Ouch-ooch-ouch." Abel stepped back on the mat and continued to wrestle. He lost the match. And because he was correct about something breaking—there was a hairline fracture of his big toe—he wouldn't get to push against Iowa State three days later.

College wrestlers major in pain. If there's a more punishing sport, I'd rather not hear about it. At Oklahoma, Stan Abel owns his wrestlers' bodies for six months out of the year. One season, the coach thought it would be a great idea for his team to meet in the football stadium each morning and race up the stairs. Mayan architects would have shed tears over the stairs at Oklahoma Memorial Stadium. Since the coach understood that vertical running might interfere with classes, he scheduled the concrete sprints for 6 a.m.

Frankly, Abel isn't one of those coaches who remind you of prison guards. He smiles easily, tells a terrific story and uses all of the language he can. I particularly liked his description of one wrestler who won a national championship: "He was luckier than a three-peckered rabbit."

What I hope is clear by now is that wrestlers don't have an easy time. They run, pump iron, jump rope and are constantly stepping on scales. Don't confuse any of that with formal practice. The wrestlers are shut in a room heated to about a hundred degrees for better than two hours. The drills are arduous and repetitious. Much rolling on the mats. Leg bandages everywhere. When they're done, they all want to get through the door at the same time. The scale is waiting for them.

Why do people bother? I put the question to several wrestlers during my visit to the Norman, Oklahoma, campus. The answer I heard most often was their older brothers did it first.

Darren Abel, of course, could point to his father. The old man was a 130-pound sophomore at Oklahoma 25 years ago, when he was beaten in the finals of the NCAA championships by a sophomore from Iowa State named Les Anderson. "I wasn't the best athlete at my weight," Abel says now. "I was just the best at taking advantage of what I could do. And I had my priorities. It was important for me to be a national champion." So he ran eight miles a day, every day, his junior year. And when the NCAA finals came around again, he met and defeated Anderson.

The winners and losers adjourned to a motel room to celebrate the end of the season and graduation. "We got drunk," Abel says, "but I wasn't as far gone as the other guys. They passed out, and I dragged them down to my car and threw them across the hood like deer." He drove the Iowa State wrestlers back to their hotel, hoping no one would notice. But since pulling wrestlers off fenders is probably noisy work, he attracted the attention of the Iowa State coach, Harold Nichols. "Here they are," Abel told Nichols. "They can't wrestle, and they can't drink, either."

The Iowa State Cyclones continue to be archrivals. Nichols is still the coach; Les Anderson, his assistant. Oklahoma, Iowa State, Oklahoma State and Iowa make up college wrestling's big four. One or another of that group has won the NCAA team championship for the past twenty years. "They aren't going to fire you if you don't win the nationals," Abel says. But go a few years without beating one of the big four in a dual meet, and they might stop laughing at the story about the wrestlers on the fender.

Oklahoma was pounded by both Iowa and Oklahoma State this season. Abel's last chance for a score is the upcoming meet, at Norman, against Iowa State. "A month ago," he says, "we would have kicked their butts up around their necks. Now they've got the best team they've had all year and we're in one of our weaker positions. I'm hoping to outfox them."

The toe injury to his son, a 150-pounder, has forced him to juggle. He's moved Darren Higgins, a sophomore who usually wrestles at 142 pounds, to the 150-pound class. Clint Burke, a 134-pound All-America, has been pushed to 142 pounds. At 134, Abel will be gambling on Glenn Goodman, who has wrestled only once the entire year.

Goodman had thought his season was over. "I quit watching my weight," he says. "I was writing it off as a bad year." The telephone call from an assistant coach came Wednesday afternoon. "He said home about. He won a few more matches than he lost. When he showed up this year, he said, the new assistant coach seemed to take a personal interest in him. "Lanny held up a broomstick and said this is what I would look like," Mangrum recalls. The prospect excited him. The wrestler and the young coach worked together, jumping rope 500 times, making round trips to the sauna. "Crazy workouts," Mangrum says now. He lost six pounds in one hour. But he never reminded anyone of a broomstick. The last straw came just before Christmas.

Davidson, he says, didn't particularly care that it was the end of the term. "We were studying for finals, brown-nosing our professors for a little credit, handing in papers. And the way I type"—he pokes at the table with one finger, and then another—"I told Lanny I needed more time. He said, 'Fuck school. We got a national championship to win.' " There were meets over the Christmas holidays, but Mangrum decided to visit his family. "I missed the first few days of practice after the holidays," he says. "I guess I was sort of hoping they'd kick me off the team."

He wasn't prepared for how it was done. Davidson, the wrestler says, removed his name from above his locker. "He told Glenn Goodman, my roommate, 'I threw Mangrum's name in the pisser, and we're all gonna piss on it.' " Mangrum takes a sip of his rum and coke. "The way I feel now, I'm a little down on Oklahoma wrestling."

★   ★   ★

The next time I see Goodman, the team is lining up for the Friday weigh-in. I congratulate him on his new cheekbones. Goodman smiles. "I feel shitty," he says. There was a team meal at a local pancake house—"but after you don't eat for a while, food doesn't look that good to you," Goodman says.

That night, while his wrestlers roll around the mat, limbering up for the meet, I sit with Abel. "Goodman said he'd make the weight and I said, 'They don't give you a medal for that. You've still got to win the match.' He's in a rough situation, but he knows he's good. There's no doubt in my mind he's gonna win. I know this much: We've got to get two wins from the three weights I played around with: Goodman, Burke and Higgins." He stares at the wrestlers on the mat. "If Goodman don't win his match, we're in shit city."

Well, Goodman lost. Burke won, but Higgins was another loser. So much for outfoxing Iowa State. But the heavier weights came through brilliantly, and Oklahoma came up a winner.

After the meet, Goodman was one of the last to leave the locker room. I found him pounding a fist against the top of his foot. "It's cramping," he said. He was fighting cramps all through the match. "I felt terrible. I can't lose weight like that and wrestle."

The match had ended an hour earlier, and the coach was still on the arena floor. "I made a mistake on Goodman," he said. "I saw it right away. He was listening to the sound of his body so much, he

'You'd better not eat lunch,' " Goodman recalls. He weighed 149 pounds when Abel made the decision to send him in at 134. Since the wrestlers weigh in at 2:30 the day of the match, Goodman would have 48 hours to lose 15 pounds.

He is sitting on the bench in front of his locker, wearing a red wool cap over his full head of curls, a rubber suit, sweats, a T-shirt and shorts. The jump rope he has been using in the heated wrestling room is at his feet. He pulls the sleeve of the rubber shirt away from his wrist and perspiration sloshes out.

"See what you're doing now?" Abel says, pointing to a small puddle. "I wouldn't let that sweat die. You ought to run till you lose 10 pounds. Not run, trot." The coach trotted for about a dozen steps. "That's all you've got to do. Do that for about two hours right now. Try it. One time in your life."

Goodman nods. "Do it for a hundred laps," Abel says. "Count a hundred sweat beads off the end of your nose. Do fifty more laps and count fifty more sweat beads. That's how I did it. It'll seem like forever, but it'll go faster than you think." One last suggestion: "Lose ten pounds tonight and go on home and eat your little bowl of soup."

★   ★   ★

Clinton Burke is picking up four pounds to wrestle against Iowa State. He actually ate breakfast the day before the match. Lunch and dinner, he's found, are also meals. "Eating three a day is unusual," he admits.

Burke hasn't been satisfied with his season. Abel had brought in a new assistant coach, Lanny Davidson, whose prowess he praises, to run the practices. Abel describes Davidson's coaching technique as something close to "a marine drill instructor. He'll tell a guy, 'Hey, dickhead, pay attention.' I'm making up the terminology, but that's the kind of thing he'd say."

The language, whatever it was, disturbed Burke. He was willing to put up with the normal routine—"constantly watching your weight, getting your head beat in during practice"—but this assistant coach was a new sound. Prior to one match, they got into "a little scuffle," and Burke took a swing at Davidson. Davidson wanted Burke thrown off the team; Abel's compromise was a suspension.

While I am in Oklahoma, Davidson is in Russia, coaching a touring American team. But he's left behind more than the scene with Burke.

Take the case of Mike Mangrum. Four years ago, Abel, who describes himself as a sensational recruiter, turned his considerable charm on him. "I was the best prospect in the country at my weight," Mangrum tells me in the back room of O'Connell's, an important Norman watering hole. From time to time, Abel would call Mangrum, who was still in high school. "He'd give you that big 'Hello, Stud.' It sounded so great when he said, 'What's right? The Red and White.' "

Mangrum's first two seasons at Oklahoma were nothing to call didn't use his technique."

Abel delivered a few words to Goodman after he was done wrestling. "I told him he made a big sacrifice with the weight, but he didn't show me much courage out there. I wanted him to feel some shame, some grief. I wasn't singling him out; just wanted him to know what was on my mind. He may be starting for us next year." Goodman would have wanted to hear that last part. I didn't have the heart to tell him.

The World is Watching Carl Lewis

OLYMPIC TRACK AND FIELD

By *GARY VAN SICKLE*

From the Milwaukee Journal
Copyright © 1984, Milwaukee Journal

The world waits for Carl Lewis. That is the way Carl Lewis likes it. That is the way Carl Lewis must have it.

So nobody was really surprised last week when Carl Lewis, the man who expects to win four gold medals, was more than 30 minutes late for a press conference the U.S. Olympic Committee scheduled for him.

"He's keeping writers from how many countries around the world waiting?" asked Jerry Green of the Detroit News.

That's the idea. Gary Smith's superb article in Sports Illustrated's special Olympic issue caught Lewis' mood perfectly with the headline: "I do what I want to do."

That's all he's ever done. That's all he cares about. That's all he knows: What he wants to do.

What Carl Lewis wants to do next is win four gold medals at these Summer Olympics, become an athletic hero the size of Jesse Owens, get incredibly rich and famous, act and sing. In short, he wants the world to watch him—like they did Saturday night when he won his first medal, in the 100 meters.

Oh. One more thing. He wants to run the hurdles, too. He announced that last week. Since the world was watching.

"I am considering hurdling," Lewis said in answer to a question about what he'll do in 1985. "I haven't done it in years. I think it would be fun. It's an added challenge. I'll start at the bottom and see how well I can do."

Another way to keep the world watching. And waiting.

★   ★   ★

"*ABC paid $225 million for the rights to the Olympics, and other* *corporations paid millions to be part of it. What we're talking about is miniscule compared to that."*

—Carl Lewis

"Money has nothing to do with my goals."

—Carl Lewis

★　　　★　　　★

Money will be the result of Lewis' goals. He is very intelligent, and very motivated to set, and reach, high goals. Though his education has been interrupted by his athletic career, he plans to finish his degree at the University of Houston. He lost his eligibility there due to a history exam that he said he turned in, but his professor never found.

Lewis has set himself up as practically a sure winner, even more so than high jumper Dwight Stones, who boasted how he would win in Montreal in 1976, and then placed third. Lewis has shrewdly refrained from sounding boastful.

Clearly, he expected to win the 100-meter dash. And he expects to win the 200-meter dash, the long jump—his best event—and to be part of the winning 4x100-meter relay team.

After the U.S. Olympic Trials, he was asked if it was realistic to think that he could win four gold medals, a feat that Owens accomplished in 1936.

"As long as we don't drop the baton," he said.

The pressure he has put on himself, perhaps, is calculated. He will be a large-as-life hero if he succeeds, the kind only television can make. If he fails—can you call three golds and a silver failing?—he will be an even bigger news story. For publicity, he can't fail. In his own mind, he can't fail, either.

"I have a God-given talent, and I will try my best," he said. "If I run my best, and get four bronze, or even no medals, I won't see that as a failure. All I have to know is I competed at my best, and I can't fail.

"Doing my best is the most important. If I don't, I won't win."

Winning Olympic gold medals is important to him and to what he wants to do. Olympic heroes, such as Mark Spitz, Bruce Jenner and Eric Heiden, get chances to be in television and movies.

And the world will keep watching him.

★　　　★　　　★

In a poll taken one month ago by a New York public relations firm and published in The Los Angeles Times, 62 percent of those polled couldn't name a single Olympic athlete who would be competing in Los Angeles—including Carl Lewis.

★　　　★　　　★

Two weeks from now, if all goes as planned, Lewis may be a household name. Beyond his outstanding physical skills, he also has outstanding mental preparation. He is able to stay relaxed when he sprints. In a 100-meter race, just a few blinks of the eye, where the finish line is only moments away, staying relaxed is among the most difficult feats in track.

"You have to be mentally strong," Lewis said. "Up to now, it's been 99 percent mental and 1 percent physical. At the Olympics, it's 100 percent mental.

"One thing I do is I've always been very low-key. I stay very relaxed. I know I've trained excellent. I've been undefeated this year. Once you're here, you just duplicate what you've worked on in practice. The mystery is taken away in training."

For all of Lewis' training and his excellence, he doesn't hold any world records. The talk of his breaking Bob Beamon's long jump mark of 29 feet 2½ inches has, so far, been just talk. Lewis has consistently jumped in the high 28-foot range, near 29 feet. It is presumed to be a matter of time until he surpasses Beamon. It isn't doubted that he might someday break 30 feet.

"Between now and when I retire, I'll have 100 shots at a record," Lewis said. "You only get one shot at the Olympics. Everyone feels more joy in an Olympic gold than in a record in just another meet somewhere.

"I'm not a person to chase world records. It (Beamon's mark) definitely can be broken at sea level (Beamon did it in high altitude in Mexico City in 1968). Here at the Coliseum, it would be difficult because of the swirling winds.

"Also, I'm concerned with four events, not just the long jump. I feel the world record is in me, and the talent is there. When the time comes, the time will come."

When the time comes, Lewis will share his success with his family, his coaches, his god. He doesn't have a lot of friends. When you do only what you want to do, you don't make many friends. So he is a loner.

He isn't staying at the Olympic Village here, against the orders of the USOC. He can't go anywhere without being inundated by autograph requests from other athletes, he says.

Other Olympic athletes are largely unsympathetic to his problem, since Lewis usually wears bright, attention-getting clothes, often with his name in large letters on his back. And they're a little resentful of all the media attention he gets.

"If anyone should be leaving the Village, it should be me," said Tonie Campbell, a USC hurdler who is from nearby Carson, California. "I live only a few miles away. But we're competing as the U.S. team, not as individuals. This is a time when we all come together and get each other psyched. We're here to help each other."

Campbell didn't mention Lewis' name. He didn't have to. His meaning was clear.

Perhaps because Lewis does not make close friends, he feels he must prove himself to them, prove himself better than them, prove that he doesn't need them.

He must make them watch him.

★   ★   ★

"I open up the paper and I see everything—kayaking, canoeing—

but no football (soccer). The rest of the world doesn't care about Carl Lewis and his four gold medals."

—Alkis Panagoulias,
U.S. soccer coach

Carol Lewis, Carl's sister, also is an excellent athlete and is favored to win the women's long jump. She sat at the head table at the press conference here. So did Carl's mother and father, Evelyn and Bill.

"We're very proud of Carl and Carol," their mother said. "It's a wonderful feeling."

"As a spectator, and as part of the procedure we used to get Carl here," his father deadpanned, "I feel great."

Playing sports, running track and field, is all Carl Lewis has ever wanted to do. They're what make him happy. The would-be hurdler, singer, actor, car enthusiast and crystal collector still enjoys track and field the most.

So much so, that he may compete again in the 1988 Olympics in Seoul, Korea.

"In the past, I have said strongly, no, but this is such an experience, it's difficult to relive," Lewis said. "I might stay around. It's been a great experience.

"If it's possible to duplicate this feeling, I just might."

First, however, are these Olympics, and the little matter of four gold medals.

"I've been watching the Olympics all week," Lewis said. "I've gotten quite a lot of joy to see the gymnastics team and swimming relay team, which was the most exciting event. It's given me a good feeling.

"I'm anxious to get started."

The world is waiting. And watching. That's just the way he wants it. That's just the way he must have it.

Cubs: One Race Won, Another Still Waiting

BASEBALL

By *MICHAEL WILBON*

From the Washington Post
Copyright © 1984, Washington Post

As a child, it was always difficult for me to understand why my family never went to Wrigley Field. Sure, my brother Don and I lived on the South Side of Chicago, which by birthright and territory made us White Sox fans.

But no matter how far south you lived, if you were black you rooted for Ernie Banks, Billy Williams and Fergie Jenkins, which meant you rooted for the Cubs, too. You rooted from home, though, because black folks didn't go to Wrigley Field.

Even now, if you look closely at the screen when the Cubs are on television and the cameras pan Wrigley Field, you won't see more than a couple of dozen black people on any given day. Dozens of Cubs fans have been interviewed on network television since the team won the National League East last week, but I'm still waiting to see one who is black.

The more years you go back, the fewer blacks you could find at Wrigley Field. My father came to Chicago from Georgia in 1946 and my mother from Tennessee in 1942; neither had been to Wrigley Field in 1969.

I was 10 years old in 1969, the first summer of division play, and the Cubs were ripping through the National League. We spent many afternoons and nights in Comiskey Park watching the White Sox (Walt Williams and Bill Melton even came to our Little League opener) but I wanted to go to Wrigley Field to see the vines. My brother and I asked my parents about going to see the Cubs. In person.

We wondered why they'd never been there and why few, if any, of their friends had gone.

They told us that it was all the way across town on the North Side, 20 miles away. Black people didn't live on the far North Side and still don't, for the most part. And Chicago isn't the type of city where you just wander around in foreign neighborhoods.

Chicago was about the most segregated big city in the country, my parents explained. Still is. And black people just don't make a practice of going to Wrigley Field.

My mother was diplomatic about it, my father was less so. He said he never wanted to go to Wrigley Field. The Cubs were a racist organization, he said, and didn't want black players. They never paid Ernie Banks—the great Cub ever—even half of what he was worth and wanted to cut his salary $5,000 once after his home run production slipped.

And you could always talk to older black people on the South Side and hear stories about how they tried to go to Wrigley Field in '47 and '48 to see Jackie Robinson play and got harassed by whites.

But all that was put aside for a day and my parents decided we would go to Wrigley Field to see the Cubs. My father got tickets to see the Atlanta Braves on a Saturday afternoon in June. Don and I told everybody we were going to Wrigley Field, "taking the 'L' train, too," and nobody could believe it. Kids in the neighborhood wanted to know if we'd be gone overnight.

We went anyway. Henry Aaron hit a home run, the Cubs won and I didn't see another black face in the stands other than an Andy Frain usher.

I remember the elevated train trip to Wrigley and how the train started off all black, but had changed to stark white by the time we got well into the North Side. I remember how tiny the park looked, compared to Comiskey. I recall that we sat in upper-deck box seats just beyond first base and some people stared. We took the train back to the South Side and I don't remember having a strong desire to go back there right away.

I watched the rest of the games on television in 1969. The Cubs blew that big lead to the Mets in September and the whole thing was just painful. I think it was the last time I actually cried.

My parents haven't been to Wrigley Field since. I went a lot after that, once I got to high school. Many times I went by myself because black friends didn't want to go, except when Bob Gibson of the Cardinals would hook up against Fergie Jenkins, and a few more black faces than usual would show up.

Once, on a hot summer day in 1976, I let my high school sweetheart talk me into doing something I said I would never do: sit in the bleachers. After the first trip to Wrigley, in 1969, I had seen other black people in Wrigley, but never in the bleachers, where lots of young rowdies sat—many of them what I considered rednecks.

We sat in the left-field bleachers, and a white guy near me, wearing the yellow hard hat of the Bleacher Bums, said politely, "We don't get many black people sitting out here." He knew loads about baseball and offered to buy us beer every couple of innings. But after five or six innings of being uncomfortable (and paranoid), I had found different seats.

The next season, I decided not to go to Wrigley at all. It was 1977, the year the Cubs reportedly wouldn't give Bill Madlock, who had just won his second consecutive batting title, a raise to $185,000. Cub management said he wasn't worth that much money.

They traded Madlock, who is black, for the fading Bobby Murcer, who is white, and paid Murcer $330,000.

My father had always said the Cubs would rather lose with mediocre white players than win with good black ones and it would be all right as long as a million white people a year showed up at the park. I always thought he was wrong.

But after the Madlock/Murcer deal, it looked to me as if he were absolutely right. You'd think back to some other trades—young, fleet, promising Lou Brock for Ernie Broglio, for example, and wonder if it was just the Cub management being typically inept, or if it was motivated by other factors.

What the Cubs have long represented, and why so many people adore them, still isn't clear in my mind. Certainly, American sports fans love the underdog and the Cubs are certainly that, with no title of any kind since 1945 until they won the N.L. East last week.

But part of the charm, at least for white Chicagoans, seemed to be that the Cubs represented the city: conservative, slow to change. And though Wrigley Field is the most beautiful park in baseball as far as I'm concerned, the whole setting is backward and old-timey and reminiscent of a period—the good old days—which held nothing good for black people.

Earlier this summer I went to Wrigley Field on assignment. The bleachers were packed an hour before the game, and I looked in my binoculars. Still no black faces.

There's a lot about Cub history that doesn't sit well with me. But they're my team, too. Always have been. I wore Ron Santo's number in Little League.

Before the season I even persuaded my father to give the Cubs another chance. This was new management and it did trade for Gary Matthews.

So when the playoffs begin Tuesday in Chicago, I'll be there. It will be warmer in the press box, but there's only one place to watch batting practice. From the bleachers. This Cub fan will be there early.

Come See the Dinka Dunker Do

COLLEGE BASKETBALL

By *FRANZ LIDZ*

From Sports Illustrated
The following article, "Come See the Dinka Dunker Do" by Franz Lidz, is reprinted courtesy of Sports Illustrated. Copyright © Time Inc., December 10, 1984.

As morning broke on the third day of his month-long clinic with the Sudanese national basketball team in the summer of 1982, Don Feeley, the coach at New Jersey's Fairleigh Dickinson University, stood on a scruff of hill in Khartoum and caught his first glimpse of Manute Bol. In the bright sun, Feeley watched Bol, all 7-feet-6 of him, loom over the outdoor court like a giant exclamation mark.

"Who's *that?*" Feeley asked the other Sudanese players.

"That's Manute," they all chorused.

"Boys," said Feeley after a long pause, "from now on we're going to play a very different game."

It had taken Bol, a Dinka tribesman, six days by train to travel the 600 miles to Khartoum from his home village of Gogrial in the savanna country west of Sudan's vast, central swamp, the Sudd. Basketball was a relatively new game to Bol, who had been playing it for two years around Gogrial, but Feeley was struck by the way Bol could dunk while standing on tiptoes and touch both sides of the backboard simultaneously. "Manute (pronounced sort of like minute, as in tiny) had a 6-foot wingspan," recalls Feeley. Probably because Bol distributed all that body on a mere 190-pound frame, Feeley's expectations for him were modest: "I thought of him more as the next Bill Russell than Wilt Chamberlain."

Feeley showed Bol which basket he should slam balls into and which basket to bat them away from. Now, Bol has it down pretty well. Since that fateful journey to Khartoum, he has followed the bouncing ball to Cleveland and Connecticut, where he's now a freshman at the University of Bridgeport. In his college debut on November 19 he scored 20 points, had 20 rebounds and blocked six shots in a 75-63 victory over Stonehill College of North Easton, Mass. At the end of last week he was averaging 19.8 points, 16.5 rebounds and 8.5 blocks through four games, all of which Bridgeport had won.

Feeley returned from the Sudan, and after the 1982-83 season he was let go by FDU. So he steered Bol to Cleveland State, where Feeley's buddy, Kevin Mackey, was coach. But, like many Dinkas, Bol didn't know how to read or write, which made it difficult for him to meet the academic requirements necessary for basketball eligibility. So Feeley sent him to nearby Case Western to learn English. Bol, obviously a fast learner, soon knew his new language well enough to understand that at Division I schools, the NCAA docks a player one year of eligibility for every year he is over the age of 20. Although Bol's passport indicates he's 21, some doubt its veracity. No wonder: The same document lists his height as 5-2. Bol explains, "When they measured me, I was sitting down."

Feeley, who's looking for another coaching job, lives near Bridgeport and suggested Bol come East this fall. As a Division II team, Bridgeport isn't subject to the strict eligibility rules that Cleveland State is. Bol can play four years for the Purple Knights, and he can also continue studying English. Bridgeport is one of 21 schools in the U.S. that offer a program in English Language Skills.

Around the Bridgeport campus Bol was at first treated like a UFO. Reported sightings would be disbelieved until each astonished skeptic made his own observation. "I thought Coach (Bruce Webster) was joking when he said I was getting replaced by a 7-6 Dinka," says 6-4 junior Clarence Gordon, the Purple Knights' starting center last season. "Manute was sitting down when I met him, and then he got up and started to . . . *unfold!*"

Not since the old showman P.T. Barnum discovered Charles Stratton, a.k.a. Tom Thumb, in Bridgeport in 1842 has a spectacle so astounded the local gentry. "When Manute walks into Famous Pizza, everyone stops eating," says Webster. "He's E.F. Hutton."

If Bol is a sight in a pizza parlor with his knees propped up around his ears, you should see him in the university's Harvey Hubbell Gymnasium. He dribbles down the floor on spindly, Q-tip legs, massaging the ball with long, sleek fingers.

Bol has a watchful reserve and an imperious smile that's almost as thin as his frame. He speaks proudly in Dinka and Arabic as well as his improving English, and from a great height, his head thrown back for a better view of the ceiling. Bol doesn't do much he doesn't want to do, but his teammates say that if they cajole him and treat him with respect, they couldn't have a better friend.

He tends to show the same disdain for strangers that Dinka herdsmen display toward the 60 or so species of mosquitoes that inhabit the Sudd. "Getting Manute to give an interview," says Webster, "can be like pulling teeth." Which would not be easy with Bol, who is missing 15 choppers. He sacrificed four or five in a tribal ritual that marked his passage to manhood at age 14. And he lost a few more four years ago in his passage from backcourt to frontcourt. "The first stuff I ever try," he recalls, "the ball go *salm-dunk!* in the basket." And his front teeth went *bam thunk!* on the rim.

Bol got his first face job at 14. In a sort of Dinka Bar Mitzvah, an elder carved three lines across his forehead. The English translation of Manute is Only Son, and indeed he's the only son of Madot and Abouk Bol. But back home some of his friends still call him Raan Cheg. That's a Dinka joke. Raan Cheg means "short stuff."

Sudan is the biggest country in Africa, about one-third the size of the continental U.S. From the harsh desert that borders Egypt in the north, it runs through desolate stretches of scrub and grassland to the marshy waters of the Sudd and then to the green uplands along its southern border with Uganda. Before Bol began playing hoops, he had led the traditional life of a seminomadic Dinka herdsman. In summer, when the White Nile-fed Sudd would flood to the size of Maine, he would take his cattle to the higher ground of his village. He would also head for the swamp during the winter drought. The nearest city was Wau (pronounced wow), which, according to Bol, resembles Bridgeport. "Both have trees," he says.

Giraffes used to trample Abouk Bol's vegetable garden, but Manute was more concerned about the lions and hyenas that pounced on his father's cattle. The Dinkas revere cattle: They sing their praises in songs, drink their milk and blood, trade them for wives and other essentials, and warm themselves by burning cattle dung. "I protected the cows by talking," Bol says. "Lions would not attack if they heard my voice." Or maybe they were surprised to hear the voice coming out of a mouth that was seven feet in the air. Actually, in the Bol family, 7-6 is not all that outstanding: Ma Bol was 6-10 and Pa Bol was 6-8. Grandpa Bol Chol, chief of the Thwig tribe, is said to have been 7-10, but he was born too early to be discovered by American hoop recruiters. Bol's sister, also named Abouk, who has never seen a basketball, is back home tending his 150 cattle. She's 6-8.

What Bol says he misses most about Sudan is the milk.

"Milk?"

"American milk, plecchh!" he roars ruefully. "Pasteurization! Homogenization! Skim! White! Tree milk!"

Lately, Bridgeport has been milking this tree for all he's worth. Despite the fact that the Purple Knights had a losing record the last two years, they're now talking national title. Normally, Bridgeport can't even sell out its annual game with archrival Sacred Heart. Now there isn't an empty seat for an intrasquad scrimmage. Nearly 1,800 fans jammed Hubbell Gym for the home opener. To paraphrase Jimmy Durante, they came to see the Dinka dunker do.

And dunk he did. He showed a splendid sky hook, a fabulous fadeaway hook and stuffed more baskets than an old Connecticut River tobacco farmer. "You can't zone or zone-trap Bol," moaned

Stonehill Coach Ray Pepin after the Chieftains' loss. "We should have stuck our 5-8 point guard on the shoulders of our 6-6 center."

Feeley had been so high on Bol that he talked another friend, Jimmy Lynam, coach of the Los Angeles Clippers, into picking Bol in the fifth round of the 1983 NBA draft, sight-unseen. The NBA voided the pick because Bol was under the legal draft age of 22 for foreigners who haven't attended college. "Manute's problem is that he lacks stamina and endurance," says Lynam, who later scouted Bol and insists he's 7-7. "He needs body strength and body weight."

Bol could stand to put another 30 to 100 pounds on his frame. But then this is a fellow whose life has been marked more by abstinence than excess. As a teenager, he once subsisted for four months on milk. Bol now inhales pizza, spaghetti and chicken, and quaffs a few cans of Nutrament a day. And Webster has him on the same sort of weight program that Ralph Sampson did at Virginia.

Webster is understandably euphoric. "In my wildest dreams, I wouldn't have even asked for a guy 7-6," he muses. "I'd say, 'Just give me somebody 6-9 or 6-10.'

"I mean, why be a hog?"

Larry Holmes: At Home in Easton

BOXING

By ROY McHUGH

From the Pittsburgh Press
Copyright © 1984, Pittsburgh Press

His routine is to run three miles after breakfast, shower at the office and go to work. He works all day, behind a door on which one brass plate says "Larry Holmes/President" and a plate just below it says "Private." A receptionist shields him from skeptical intruders.

At home in Easton, Pennsylvania, Larry Holmes is addicted to taking care of business, which plunges him often into single-handed combat with the telephone. Holmes has a policy, or maybe just seems to, of answering every call. An exception not long ago was the call his brother Jake intercepted: "If Larry can let me have a million dollars . . ."—needed, the man said, "to put me back on my feet." Jake Holmes said it wouldn't be feasible. Larry Holmes, at his desk, remained ignorant of the chance to do good.

For office attire in the summertime, he favors short-sleeved shirts, open at the neck, and gray or blue slacks. He is 6-feet-3 when he gets out of bed and 6-feet-5 with a lift from the heels of his boots. Whether he needs one or not, he looks for an edge. Although his office is windowless, admitting no sunlight, he opts to avoid eyestrain by wearing tinted glasses.

Trophies and photographs decorate the walls, tangible confirmation of who he is. A hundred-dollar bill in a frame serves an initially less-obvious purpose.

Recently he entertained visitors in his office. There were ice-breaking remarks about Easton, where Holmes grew up, where he lives in a million-dollar house and where his various activities stimulate employment. It's a picturesque city of 27,000 nestled at the fork of two rivers, the Lehigh and the Delaware. The rivers are narrow; they flow between thickly wooded bluffs. An obelisk memorializing the Union dead of the Civil War rises over Easton's town square. Modestly, Holmes acknowledged the scenic qualities and pastoral charm of Easton. "It's a quiet place," he said. Then he smiled, showing a space between his two front teeth that somehow makes him look guileless. "And I own it."

The smile invited laughter, which was forthcoming.

Beyond the closed door, the receptionist's voice in counterpoint with that of another woman could be heard. Leaning forward, Holmes pushed a button on the intercom. "Tell my wife to come in," he said.

Her name is Diane; she's as slender as a fashion model; jeans and jerseys still become her. "I didn't know I was talking so loud," she said.

Holmes swiveled around in his chair. "Any money on you? Give me a hundred dollars."

She emptied her purse, tens and twenties fluttering onto his desk. Holmes scooped them up.

In a spirit of carefully emphasized levity, someone made bold to chide him for putting the bite on his wife. His attention was called to the hundred-dollar bill on the wall—legal tender, certainly.

That hundred-dollar bill, Holmes replied, was going to stay on that wall.

For its sentimental value?

Holmes smiled as he had before, telegraphing a punch line: "It reminds me I'm not broke anymore."

★   ★   ★

Since way back when, in colonial times, Easton has had its share of distinguished sons. First there was George Taylor, who pledged his life, his fortune and his sacred honor to the principles embodied in the Declaration of Independence, affixing his signature to it. Edwin Binney invented the Crayola, Hugh Moore the Dixie Cup and Samuel Phillippe the split-bamboo fishing rod in Easton. George Wolf was a governor of Pennsylvania. Transcending them all as a public figure, transcending them all in renown, is Easton's current leading citizen, the heavyweight champion of the world, Larry Holmes.

To be sure, he is not the one and only. In the never-never land of prizefighting, with politics the fertilizer, champions spring up everywhere as common as crabgrass. Among the heavyweights right now, we have Gerrie Coetzee, champion of the World Boxing Association and Tim Witherspoon, champion of the World Boxing Council, whose champion, until last December, was Holmes. How Witherspoon came to be his successor is a complicated story, as we shall see. It was not by defeating Holmes in the ring. No one has ever done that. In any case, no sooner was Holmes a man without a title than a new organization called the International Boxing Federation handed him one, seemingly the purpose of its existence. That much said, the IBF has the only authentic champion. Witherspoon and Coetzee are pretenders; Larry Holmes is the real thing. He's the only true champion, the undefeated champion: 45 fights in 11 years and his hand raised 45 times.

But in quite a different way he is leaving his mark on Easton. His hometown knows him as Larry Holmes the civic booster, Larry Holmes the tycoon. There are Holmes aficionados, 150 at the most, who faithfully follow him to Las Vegas or wherever for all of his major fights. The stay-at-homes in Easton have been able to catch his act only once—in 1976, before he was champion, when they packed the Lafayette College field house for his eight-round destruction of Jo Jo Gholston. It was the one time Holmes has performed in Easton, and his purse that night went to the St. Anthony's Boys Club. In the dawn of the big-money age, St. Anthony's was where Holmes learned his trade, from which he since has extracted, to use the rough figure his accountants supply, "around" $48 million. A lot of it Holmes can't touch. He has put large sums into annuities. He is not by any classic definition a spendthrift, but he indulges himself on occasion, having accumulated more automobiles than his garages—there are two of them—will contain. The total, if he remembers correctly, is 13, including the obligatory Rolls, the obligatory Mercedes and the obligatory BMW. His white stucco house, a modified A-frame designed from his own sketches, cost $500,000 to start with and another half-million in add-ons such as the motorized skylights, a wing that would hold any two of the adjacent houses in the middle-class neighborhood where Holmes elected to build, and a cabana. Still there is something left to invest, and when Holmes has spare cash he thinks of Easton.

It wasn't always like that. Two years ago or more, fenced in, as he perceived it, by the establishment and the city administration of Easton, he moved his corporate headquarters, Larry Holmes Enterprises, across the Delaware River to Phillipsburg, N.J. He moved his sportswear store into the Best Western Commodore Inn he had purchased in Phillipsburg, changing its name to—what else?—the Larry Holmes Commodore Inn. He closed his nightclub, Round One, and his restaurant, the Four Corner Lounge. Easton and Holmes were on the outs.

The election in 1983 of Salvatore Panto as mayor reconciled them. "The mayor's my buddy," says Holmes. "The mayor's my friend." At 34, soon to be 35, Holmes is two years older than the mayor. When they were kids they were neighbors in a racially mixed housing project on Easton's South Side.

Holmes, after reaching the seventh grade, dropped out of school. He took the jobs that are open to an incompletely educated young black: he shined shoes and washed cars. Later, there were semi-skilled jobs in a carpet factory and an iron foundry, which was opportune. Holmes had become a father. He supported three daughters and their mother, who was not, and never would be, his wife. He still does.

Sal Panto and his family left the project when he was 10. He finished high school, got through Kutztown State College and took a master's degree in social studies at Lehigh. Back in Easton, Panto taught social studies in junior high. St. Anthony's Boys Club appointed him to its board of directors. Holmes, 22 now, was representing St. Anthony's as an amateur boxer. He turned pro, but Easton is not a fight town. Holmes needed money to commute between Easton and Scranton, which was always a fight town, and Panto helped raise it. On March 21, 1973, Holmes launched his pro career by winning a four-round decision from Rodell Dupree in Scranton.

★   ★   ★

"To me," Sal Panto was saying, "Larry is still the same guy. He hasn't changed. I was with him for two hours last Saturday afternoon, and it was Larry and Sal, not the champ and the mayor."

The mayor looked dapper in a blue cotton washable suit, stylishly wrinkled. His wood-paneled office in City Hall is attractively hung with Larry Holmes fight posters.

"Larry's a real gentleman," he said. "One of the nicest people I know. I don't believe he's ever wanted to hurt anybody. He could have *killed* Muhammad Ali in that fight. It was depressing for me—I was always an Ali fan—but I think that Larry does more for the championship belt than Ali did.

"He lives a very clean life. He helps this community. He has a Larry Holmes Kids' Day every year. Gives away T-shirts, hot dogs and soda. He sponsors a 10-kilometer race called Run with the Champ. He sponsors teenage dances at his training center."

Does Larry Holmes have a talent for business?

"He has a talent for dealing with people." From his memorabilia display on the wall, the mayor took down a prized photograph. "This is Larry getting an award as one of the 10 most outstanding young men in the United States. The Jaycees of America gave it to him. I'm a past Jaycee president in Easton and I recommended Larry. He received the award in Tulsa—1980, as I recall—and this was where we really got close."

Panto's index finger tapped the edge of the picture frame. "I think it is safe to say that Larry has it in him to be a successful businessman for the rest of his life, and I'll tell you why. At this black-tie affair down in Tulsa, the other nine recipients were scientists and academics and so on. David Stockman got one of the awards. He was still a congressman then, not the head of the OMB (Office of Management and Budget). Well, this hydrogen scientist spoke first, and he was using a lot of big words. I glanced at Larry, sitting next to me. 'Did I tell you they expect you to say something?' He said, 'Yeah, OK. No problem.' The second guy was another good talker. I leaned over to Larry again. 'Do you have something prepared?' We said, 'No. I'm gonna speak from the heart.' I was getting nervous. We had two more speeches to sit through, and then it was Larry's turn.

"And he brought down the house, three standing ovations. I said,

'Champ, I've got to apologize.' He asked me what for. I said, 'I didn't think you could do it.' He said, 'Well, Sal . . . you grow up.' "

★   ★   ★

The mayor before Panto, another young man—35 when Easton elected him—was Philip Mitman, whose great-great-great grandfather opened a jewelry store in Easton 200 years ago. Called Bixler's, it's still there, an exceedingly elegant store, and Mitman runs it. His other great interest, historic preservation, clashed from time to time with Larry Holmes' ideas.

One was to build a restaurant on Larry Holmes Drive, the river road renamed for him in 1982, four years after he won the WBC title from Ken Norton. Sal Panto, who saw the plans for the restaurant, thought it would be a "very nice" family-type place. Phil Mitman envisioned "a fast-food chicken restaurant" on one of the most desirable pieces of ground in Easton. Mitman's view carried more weight with the redevelopment authority, and property values on Larry Holmes Drive have not fallen.

Neither have they increased, some might say. There were other disagreements and failures of communication, ending when Mitman declined to run for a second term. Says Dick Lovell (accent on the first syllable), the publicity director for Larry Holmes Enterprises: "Easton's a funny town. They don't really seek investors. When someone comes in and makes a proposal, nine times out of 10 they turn it down because it's not what they want. But now Mayor Panto is saying, 'Let's not turn away investments, let's encourage them.' " Panto's encouagement brought Larry Holmes Enterprises back to Easton. "The mayor before him was historic," says Holmes, "and I'm jet, man. I'm flyin'. I'm movin'."

Flyin' and movin', Holmes has remodeled his two-story brick building on Northampton Street, the main drag in Easton, and will shortly reopen the restaurant and nightclub directly below his executive suite. A nightclub in the square, two blocks away, is on the drawing board, too, and his Larry Holmes Parking Authority continues to function. It's a lot across the street from Larry Holmes Enterprises, not often supervised by an attendant but with a sign that reminds customers: "Parking $1. No Exceptions!"

In the words of its executive vice president, J. Michael Dowd, the Two Rivers Area Commerce Council of Easton "couldn't be more thrilled" about Holmes's return. "It has enormous positive impact, enormous psychological impact," says Dowd. A 1983 Washington Post story referred to Easton as "old and dying," but Sal Panto now talks of "a brand new attitude with Larry moving back." Easton, he declares, is "seeking a lot of regrowth."

★   ★   ★

Depending on whether or not, and for how much money, Holmes will fight Gerrie Coetzee, Easton may see a lot more. For Holmes, looking toward retirement and his role in the Easton power structure, a fight with Coetzee was the centerpiece. "It would put me right over," he said.

It would put him right over if there were fewer wild cards in the deck. An on-again, off-again proposition, it was off again, or at least in abeyance, as he spoke. Like the arms control impasse between the United States and the Soviet Union, a Holmes-Coetzee fight has been one of the great unresolved issues of the 1980s, with papers signed, announcements made and preparations begun with everything certain including the date, and then all of a sudden new promoters, all former agreements invalid, negotiations starting again from scratch. Mere words, mere talk, mere announcements, it was plain, would be worthless until the moment the two fighters answered the bell.

In November, after doing a one-round number on Marvis Frazier and exposing for all time the irrelevance of bloodlines in boxing —Marvis being the son of ex-champion Joe Frazier—Holmes had vowed to Diane that he would fight no more. The script was an old one, mothballed for the next time when a man named Kenny Bounds, a real-estate developer in Dallas, offered him $3.2 million for a fight with John Tate in April and $12.3 million for a fight with Coetzee in June. Accounting for the spread between $3.2 million and $12.3 million were Coetzee's synthetic title, his South African origin and the color of his skin, which is white. Boxing still thrives on racial differences, however trumped up.

Holmes was able to pocket the $3.2 million, paid in advance, without ever lacing on a glove. Tate, pleading a shoulder injury, asked to be excused from the April bout. The World Boxing Council, meanwhile, instructed Holmes to forget about fighting Coetzee and promptly defend his title against its No. 1 contender, Greg Page. Don King was to be the promoter.

King's relations with Holmes had never been good. They deteriorated further when Holmes realized that the very best offer he would get from King was $2.5 million. Rather than accept, he would give up the title. In December he carried out his threat. The WBC matched Page with Tim Witherspoon, the winner to inherit the championship, and it was Witherspoon, in an uneventful fight.

Down in Texas, Kenny Bounds was having problems, mainly financial. He could not get up the money he had promised to Holmes and Coetzee. Months went by; the promotional rights passed from Bounds to a California group and eventually to Don King. The size of the fighters' jackpot steadily dwindled. There came a morning in Easton when Holmes, his normally pleasant face wearing a scowl, his arms tightly folded across a blue-and-silver warmup jacket, stood at the head of the asphalt path where he does his roadwork and listened to a new set of terms Don King was insisting upon, as relayed by Dick Lovell.

"The guy started out at $6 million," Holmes seethed. "Now he's reducing me to $4 million, maybe $3 million." With a shrug of exasperation, he was off down the path, his determined, slightly knock-kneed trot returning him to the realm of the physical.

★　　　★　　　★

Holmes is a tenacious bargainer. The seventh-grade dropout makes his own matches and deals, hiring lawyers to untangle the complexities. "My mother Glossie," he says, "raised hard-headed kids" (11 altogether, some born in Easton and others, like Larry, in a town called Cuthbert in southwestern Georgia; four of his seven brothers, notably Robert, who is manager of the Larry Holmes Commodore Inn, are in one capacity or another on his payroll of 125).

Misty, the oldest daughter of his early liaison, called him one day and said, "Dad, I'd like to work. I'll do anything." Her father gave her a job at Flossie's Cafe in the Larry Holmes Commodore Inn, and took her at her word. She is busing tables. When Misty turned 16, she made another request. Would he buy her a car? He would. It was no inconsiderable undertaking.

From his motor pool on Misty's birthday, he commandeered a van, his brother John Henry at the wheel. Misty and her sister Lisa piled in. It was Holmes's lunch hour, and he was hungry, but he is never without a walkie-talkie. Neither are his wife and his key associates, among them his brother Jake. Calling from the van, Holmes ordered Jake to McDonald's. "A Quarter Pounder with cheese—tell 'em not to put no onions on it—and a Coke." Holmes then directed John Henry to a Volkswagen-Dodge-Mazda lot. There he inspected car after car, soliciting no opinions from Misty, and wolfed down the hamburger delivered by Jake. Only the hamburger pleased him.

"You're putting a knife in my heart," said the orange-haired salesman as Holmes led a trek to the van. "Good luck, hope you find something," the salesman called after him forlornly. At the next stop, Holmes found something, a royal blue Pontiac Phoenix. The sticker price was $10,783. "Now show me your invoice," Holmes demanded. Producing it, the salesman told him, "I'm not supposed to do this." Holmes got the Phoenix for $9,871, with a radio thrown in.

"I'm giving it to you for $100 over cost," said the salesman.

"I never mind someone making a little money," answered Holmes.

★　　　★　　　★

The money Holmes will make with Coetzee, if he makes it, well could be his last big touch. Many black people—and not only blacks—were critical of him for consenting to fight a white South African. "I pay it no mind," he says. "I don't agree with apartheid. I don't agree with the politics of South Africa. I wouldn't fight there. I think South Africa should be blown off the map. But I've talked with Coetzee and he seems like a pretty nice guy. People can't help what's going on in their country. Coetzee can't help it because he's white and I can't help it because I'm black. We have no say. God shows the light—the direction we should go."

God shows the light, but there are shadows as well. In the project where Holmes spent his youth, a former neighbor, a woman, was bitterly complaining. "He don't come around here anymore. Everything he does, he does for the high and mighty. He ain't done nothing for welfare recipients. He ain't black no more." Her reasoning seemed to be that all black Eastonians on welfare are in some way the responsibility of Holmes.

It was perhaps no doubter of Holmes' blackness who smeared black paint on the white face of the lawn statue in front of his house, a figure wearing a jockey's cap, red vest, white jodhpurs and black boots, or who painted the word "nigger" on the white stucco wall.

Holmes has a tendency to brood about such matters if by chance he is somewhat depressed, as he was at the end of a long day on the telephone, mostly with Don King. He drove his white Harley-Davidson Special Edition Electra Glide motorcycle from the office. Diane was at home. The children, off visiting somewhere, were not. Kandi Larrie (pronounced Laree) is 4. Larry Jr. is not quite 2, but ready to join the gang claiming titles. "Who's the champ?" people ask him, and he taps his own chest. "Me!"

"Hey, Di," Holmes said. "Did you cook anything?"

She hadn't. Nor did the prospect of cooking exhilarate her. "There's some chicken," she said. "I could fry it."

"No, no, no. We'll go out and get something. I'm tired. I'm beat."

Two callers prepared to depart. Their host and hostess had shown them the sights—the tennis court, the satellite dish, the house itself, the indoor swimming pool shaped like a boxing glove. But Holmes was in a mood to share his feelings. "I'll be in court all day tomorrow, giving depositions," he confided. It's a case that involves the Coetzee match and one of its would-be promoters. "When you're on top," Holmes sighed, "people think it's a bed of roses. It isn't. It's dog eat dog. You've got cutthroats out there, everyone pushing you, and when somebody tries that with me, I could punch him out in a minute, but I don't."

Shoulders slumped, he was sitting at a table in a room between the foyer and the swimming pool. He rambled on. He told of how a boisterous crowd at his brother Lee's bar and grill was "arguing and fighting and making a lot of noise," and how he reprimanded the whole bunch, using the same epithet he had found on his wall, only not in a racial sense, because "niggers don't have no color, it's how you act," and how the incident had made him unpopular in certain quarters. He said he likes to take a drink himself now and then, not to get drunk but to relax, and for the first time in his life has been doing it—once a month. Stress is no respecter of persons.

But the problem with being a multimillionaire is that your troubles are seldom interesting to those who are not multimillionaires. Brightening, Holmes said, "Did you see my bell?" He was suddenly cheerful. "My Madison Square Garden Bell?"

It was on the wall in the sunken living room, next to his WBC championship belt, which is gold turning green, and the belt Don

King gave him, worth $40,000 with Holmes' name spelled out in diamonds and rubies and emeralds. Gleaming like new, the bell is supposedly the first ever used at ringside in the original Garden, said Holmes. It was being auctioned off in Las Vegas, and he'd been drinking a little wine, and when the auctioneer said, "Do I hear $100?" he immediately bid $2,000 and the auctioneer immediately shouted, "Sold!" Holmes got the worst of the transaction, he knows, but the auctioneer wasn't Don King.

"Hey, Di," he said. "Let's go for a motorcycle ride. Put your jeans on. We'll ride over to Bethlehem and get hamburgers."

As it happened, they rode across the bridge to New Jersey and dined with more pomp at the Larry Holmes Commodore Inn.

Tackling the Odds

COLLEGE FOOTBALL

By *JON MASSON*

From the Colorado Springs Sun
Copyright © 1984, Jon Masson

Gladys Southall knew something was up when two somber individuals entered her hospital room in Loveland on that September day 22 years ago.

Not something wrong, mind you. Gladys Southall doesn't look at life in that way. She *knew* what Dr. James Brown and her husband, Herb, had to tell her.

Call it a mother's intuition.

The seventh of Gladys and Herb Southall's eight children wasn't like the others. He was born September 22, 1962, without a complete right arm, the limb ending just below the elbow.

"I think the Lord prepared me," Mrs. Southall said. "Two weeks before in Loveland another family was there and they had a little boy who had it on the opposite arm. He walked in front of me and walked back and forth. I just thought, 'The Lord is telling me.' People look at me kind of strange when I say that. But he prepared me."

★　　　★　　　★

Tom Southall circles under the plummeting football, catching it with relative ease. He flips the ball to the referee, who is still signaling the touchdown reception at leaf-covered Washburn Field on the Colorado College campus.

Not a bad catch, considering Southall snared the elliptically shaped ball with one arm. He wasn't being a hot dog (sports parlance for showoff). He really didn't have another choice.

"I'm just different because I don't have two arms," said Southall, a senior at Colorado College. "Other than that, everything is normal."

Normal. That's the way Southall wishes life to be.

"Everything is always 'the one-armed football player,' " he said. "It would just be nice to be the football player from Steamboat

Springs. But I realized that's the way it is, so you can't complain about it.

"You're talking to me mostly because I play football still and I have one arm. And it's not something you see every day."

Especially when oftentimes he is the best player on the field. He's a key figure on the Colorado College football team, playing a running-back position.

"Tom Southall has been an outstanding player for us ever since he came here," said Jerry Carle, in his 28th year as Colorado College's coach. "He's a super football player and super leader. He's not a very big kid. He's subject to being banged around. We can't afford to play this year without Tom Southall. Tom Southall has to be healthy and contributing his usual 150 percent."

Teammate Scott Driggers said, "He's the best athlete I've ever played with in any sport. It's really amazing what the guy can do. I don't know what you can say about him. It always feels great to give the ball to Tom. You know he'll make something happen. He is the most liked and respected on the team. He's outgoing but not obnoxiously so. I've not met anybody who has a bad thing to say about him."

Describing himself isn't quite as easy for Southall. Minutes pass before he responds.

"I don't know," he said. "I'm pretty mellow. I just like to have a good time. Even at practice I like to joke around a lot and keep everybody going."

The mischievous twinkle always appears present in Southall's blue eyes. He's a prankster. A clown. Ready with a joke. Ready to be the butt of one.

"It takes awhile to get a nickname," he said, sitting in Rastall Center, the Colorado College student union, and wearing his Steamboat Springs sweatpants. " 'Captain Hook' was my nickname in high school."

With that remark, Scott Campbell, another teammate, popped his head over a nearby couch and away from the television screen. "How come?" Campbell said, with his best quizzical look.

"Because I was a pirate," Southall said, and the room filled with laughter.

★   ★   ★

Southall has gone about life filled with laughter. He isn't handicapped by what some would consider a handicap.

The 5-foot-9 ("OK, 5-8¾"), 157-pounder was a 12-time letterwinner in track, basketball and football in high school. He rushed for more than 300 yards a half dozen times in high school. In his junior year, he gained 412 yards on 28 carries in a state semifinal win over Sheridan High School. Generally, 100 yards rushing in one game is considered an excellent performance.

His high school track team won the state title three times; the football team won it once.

At Colorado College, he also runs track—performing in the long jump, the triple jump and on relays.

He has appeared on the television show, "That's Incredible." ABC recently featured him on a halftime show during the Oklahoma-Texas football game.

He's rush chairman for the Kappa Sigma fraternity. "Of the five fraternities, ours is the least stereotypical—I think that's a word," he said.

He's a 3.5 student majoring in business economics and working on his thesis. "If I work, I want to work in an accounting firm—be a CPA-type person," he said. "I don't think it would be dull. But everyone says I'm not the numbers type."

He drives a beer truck for a summer job. "I drive a stick with no trouble," he said.

And he's popular. Popular with the girls. "I learned in high school you don't mention girls because it will always backfire," he said. "If you say something nice, they say, 'Ooooooooo.' And if you don't say something nice. . . . I try not to talk about girls. If you want to look back on an article in 50 years, you don't want to say, 'God, why'd I talk about her.' "

He's happy-go-lucky. Just a normal guy.

★   ★   ★

"He was very young," Gladys Southall recalled. "He was going into kindergarten. He was taking a bath and I heard heavy sobs. I walked in and he was washing himself. He said, 'But why?' and held out his hand—his stub. Tears were really pouring out.

"I said to him that God must have thought he was special and that he had a cross to bear. He doesn't like the word special. How do you answer a kid when he says, 'Why?' "

He used a prosthesis, a mitten with a blue thumb, until the third grade. But he wasn't too keen on that mitten. It was a pain in the neck for the active youngster to take it off for recess, then cleanse the elbow area, put the sock back on and put his shirt back on. Finally, the prosthesis was history.

"For Tommy, it was the best decision," his mother said. "For others, I don't know."

Southall said, "I had to go to Children's Hospital in Denver when I was a little kid. That's where I learned how to tie my shoe and stuff. Just growing up I had to learn how to play football or basketball or whatever. I had to work on my own.

"Looking back on it, I don't remember having to stop and worry about it. I just figured out how to do it. I don't really remember having to sit down and think about it. It pretty much just came to me. I knew what I could do and couldn't do and went from there.

"I've had to work harder just to get where I am. I don't know if I would have worked as hard having two arms."

His family didn't treat him any differently.

"It was a very difficult moment when Dr. Brown told me," said his father, Herb. "It all blew over pretty quickly. One of the things that brought me to my senses was one of my customers had a child who was a mongoloid. There was no hope for that child. It forced me to realize that different people come in different-size packages."

On the family refrigerator was the saying "Love is the family together."

"He doesn't tell this story," Mrs. Southall said about her son. "He was mischievous and I was cooking or something. I said, 'Young man go sit in the corner and go twiddle your thumbs.' At first it was pretty sad to say that but then the rest cracked up. And Tom was in the corner and he was twiddling his thumb. At that young age he was able to take the joke."

Southall would watch older brother Richard, also an all-state performer in high school. "I used to get in trouble because I'd stop on the way from kindergarten and watch him at junior high practice," Southall said. "I grew up watching him play. He was kind of my hero growing up."

Richard helped Tom learn how to catch. To make those easy catches, he blocks the ball with the stub and controls the football with his left hand.

Theirs was a family together. "They brought up a good family, a good Catholic family that went to church all the time," Southall said of his father, who now works in the purchasing department of a coal mine, and of his mother, a bookkeeper.

"When I was a little kid they just stressed honesty and just being nice to people—treating them how you'd want them to treat you. In Steamboat, I knew the little kids were really looking up to me. I watched what I did. I made sure that whatever I did I would be proud of and they would look up to it and respect it.

"It helped having a big family because there were a lot of people to play with and a lot of support from everybody."

His parents' philosophy came across well to Southall. "We never said they can't do something," Mrs. Southall said. "I believe you can do anything."

She remembers Southall's brief grade-school wrestling career. He was called once for an illegal hold—because the referee said he had clasped his hands together. "I never could get that one," she said.

Sometimes Southall will amaze—try to dribble a basketball and fire in a shot with one arm, or catch a kickoff and ward off 11 tacklers. "You do forget he has the one arm," his mother said. "He isn't the one-armed football player, he's a football player."

★　　　★　　　★

Southall likes to reminisce about the good old days at Steamboat Springs High with Scott Clementson, who, with Southall, co-captains the Colorado College football team.

But Southall thinks about the future, also. He has dreamed about the pros.

"I think about it especially with scouts looking at Drigs (Scott

Driggers)," he said. "That would be nice if I had the opportunity. I'd put everything on the back burner for a while."

But that's farfetched. He's not kidding himself.

"My family let me know, 'Don't plan on playing professional football or having that be the only thing you want to do in college,'" he said. "Then your four years are up and you are not prepared to go anywhere. That's everybody's dream to play ball for a big school. It would have been nice but if you don't make it big in sports. . . . You had to make sure you were prepared to do something else."

Tom Southall is prepared. Just a normal kind of guy.

Gibson's Two Homers Win Series for Tigers

BASEBALL

By _THOMAS BOSWELL_

From the Washington Post
Copyright © 1984, Washington Post

Finally, with two huge swings of his bat, Kirk Gibson put the 81st World Series out of its misery and sent the Motor City into urban ecstasy—i.e., riots.

Twice Gibson sent homers deep into the upper deck here in Tiger Stadium this evening. Once, he scored from third on a daring Krazy Kirk dash on a 200-foot pop-up.

When the ragged curtain dropped on this shaggy anti-Classic, the Detroit Tigers had their first World Series triumph since 1968. And Gibson had given an electric five-runs-batted-in performance that disguised the aesthetic grotesqueries in Detroit's 8-4 victory over the San Diego Padres in this fifth and final game.

The last contest of a superb Tiger season combined almost all the proper threads. The Tigers, one of only three wire-to-wire pennant winners in history, closed their show exactly as they began it, winning the Series, four games to one. Detroit started the season 35-5. It went 7-1 in the postseason; multiply that by five. When the Tigers needed to be good, they were great.

All the Tigers' central figures shared the closing stage.

• Gibson, who was the American League playoffs Most Valuable Player and Detroit's hidden superstar all year, hit a 430-foot, two-run homer in the first inning and a 420-foot, three-run blast in their last at-bat of the year, turning Trumbull Avenue outside Tiger Stadium into a riotous Damnation Alley. For five years Gibson, an All-America football player at Michigan State, has been the symbol of the Tigers' enormous physical potential but unpolished and sometimes uptight play.

• Sparky Anderson became the first manager to win the Series in both leagues.

"I'm glad that today we finally played like we can play . . . the saddest thing to me is that my daddy can't be here," said Anderson, who has aged years this season under the double pressure of his father's death in May and his team's everything-to-lose league lead.

• Aurelio Lopez retired all seven men he faced, four of them on strikes, to get the victory and finish a 12-1 year. "This is the most beautiful moment in my life," he said.

• Lopez's fellow superstar reliever, Willie Hernandez, gave up an eighth-inning home run to Kurt Bevacqua that cut Detroit's lead to 5-4 and gave this town heart flutters, but staggered to his 35th save of 1984.

• Lance Parrish greeted reliever Goose Gossage with a seventh-inning homer even as the crowd of 51,901 sang, "Goosebusters."

• Finally, slick shortstop Alan Trammell, who hit .450 against the Padres, won the Series MVP award. "We've really grown the last two years," said Trammell, who's endured many frustrations here in recent years and who, within the next week, will face knee surgery and, perhaps, shoulder surgery as well. No, you never know when you'll pass this Series way again.

It was even fitting that, in a Series in which Bevacqua and Marty Castillo had game-winning homers, the game-winning RBI tonight went to Rusty Kuntz on a tiny pop-up.

Of all these days' fitting scenes, the best scripted was Gibson's three-run homer in the eighth that settled all doubts in this town that has had only one other champion since 1945.

After all the buffoonery of the past week, after the goofball plays and hours of yawnball, Gibson gave this Series an emblematic moment that combined Tiger heroism and incompetence.

Gibson, the Tigers' most physically gifted player, already had smashed a two-run homer in the first inning off Mark Thurmond, who got just one out and thus personified a San Diego starting rotation with a 13.94 World Series earned-run average. Gibson already had scored the tie-breaking run in the fifth on that meek pop-up by Kuntz that San Diego's right fielder lost in the clouds.

Now, with the Tigers clinging to a 5-4 lead in the eighth with two men on base, Gibson laid his enormous strength into a heater by Gossage. He rocked the ball 20 rows into the right-field stands to finish the scoring, finish the Padres and finish a final game that was both exciting and fundamentally awful.

How awful?

Awful as Garry Templeton standing inches from second base but forgetting to put his foot on the bag on what should have been a force play, two batters before Gibson's homer.

Awful as pinch-runner Luis Salazar, the potential tying run, taking it upon himself to steal and getting picked off in the Padres' eighth.

Awful as Anderson yanking Lopez when he was overpoweringly

sharp and replacing him with a tired Hernandez, who almost blew his two-run lead.

Awful as Padres Manager Dick Williams replacing a razor-sharp Craig Lefferts (two shutout innings and a 0.00 October ERA) in mid-inning after a strikeout so he could wave for Gossage, who had a 13.50 Series ERA. "If I had just done my job," Gossage said, "we probably would still be playing now."

The worst of all the awful decisions was the last. Williams actually had ordered that Gibson be walked with first base open. However, Gossage summoned his manager and talked him out of the rational move and into the emotional "I can get this guy, Skip," school of baseball.

Poor Andy Hawkins, who allowed one run in 12 Series innings, may have taken the loss, pinned on him by Kuntz's "sacrifice fly," but Thurmond and Gossage were the real culprits.

This game was a prototype of the whole Series in almost every way.

The Tigers scored three runs in the first inning, the eighth straight time that they took the lead in this postseason with runs in the first (six times) or second innings.

Lou Whitaker singled, Trammell forced him and Gibson sent the first pitch—a waist-high gopher ball—15 rows into the upper deck, far above the 370-foot sign. Parrish, Larry Herndon and Chet Lemon singled, sending Thurmond to the shower.

As has been the case throughout the postseason, the Padres showed their grit in battling back—this time to a 3-3 tie. Steve Garvey, who'd managed only one RBI in 17 Series games, drove home a run off subpar starter Dan Petry with a two-out infield hit in the third. In the fourth, Bevacqua walked, Templeton doubled, Bobby Brown lined a sacrifice fly to center and Wiggins delivered a two-out RBI single to throw the game back to square one.

If this game had one key play, besides Gibson's turn-out-the-lights homer, it came in the Tigers' fifth.

Gibson—who else?—smashed a hit off the glove of diving Graig Nettles at third, then alertly took second on a long fly by Parrish. Herndon walked and, with Lefferts in the game, so did Lemon to load the bases.

Kuntz, a .234 hitter this year and the most unlikely of heroes, lofted his pop-up to short right. Gwynn never moved: "Lost it when it got above the roof." Instead of Gwynn cruising in for an easy catch and quick throw to the plate (on which no runner would have tried to move), Wiggins had to make a back-pedaling catch and a weak, off-balance throw to the plate.

Gibson, once among the game's worst baserunners and still its most aggressive one, scored easily for a 4-3 lead.

All that remained was the over-managing sweepstakes.

Williams waved for Gossage as Lefferts finished his 10th consecutive inning of shutout pitching with a whiff of Gibson to start the seventh. Parrish's liner over the left-field scoreboard on Gossage's second pitch made it 5-3.

Anderson countered with a parallel gaffe. Lopez had been perfect, but he wanted better. Hernandez entered and started throwing line drives. One was caught, one by Bevacqua went into the upper deck in left and one was a single. That 5-4 lead didn't look a bit safe.

That's why the Tigers' eighth mattered so much. Gossage walked the leadoff man. Templeton fell asleep and never put his foot on second as Nettles made a great play to get the lead man on Whitaker's sacrifice attempt. Trammell moved the runners with a bunt.

Then came the obligatory walk to Gibson and the battle between Gossage and Parrish.

It never happened. Anderson held up four fingers to Gibson, meaning, "They're going to walk you." Gibson put up 10 fingers, meaning, "Ten dollars says they don't and I get a hit." Anderson took the bet. Smart man.

Two pitches later, a fellow who probably shouldn't have gotten to swing was this town's hero of heroes.

Detroit could begin trashing itself and a comedy classic had ended.

Matter of Grit: Hazzard Era Begins at UCLA

COLLEGE BASKETBALL

By *MIKE LITTWIN*

From The Los Angeles Times
Copyright © 1984, The Los Angeles Times

It's basketball season and they're introducing yet another era at UCLA, where eras are beginning to stack up like so much cordwood. There's enough now for a funeral pyre.

This time, though, is different. This time is like no other time.

This time, UCLA hired itself a bulldog, one who has been tugging on the school's pant leg for years, growling for attention. The teeth marks, and the coaching job, belong to Walt Hazzard. They're going to have to work to get rid of him.

In the post-Wooden era, coaches generally have stayed at UCLA just about long enough to get their names on the stationery and the lips of courtside critics. Then they disappear, usually under cover of night.

When the latest in the long line of coaches made his getaway and there was no immediate place to turn, there was the bulldog, his teeth still clamped onto UCLA. He got the job, by default as much as anything else. And now, no one is going to run Walt Hazzard off. He's going to be there when morning comes.

Gene Bartow was too thin-skinned. He couldn't take the pressure. Gary Cunningham never really wanted the job. Larry Brown didn't know what he wanted—until it was too late. Larry Farmer, who waited a lifetime to be UCLA's coach, wasn't ready when he finally got the call. In nine seasons, four coaches. None of them got fired. They all ran.

For different reasons, each was the wrong person for the job, and now Hazzard, the original Bruin, co-captain of the first NCAA championship team under John Wooden, will get his shot. History aside, there is little enough to recommend Hazzard. He has never coached on the Division I level, and he left behind him in the Division II and junior college ranks a record which, though successful, is not exactly spotless.

Hazzard pushes, though. He works. He gets noticed. He latches on. He helped recruit for UCLA, and he was involved in fund raising. He was sometimes a critic, and Larry Brown thought he was bad for the program. Twice, Hazzard had been considered as an assistant coach.

Hazzard has always pushed. When he was 14, his family moved to Philadelphia from a small town in Maryland. Almost the first thing Hazzard did was head for Haddington recreation center, a legendary playground that spawned Wilt Chamberlain, among others.

"He'd come and watch us play," recalled Sonny Hill, a mentor for many Philadelphia playground regulars. "He was always there. When we didn't have enough players, we'd let him play. He was good, and he worked so hard. He made it so you had to pick him."

That same year, he went to coach at Overbrook High School, carrying with him the Converse basketball yearbook featuring pictures of each state championship team. The year before, as a freshman, Hazzard had played for the Maryland state champion. His picture was right there in the book.

"I just wanted to be able to prove who I was," Hazzard says now.

The proving continues.

★   ★   ★

Walt Hazzard, 42, drives to work in a new sports car, pulls into the parking lot across from the Wooden Center and heads for his office. Across the way is Pauley Pavilion, where Hazzard's UCLA team plays basketball.

For Hazzard, each day is a pleasure, each day a reminder that anything is possible. It's not a bad place to begin your career as a Division I coach.

"I get the same feeling every time," Hazzard said, lounging in his office, dressed in blue and gold warmups, being the UCLA coach. "It's exhilarating. You know where I came from, and now I have all this."

All this is all Hazzard ever wanted—all that comes with being the UCLA coach. Where he began coaching was Compton College, a low-budget junior college operation where the coach and his assistant, Jack Hirsch, swept the floor before practice because there was no one else to do it.

"One day when I first got here, they asked me if I wanted a regular bus, vans or station wagons," Hazzard said. "I asked them where we were going and they said the airport. Jack and I just broke out laughing. Jack and I were used to getting a requisition, getting the keys and sleeping with them. We'd get in the bus, with straight-back seats, and go wherever we had to go. To Bakersfield, Santa Clara. We didn't have to worry about stopping in any fancy steak houses. McDonald's was right in our budget.

"It's a different world now. I get a menu to select the pregame meal. I can have a party catered at the faculty building. I can have a party catered at my house. Five years ago, I was driving a Mazda. Now I'm driving a Mercedes. I like that."

It's with a certain wonder that Hazzard talks about his job at UCLA, the job that four others left prematurely. None of them had seen what Hazzard had seen. Larry Brown complained about the paint in his office. Walt Hazzard is happy to have an office.

"Dues are overrated," said Hirsch, who has been Hazzard's assistant for five years and his close friend for more than 20. "How many coaches can say they've swept rats out of the gym, or who have had players with bullet holes in their bags, or who had players who didn't have enough money to buy jockstraps? Who had to sweep the floor? That's paying dues. Sure, we got here quick. It ain't a 20-year progression, starting in junior high school. You can say it's a fantasy and I guess it is, but it was also a lot of hard work."

It was also a lot of luck. You may recall at least part of the story. Hazzard and Hirsch were being recruited from Chapman College in Orange by UCLA to be Farmer's assistant coaches. There was some feeling, in fact, that they were being dumped on Farmer.

Suddenly, days after agreeing to a two-year extension to his contract, Farmer quit instead, and Athletic Director Pete Dalis, figuring he had to have a coach right away, chose Hazzard.

A lot of people were surprised—the hiring was the talk of the town in Seattle, where the nation's coaches convened for the Final Four the following week—but no one was more surprised than Hazzard himself.

"My son from Stanford was at home, and he kept repeating, 'Compton to Pauley, Compton to Pauley,' " Hazzard said. "The more he said it, the more unbelievable it sounded. I had never heard anything like it."

It was crazy, but somehow it seemed all planned. It was just a crazy plan that had somehow worked.

Where to begin? How to explain?

A product of Philadelphia's playgrounds and championship teams at Overbrook, where he was city player of the year and student body president, Hazzard was the point man in what would become a migration of city kids to the West. The 6-foot-3 guard signed on with UCLA, after a year at Santa Monica College, and became an All-America, Player of the Year, Olympian, a territorial draft pick by the Lakers. A hard-nosed player, and smart, he was a coach's dream.

His years at UCLA were perhaps the best of his life. He played for five teams in 10 NBA seasons, some of them better than others. He was an All-Star, and he was waived. He averaged 24 points a game once, the season after the Lakers had failed to protect him in the expansion draft.

He warred with one owner, who, Hazzard said, had touched his wife improperly. "I told him I'd kill him," Hazzard said. In another city, Hazzard set up clinics for underprivileged children. He has had foundations created in his name.

He has large hands, large feet—he used to wear Chamberlain's shoes—and round eyes that can flash in anger. "Intimidating," Hirsch calls them. His voice is gruff, a dry rasp that Hazzard's wife, Jaleesa, said sometimes scares babies. "That drives him crazy," she said, adding that some people think "he must be some kind of ogre, and he's one of the sweetest people you'll ever meet."

Said Hazzard: "It gives people the wrong impression about me. The way I look, the veneer, the fact that I don't smile, that's just Philadelphia."

Where one side of Hazzard ends and the other begins is not always clear. He can be charming or the eyes can flash. On the floor, however, he was a fighter who always tried to give more than he took. He expects his teams to act accordingly.

In his first time on national television, Hazzard was tangling with Tommy Heinsohn. Teammate Elgin Baylor told Hazzard he should quit basketball and head straight for the Olympics. Baylor said he'd be glad to manage him.

"He was a battler," said Al Bianchi, who coached Hazzard in Seattle. "He didn't take anything from anyone."

There's a picture on Hazzard's office wall, taken at 4 a.m. one fall night in Seattle. It was the night Bianchi had traded him to Atlanta, one day before the season began, one season after he had been the team's best player.

It shows Hazzard cleaning out his locker, leaving someplace else behind.

"You don't forget those times," he says. "You don't forget the hurt."

He hasn't forgotten the 21-61 season in Buffalo, or the time he got waived and read about it in the newspapers.

The pro career began to unravel in Atlanta when he became a Muslim. In those days, that was more than a religious conversion, it was a political statement. A year later, in Buffalo, word got out that Walt Hazzard had became Abdul Rahman.

"That was it for my career," Hazzard said.

It was a difficult time, but it shaped the man. He says now that he was used, that he didn't have a clear understanding of what he was doing, that his status as a professional athlete was exploited by those he trusted in the Muslim movement.

"I didn't conduct myself in the best way," Hazzard says now. "You know how you get into something and you have that zeal. I got overzealous. I never had a clear understanding of what was going on. As I studied on my own, I learned a lot of things they told me weren't true.

"I went to Mecca my first year, alone. I didn't know one word of Arabic. I was there for the big Friday prayer and I didn't know anything. I didn't even know how to pray. The people who suggested that I go said I knew more about Islam than the Arabs.

"I had to think about that because I didn't know anything. If they know less than me, I'm in trouble. I was wondering how I was going to get through this when a little boy, 7 or 8 years old, stood next to me, and I just did what he did."

Later, he went to Libya at the behest of Col. Moammar Kadafi, and that woke him up some.

"I was used, no doubt about it," Hazzard said. "I was naive. To tell you the truth, I didn't have a clue."

That was all prologue, though, no more than part of the circuitous route that would one day lead him back to Westwood.

In 1977, his NBA career over, Hazzard returned to UCLA to get a degree. He took that time to renew his friendship with Pete Dalis, who was years from becoming athletic director. That was portentous bread being broken.

After graduation, Hazzard spent a year as an entrepreneur—"I lost a lot of money"—which convinced him that what he should be doing was coaching. He changed his name back to Walt Hazzard, figuring that he could practice his religion without going around as Abdul Rahman and that Walt Hazzard had a better chance of landing a job. He found one at Compton for two years, then another at Chapman for two more years. Finally, Valhalla.

"I always wanted to coach," Hazzard said. "I always wanted to be at UCLA, but I'm not sure I ever let myself believe it would happen."

It's harder to believe how it happened. Not everyone is willing to talk openly about it, but this is what can be pieced together.

Larry Farmer was struggling, his team losing an alarming number of games. There was talk, among some of the alumni anyway, that Farmer should be removed. Farmer's friend, Sam Gilbert, wanted to make certain that wouldn't happen.

Gilbert, a widely known UCLA booster who was once accused of helping basketball players in violation of NCAA rules, reportedly went to Dalis and asked him what could be done to help Farmer. They arrived at the same conclusion: Farmer should change assistant coaches. The names of Hazzard and Hirsch came up, and those names started appearing in the newspapers.

"No one had even talked to us and we were reading our names," Hazzard says. "We didn't know what was going on."

Farmer was reading them, too, and was as confused as anyone. After talking with Dalis near the end of the season, though, Farmer agreed that new assistants had to be hired. A change had to be made.

Said Dalis: "He told me he wanted someone who had professional experience, with a UCLA background, someone who had been a head coach, someone who had national contacts. Basically, he ended up describing Walt Hazzard and Jack Hirsch."

Farmer won't say that Hazzard and Hirsch were thrust on him, but neither will he say they were his first choices. At that point, uncertain whether to leave or to stay, Farmer was of two minds on almost everything.

"Sometimes he was uneasy about them, and sometimes he seemed very eager to have them," Dalis said.

He had his first meeting with Hazzard and Hirsch at Gilbert's office in Encino. "Just a matter of convenience," said Farmer, who continued to meet with Hazzard to discuss Xs and Os while Hirsch and Dalis were talking dollar signs.

Days went by with no decision. Chapman was waiting with a five-year contract for Hazzard, and Athletic Director Walt Bowman wanted an answer. When Farmer announced he was staying, Hazzard figured he was ready to go to UCLA as an assistant. Then Farmer did his disappearing act, leaving everyone in limbo. Finally, Farmer quit, leaving Dalis in a bad way.

He did not want to wait, and there, for the taking, was Dalis' friend Walt Hazzard.

"I had watched his teams play and I had seen their level of intensity," Dalis said. "I was impressed with his system. . . . I was impressed that Walt started from the bottom up because he believed so much he wanted to be a basketball coach. His teams are hard-nosed, pressing, goal-oriented, which is really reflective of Walt.

"The issue of timing was the most important thing. Given all that information, I decided to hire Walt."

So, the improbable happened.

When he starts thanking people, Hazzard can probably begin with Gilbert, who, when asked to comment on his role, angrily declined comment.

★   ★   ★

"It doesn't figure," said Hirsch, who is Hazzard's alter ego. "He's black, that's one strike against him. He's a Muslim. That's strike two. It's pretty incredible that Coach Hazzard got this job."

There were some other possible strikes as well. Hirsch has been there alongside Hazzard for all of them. Chapman's Bowman said that Hazzard and Hirsch were virtually co-coaches. Although Hirsch protests—"We're not Batman and Robin"—it is true that it is nearly impossible to separate them. "He spends more time with Jack than he does with me," Jaleesa said.

When Compton came calling with Hazzard's first coaching job, he accepted immediately. He didn't want to hear about any problems; he wanted a job. To that point, the only teams he had coached had been in youth basketball. He needed a better forum to judge his methods, which are, he freely admits, the methods taught him by John Wooden.

The first thing he did after taking the job was call on Hirsch. "He wasn't doing anything, just sitting at home watching the stock market," Hazzard said. "He needed something to do."

A self-described millionaire, Hirsch said he retired at 28 to a life of luxury and, it turned out, boredom. He says he's an abrasive New York whose family came to Los Angeles when he was in high school, where he sat out one year because he didn't get along with the coach. He went to junior college and then was a co-captain for UCLA's championship team.

"There hasn't been a thing I haven't seen, done, tried, experimented with," Hirsch says of himself. "That's one of my better qualities."

He's also a cynic who always sees the down to Hazzard's up. While Hazzard likes to think of the UCLA season as an opportunity to overcome the lowered expectations, Hirsch says, "It will be a miracle if we can play .500."

"They're complete opposites," Jaleesa said. "Maybe that's why they get along so well. Walt is always upbeat, and Jack always sees a disaster coming."

Hirsch remembered how he became Hazzard's assistant. "When Walt asked me to come to Compton, I said, 'Are you crazy? I don't want to be the White Shadow,' " Hirsch said. "He says, 'Come on, spend a day with me. See if you want to do this.' I went there and fell in love."

Two years later, they left it all behind to take the job at Division II Chapman, a small liberal-arts college where, according to Jaleesa, everyone "looked like Ozzie and Harriet."

It was an adjustment. "Walt had to be the black shadow," Hirsch says.

Not everything went smoothly in those four years, and there were lessons to be learned.

In Hazzard's first season at Compton, he used an ineligible player and had to forfeit nearly the entire season.

"I learned a lesson there, about being organized on and off the court," Hazzard said. "But if we had had a magnifying glass, I don't see how we could have caught that one. The player played three games a couple of years before. It cost me a season. It hurt."

In Hazzard's second season, he was sued by Julia Coleman for back rent on a house where eight past, present or redshirt Compton College basketball players were living. She claimed that Hazzard was subletting the apartment, which would be in violation of college rules. Hazzard said he was only collecting the money and paying the rent.

There was a suit and a countersuit by Hazzard that is still in litigation. Compton College investigated and allowed Hazzard to take his team to the playoffs.

"The players were late with the money," Hazzard said. "If I was subsidizing them, I was doing a poor job because I would have gotten the money there on time. I was not going to pay their rent for them.

"It was part of a learning process. I learned you can't trust everybody. She came to me, wanting to rent this place. People have hidden agendas."

Efforts to reach Coleman for comment were unsuccessful.

It was no problem getting a reaction from Hirsch, though. "I don't think Coach Hazzard knows how to be corrupt," he said. "You want to know why? You have to be smart to be corrupt. That's not an insult. I mean, smart enough to get an agent, tuck him away. All Coach Hazzard knows about is basketball. . . . When I say nothing, I mean nothing."

At Chapman, there was a night at Wright State, in Dayton, Ohio, when Hazzard's team walked off the court, a near disaster.

The game was already out of control, Wright State leading by 31 on its home court when, with a little more than 5 minutes to play, Nigel Wallace, Chapman's star player, fouled out and then began a prolonged conversation with an official. The official told Wallace to leave, saying that if he didn't, the game would be stopped.

"I started to walk out on the court and my players started leaving the floor," Hazzard said. "A team had walked off the floor there the year before, and I made the mistake of talking to them about it. I was never going to take my team off the floor, I never would. But that was a good lesson for me. You have to have your team under control and you can't put things in their minds that are going to elicit a response that you don't want."

The game was called, and it took 20 minutes to get it started again. Wright State Coach Ralph Underhill said he isn't certain about Hazzard's intentions.

"I told him, 'Walt, you can't take your team off the floor,' " Underhill said. "By that time he had regained his composure and wasn't going to take them off. . . . From talking one on one with Walt, I could see it was a matter of frustration. He didn't take the team off, but he might have had that feeling for a minute.

"I know that you couldn't pull that stuff at UCLA and last."

At Chapman, Bowman talked to Hazzard about his conduct. "He had some maturing to do," Bowman said. "But we were very happy with Hazzard and Hirsch. We were lucky to have them."

That was the combative Hazzard, angry because his team was losing, angry because he thought the officials were contributing to that defeat. It is a mistake, though, to try to fit Hazzard neatly into any one category. That same night, after the game, he went up to the stands to confront a fan who had been heckling him.

"He thought I was going to fight him," Hazzard said, smiling in recollection. "I shook his hand and asked him if he enjoyed the game. . . . Everyone broke out laughing."

★   ★   ★

If you want to know about Hazzard, you have to go back to Philadelphia. He didn't grow up on any mean streets. Son of a Methodist minister, he grew up going to church and going to school and playing basketball. More than anything, he played basketball.

Every day he dribbled to the playground—lefthanded. Always gotta work on the left hand. Ray Scott would be there and Wally

Jones, Paul Arizin sometimes, Alonzo Lewis, Guy Rodgers, Wayne Hightower.

John Chaney, now the basketball coach at Temple and then Hazzard's high school gym teacher at Overbrook, was there, too. He looked after Hazzard in his own way.

"The first time he came in the gym at Overbrook, his eyes were as big as marbles," Chaney said. "I'll never forget what he looked like when he opened that door and saw a brand new world for himself.

"He'd come running down the stairs at study hall, telling me, 'Let's go, let's go.' We'd go to the gym and I'd never let him beat me. I'd cheat him. When he made a basket, I'd take it out. I'd never let him call fouls on me, and I called fouls on him whenever he missed."

At the playground, the games were to 20 points, 10 baskets. You make it, you take it out. At Haddington, they might get 500 people out to watch, and if Chamberlain was there that night, there could be a few hundred more.

"If you missed a layup, they talked about you," Hazzard said. "If you didn't hit the open man and shoot a jumper, they really got on you. If you came off a screen and had a jumper and missed it, well, you better not do it too many times or you didn't play. That's pressure when you're 14 years old."

He handled the pressure. He and his friend Wally Jones were schoolboy prodigies. Jones later became a pro, and a Muslim, too, changing his first name to Wali. At 15, though, they were playing alongside NBA stars, and the world seemed just fine. Jones and Hazzard hooked up on the day after Hazzard's arrival in Philadelphia. They never came unhooked. "He's my brother," Hazzard still says. "If I was around, you knew that Wally was going to be there, too."

When Hazzard is your friend, he is your friend for life. Friendship is not a sometime thing with him, it's a lifetime obligation, a joining of blood. He has been married to Jaleesa, whom he met at UCLA, for 21 years. Fifteen years and a pro career after leaving UCLA, Hazzard called on his old friend Jack Hirsch to be his assistant at Compton.

"He's the kind of person you can call up at 4 in the morning and know that he's ready to help," Hirsch says.

Hazzard doesn't let go. Not of Philadelphia, not of his friends. Especially not of UCLA.

★   ★   ★

So now, the Hazzard era. He had a 53-9 record at Compton, 43-14 at Chapman. His teams played basketball the way John Wooden taught him: the 2-2-1 press, the pyramid of success. Now he's at UCLA, and he has a team that is perhaps less talented than any in Westwood over the last 30 years.

In the last week he has landed a top prospect from Philadelphia and he has seen his team clobbered in an exhibition game against Athletes in Action. For every plus this season, you have an idea there is going to be at least one minus.

He has worked his players hard, much harder than any of them can remember. "It's like night and day from last year," Montel Hatcher says. "We know what being in shape is now."

There is more to basketball, though, than being in shape. There is even more to it than playing hard, although that is a start. For the previous four coaches, there was pressure but there was also a bench full of talent. Hazzard is going to have to start over.

The expectations are lower this season, but they're not going to stay low for long.

"I've spent my entire life preparing for this job," Hazzard said. "I've got it now. I'm not going to waste the chance."

J.C. Snead: Bad Guy Or Good Ol' Boy?

GOLF

By *MICKEY HERSKOWITZ*

From Golf Digest Magazine
Copyright © 1984, Golf Digest Magazine

Once you have said that J.C. Snead is a real live nephew of his Uncle Sam, the connection kind of breaks down. Sam Snead is part of the glory of golf, an original, a name that ranks with Hagen, Hogan and Nelson among the Old Masters.

J.C. (for Jesse Carlyle) Snead may or may not be the least popular player on the tour today, one of the 10 toughest interviews, or one of the five most in need of a Dale Carnegie course. It is troubling enough that some people think so, and these conclusions have appeared in a distinguished national magazine (this one). I mean, has the media ever lied to you?

Of course, a lot of athletes would have taken that rap and run with it. That is, they would have advertised themselves as "The Golfer You Love to Hate," and hired Howard Cosell's PR man, and affected a scowl that would have made Mr. T look sweeter than Michael Jackson.

Do you know what would have happened? People would have started to write and talk about what a stand-up guy J.C. is, a rugged individualist. They would have dug around for the soft center under the hard crust. He might have published a book and become an analyst on golf telecasts and starred in a Lite Beer commercial.

It's the American way.

But none of this, and less, has happened to J.C. Snead. During a period of what he sees as bad press and bad karma, his game and health and purse have all suffered. In the past 12 months he has earned almost nothing in fringe monies. "I have gotten a reputation for being a hard-ass," he says, "and I think it is undeserved."

That sentence is pure J.C. Snead: direct, earthy, a little wistful. It is almost as if he had been taking a test ever since he turned pro in

1964. And now, at 42, after $1.5 million in winnings, and seven titles, and competing on three Ryder Cup teams, he had been told he was to be graded only on neatness and personality.

He had been a late-starter, coming to golf at 27, as Sam's nephew, and as a failed ex-baseball player, out of a Grizzly Adams kind of childhood. Whatever else one thinks of him, a background so distinctive should have made J.C. an unending source of what is loosely called "good copy." We can only wonder what combination of his shyness, or stubbornness, and the critical judgments of press and fans, relegated him to a lesser universe.

His wife, the former Sue Bryant, is a city girl, a product of the Florida suburbs, bright and strikingly pretty. She has her own theory about her husband's reputation. "Jesse isn't very good at game-playing," she says, "and he isn't always tactful. It all goes back to how he was raised. You're raised in this country, and if you step in mud or dirt or whatever, you say so, you don't call it banana pudding. It's sad, but on the tour it seems there have to be good guys and bad guys. And he's been labeled a bad guy."

The question is, why? What did he do, to whom and where? Even if he didn't, how does he deal with his problem? If you don't think you are the least-liked player on tour, what can you do? To paraphrase a former president of the United States, it is hardly the most effective form of public relations to cry to the world, "I AM NOT A HARD-ASS."

Yet a small irony is at work here. He openly admires the kind of sportsman whose label he doesn't want. Ted Williams, George Blanda and Bobby Knight never were afflicted with terminal niceness. Says J.C.: "Williams was the only idol I ever had. I thought he was a god." Knight is "a great coach whose players learn about life." Blanda is "another one who had to keep proving himself."

Sam Snead did not always have a saintly image, but he disarmed his critics with a quip or a story or sometimes a grin. Sam defends his nephew, although—given that famous Snead honesty, that no-bull's-wool reflex—the issue seems briefly in doubt. "The boy is his own worst enemy," says Sam. "He takes after my dad. He was a haughty sort of man. Never said a bad word to anybody. Never said much of anything.

"J.C. is a person who is kind of hard to make friends with. He doesn't want to bother people. He thinks he does the right thing by staying out of their way. I've told him, some people want to be bothered. If they applaud a shot, he ought to tip his hat or wave or smile or say hi. Don't just walk off."

The J.C. Snead story is an interesting one not only for the local color and the family connection. It is interesting because it brushes the line between writers and the people they cover, and goes to the heart of the contract that exists between the writer and you, the reader. Have we treated these people fairly and without favor, and as fully dimensional figures? Do we owe them more sympathy, or none?

Nothing has haunted and disturbed J.C. Snead quite so much as the Case of the Phantom Pro-Am. It is a tale that seems to rank right up there with the story of The Vanishing Hitchhiker. The story travels.

It has been reported as having occurred at four or five courses, but the details are fairly consistent. The money involved is described as between $600 and $750, the putt of the amateur partner between two feet and six. The pro (J.C. Snead) has ignored his partners or grouched at them for 17 holes. Then, at 18, it dawned on him that they needed this dinky putt for a birdie to win it all. Suddenly, he was Mr. Goodwrench, friendly and helpful, lining up the putt and reminding everyone: "Now, pards, if you make that, we'll win the pro-am and I'll win $750."

Given that encouragement, the high handicapper backhanded the ball across the green and into a bunker. Up yours.

The only flaw in the story is the fact that Snead swears it never happened and no living soul has ever come forward to verify it. First reported in the fall of 1983, the anecdote has followed him from Orlando to Canada to Doral to San Diego. Not a week goes by that he isn't asked or kidded about it.

Many of his fellow golfers found the story amusing. Arnold Palmer thought it was harmless and advised J.C. to go along with it. "But, Arnold," said Snead, "it never happened. And if you were the head of a big corporation, and you wanted 15 pros to play in a clinic with your best customers, would you invite me after reading that?"

Palmer said, "I see what you mean." J.C. Snead just misses—by about a quarter of a mile—finding any humor in the story or the corner it has boxed him in. "I figure it cost me at least $100,000 this past year," he says, "maybe more. The only pro-ams I got invited to were Amana and the three or four I've always done. Not a single new one. Last summer at Westchester they had five pro-ams going at the same time on Monday, and I was in my motel room. They had guys playing who couldn't qualify for a tournament. And I wasn't invited. It comes from that story."

Snead knows he should shrug it off with a casual French phrase and concentrate on his game. But the story spreads like some kind of fungus. "It hurts," he says. "I haven't even admitted that to my wife. But it really hurts to feel you're not wanted. Since this crap really started, I think I would have quit if I had something else to do. It got to the point where it was embarrassing to show up, to hear people make their little snob remarks."

Uncle Sam chips in: "When those things get going they just seem to build. It's too bad, because common sense tells you it didn't happen. That would be stupid, a man knocking off a ball when his team has a chance to win. No matter how he hates the pro, I never heard of any club golfer blowing a chance to win like that."

J.C. has a better reputation among his fellow pros on tour, many of whom seek his advice on the practice tee. "Some of the tour players such as J.C., who the public thinks are awful, are the ones the players like the most," says tour veteran Andy North. "He's a devoted family man who loves his time away from the tour and enjoys the basic things of life. To me, he's one of the most likable guys out here."

Adds Joe Inman: "What he says most of the time is the truth, but he talks sometimes when he shouldn't say anything. In our world today there are a lot of false people, but J.C.'s not one of them. If they have a war and line everybody up, I want to be on his side. He's a good person—he just never learned how to politic."

But one of J.C.'s appealing qualities is his willingness to lower his guard, and to describe a moment that may not reflect to his own advantage. "I'm sure I struck people as temperamental," he says. "In pro-ams, it was a case of wanting to win but not feeling real easy with people I didn't know. The last eight to 10 years, I always made it a point on the first green to offer my help in lining up putts or club selection or yardage. After four or five holes you generally can tell who needs help and who will accept it. If a guy takes a suggestion and seems anxious for more, I'll help him every swing I can the rest of the way.

"Then you run into guys who feel they know more about golf than you do. I corrected a banker once and he argued with me. I told him, look, if I came to you for a loan, I wouldn't expect to tell you how to determine your interest rates.

"Another time I had a run-in with John Y. Brown, before he became governor of Kentucky. He probably thinks I'm the biggest horse's ass in the world. We were playing in a pro-am in Kentucky. He's a pretty good player, a 5- or 6-handicapper, but he hit one in the rough on a par 5. No way he could hit it out of there. I couldn't hit it out of there. The grass is up to your ankles. He gets in there with a 3-wood. I said, in what I thought was a nice way, "Now, wait a minute. Take a 7-iron or something and hit down the fairway. You can get on the green in three.'

"He said, 'No, I want to hit a 3-wood.' I said he couldn't and he said, 'the hell I can't.' That kind of got me going. I bet him $10 he couldn't hit it 20 yards. His face turned red and I thought he was going to explode. He got in there and took a cut and the ball went about five feet. I mean, Jack Nicklaus or Ben Hogan couldn't have hit a 3-wood out of there. It was like trying to hit a 3-wood out of six inches of water. Can't be done. The next two par 5s John Y. put it back in the rough and he was going to show me he could hit that damned 3-wood out of there. Never did. Took himself right out of the hole each time. And I never got invited back."

At first blush, the alleged incident of the rude pro and the tanked putt might seem of only passing interest, hardly worth taking sides over. But J.C. feels he can't ignore it, believing the story to be at the bottom of his selection as The Least Favorite PGA Tour Player in a poll of 20,000 Golf Digest readers (March 1984). It wasn't the kind of cause that would send people pouring into the streets, waving their "Free J.C. Snead" placards. But he welcomed the expression of support that came from friends and even some amateurs who had gone to the firing line with him.

One such letter went to Golf Digest from Thomas R. Devlin, the president of Rent-A-Center, Inc., in Wichita, Kansas, who was in Snead's foursome the first round of the Disney World Classic in Orlando.

"I wasn't expecting to enjoy the day," Devlin wrote. "However, Mr. Snead was friendly and warm. One member of the group was very nervous. Mr. Snead went out of his way to work with him and help him to relax and feel comfortable. I was very impressed with his manner.

"The next morning, on my way to breakfast, I ran into J.C. He recognized me and invited me to go to the club with him for breakfast and introductions to some of the other pros. He was very gracious. I suspect that many people are misinformed, as I was, about him."

A congressman from Illinois, Marty Russo, also took issue with the results of the survey. Wrote Russo: "I find it hard to believe that anyone who has talked to him and gotten to know him could rank J.C. as anything but first-rate, on any scale." All of which recalls a story told by a one-time Illinois congressman named Abe Lincoln about a man being tarred and feathered and run out of town on a rail, who said: "If it wasn't for the honor, I'd just as soon walk."

★　　　★　　　★

To know or to understand the Snead who isn't Sam, it is necessary to examine the soil from which he sprang. The town of Hot Springs, Virginia, sits in a scenic valley surrounded by majestic mountain ranges on three sides. The names echo and soar and clap with thunder: Allegheny, Appalachia, The Shenandoah. It is a town that grew up around a field of mineral wells and a hotel called The Homestead.

On a clear and balmy summer day, J.C. climbed behind the wheel of a Chevrolet and headed through the hills to the airport at Roanoke, 35 miles away. He turned into downtown Hot Springs on a street with no sign. ("It's the only street we got," he said. "Must be Main Street. They built a new post office and a new bank and added a wing to the hotel. That's the only things that have changed since I was a little kid.")

At 8 in the morning the town was stirring. That is, a man in a straw hat was talking to a burly fellow outside the office of the Exxon station.

"There's Sam, now," said J.C., swinging into the driveway.

Sure enough, it was.

Sam walked over, put his elbow on the passenger-side window and said, "Thought you were leaving."

J.C.: "Running late. I'm on my way."

Sam: "All right. Did you hit some yesterday? Hit 'em better?"

J.C.: "Pretty good, but I was still turning the short iron. Right to left."

Sam: "Well, dammit, follow it along the line a little more and they won't close up as fast." He backed off a step and gave the rented Chevy a curious look. "This your car?" Assured that it was not, he nodded, and said, "Well, don't get your ass up over the dashboard, as they say."

J.C.: "I won't. Thanks."

You had to see the look on the nephew's face to appreciate the meaning of the phrase "hero worship." It was the kind of awe and affection you have seen on the faces of small boys looking up at an all-star first baseman, a look without doubts.

The fact is, J.C. barely knew his Uncle Sam when he was a youngster. He was on closer terms with his Uncles Pete and Homer. But what he really knew was the land, these roads, that bridge. He knew them inch by inch. Hot Springs was a company town and the company was The Homestead, where his father retired as chief engineer after more than 50 years on the job.

No more than 5,000 people live in all of Bath County, which includes Hot Springs, and a crime wave is when someone steals a chicken. The man talking to Sam Snead at the gas station was the brother of the fellow who manages J.C.'s farm, just outside of town. "Now that guy right there," J.C. was saying, "comes from a family of 11. That bunch was raised like somebody was raised in the 1880s. They didn't have any running water, no electricity, they hunted for most of their food, they raised a big garden and their mother canned everything."

With his golf earnings, J.C. and Sue bought two parcels of land, the Patterson place and the Jenkins place, for a total of 900 acres. They completely restored and doubled the size of a farmhouse first built in 1901, adding a second story and a master bedroom with a bathroom bigger than some of the clubhouses J.C. once changed in. It has a Jacuzzi.

A trip through those hills with J.C. turns into a travelogue. George Washington passed through town. Robert E. Lee spent the night in a house where the Cascades Hotel now stands. One of the fiercest battles of the Civil War was fought a few ridges away.

He points out his father's house, and Sam's, and the red-brick building where he attended grade school. A groundhog, odd-looking creature, skitters across the road. A hundred yards away the leaves rustle as a fawn leaps deeper into the woods. All nature seems to call.

Over there he shot his first deer, and two mountains over he killed a bear. Through those trees you can see the path where the Cherokees once came to take the mineral waters, 110 degrees, right out of the ground.

"I appreciate nature and what a good friend it is," says J.C. "I notice when we're playing golf, the guys I play with, they walk around the course and they only notice three things: the grass, the greens and their ball. That's it. They don't see frogs or snakes or squirrels or turtles. I'm always looking for something. My eyes are always working."

There have been Sneads in that valley since the 1700s, hard by the West Virginia line. They are mountain folk—you may even call them hillbillies—and proud of it. They are governed by a code that J.C. describes in this way: If you've done anything wrong and you're asked a direct question, you admit it, even if you were one of many. But you volunteer nothing.

Once he worked as a lifeguard at The Homestead and, to save his job, on the advice of his superior, he denied an act of mischief to the lady who ran the place. "You know what?" he says. "It still bothers me today, that I stood there and looked that woman in the eye and denied something I had done." He paused, then added: "That was nearly 30 years ago."

It is part of J.C.'s natural honesty, that belongs with the natural athlete and the natural outdoorsman, to not sugarcoat or nudge the myth of family fidelity.

His love and respect for Sam need no embellishment here. Just try to suggest to him that Ben Hogan had more shots or Byron Nelson more style. But into his early 20s he was never quite sure how to take him.

"When I was a kid," he says, "Sam never really made me feel comfortable. He always said something to hurt my feelings. Like, I'd slip out to one of the courses to watch him play in a tournament, and I knew he was a famous golfer and all that. I was always shy. I'd want to say hello as much as anything. He was family, and he was supposed to be the best.

"He'd see me. He'd cut a look out the corner of his eye and see me standing over there and he wouldn't say a word. And maybe a hole or two would go along and then he'd come by and he'd say something, and it would always hurt my feelings. Just the way he was. Like, 'Boy, what are you doing out here? Why the hell aren't you out caddieing and making some money?'

"I know now he didn't mean anything by it. If nobody had been around it would have been all right. But there was always a crowd around and he'd say it in front of other people and it always made me feel like a jerk, or so out of place."

As time went on, Sam realized that his brother Jess' boy was the one most like him. At 6-2 and 205, J.C. was bigger than his illustrious uncle. Both had been brilliant all-round athletes in high school and shared a love of baseball. Sam briefly played Class D ball and was once a partner with Ted Williams in a sporting goods store.

J.C. has been described as one of the finest athletes the state of Virginia ever produced. He was born in 1941, two years after Sam Snead had already blown the best chance he would ever have at winning the U.S. Open. J.C. was a triple threat in football. In basketball he averaged 26 points a game and led the team to the only state championship in the school's history. In baseball he batted .400.

He played junior college football—the first Snead ever to attend college—and signed a contract in 1961 with baseball's Washington Senators. In three minor league seasons he hit a high of .318, but broke an ankle and clashed with a manager and gave it up.

The final conflict was over a stolen glove. A gang of kids ripped off his team's clubhouse and J.C. lost a new glove. The insurance covered the cost of a new one, $40, but when the old ones were found a few weeks later buried in the ground near the ball park, the manager told J.C. he ought to reimburse the club. J.C. told him to take the old glove and put it where the sun don't shine. The manager filed a report citing J.C. for having a bad attitude.

Even after he had quit the team, the act of doing so was painful enough that he stayed in his hotel room three days before he left for home. There he faced a disappointed Uncle Sam, whose first words were: "Boy, why'd you quit?"

"I told him," says J.C., "that in baseball until someone told you that you could play, you didn't play. I decided to try golf. After playing baseball, and swinging that heavy bat, I could hit it so far it was a joke."

Three weeks after he put away his baseball glove, J.C. had an assistant's job at Purchase, New York, working for a pro named Charlie Beverage, another Hot Springs product who had apprenticed under Sam.

The first time Beverage asked Sam to check out his nephew, Sam declined. First, he had to be convinced that J.C. was serious about the game and, second, that he wasn't looking for a handout.

"When Sam first started out," says J.C., "a few guys hustled him out of some bucks. And some of the family—not mine—hit on him a few times. When you get out there and scratch from absolutely nothing, and you get something, and along the way people take some of it away, you learn the hard way and you learn quick. Sam may have a reputation for being tightfisted. He's really not. He does a lot for people that nobody hears about. That's the way people are around here.

"I had already joined the tour (in 1968) before I finally got to play a round with Sam. He was the pro at Boca Raton and I'll tell you, I was scared to death. That was just about as nervous as I've ever been in golf, the first time I played with Sam. After he found out I was really dedicated he did everything he could do to help me. Our relationship has just gotten better and better. We're not only uncle and nephew, we're friends."

A few weeks later, the Sneads played golf in Hot Springs and Uncle Sam birdied seven of the last eight holes and had his nephew down four strokes with four to play. "He's his own worst enemy," said Sam, candid as ever at 72. "Hard-headed as a damned mule. We were riding in the cart and I said, 'Just because you're mad, you follow a bad shot with another. You have to stop that.' J.C. has got ability out of this world, but it flashes on and off. Palmer told me, 'He doesn't know how good he is. He doesn't take advantage of it.' I think a lot of people on the tour envy the talent J.C. has."

They may not envy his reputation, or his temper, or a recent siege with low blood sugar that sapped his strength and weakened his game. And no doubt he could use a little of his Uncle Sam's showmanship.

But there is no pretense about him, and he needs no polls—good or bad—to tell him who he is or where he came from. He is J.C. Snead, who is never going to be Sam, who is 42 and playing for his wife and his son Jason, 5, and his own pride. He is battling to get back his health and his game and his reputation. Well, he isn't so sure about the reputation.

"I have had people tell me lately how much they enjoyed playing with me," says J.C. "They tell me I'm really a nice guy, a credit to my profession. I tell them, 'Don't tell anybody, you'll screw up my image.' "

Final Instructions

by J.B. Forbes of the St. Louis Post-Dispatch. A Francis Howell High School girls basketball coach gets together with one of his substitutes near the scorer's table for a few last-second instructions during a game in St. Charles, Mo. Copyright © 1984, St. Louis Post-Dispatch.

Study In Concentration

by Richard B. Gentile, free-lance photographer. The intensity and concentration of Boston Celtics superstar Larry Bird comes across in full force as he watches action from the sideline of a 1984 National Basketball Association game. Copyright © 1984, R. B. Gentile.

Life in the Bushes

BASEBALL

By *GENE COLLIER*

From the Pittsburgh Post-Gazette
Copyright © 1984, Pittsburgh Post-Gazette

They called this "the bushes" back when you could distinguish one part of the nation from another.

Before this nation became a power play for the Pave the World Committee, before the six-lane ribbons of concrete spread their tentacles through rural America, playing baseball was its own reward, and playing baseball in the bushes had a rustic appeal.

It is time only dimly remembered now. Baseball in the bushes has evolved into baseball in the high grass off the interstate. You have to look carefully to find what is left of an American institution —minor-league baseball played in a small-town setting.

★　　　★　　　★

On Independence Day 1984, you might be playing baseball for the Prince William Pirates and you might be on a bus at least four hours from your next game and you might be in a funk three light years from the major leagues, but you are never far from a Pizza Hut. At least you can get a personal pan pizza after 1 a.m., even though it comes with the warning that preparation time *will* be longer than five minutes.

"I can see some change in the players in that they're not as patient as some of the kids were years ago," says 61-year-old Johnny Lipon, manager of the Prince William Pirates. "Their biggest problem to me is that they pretty much want instant success. I guess everybody is like that nowadays. They give up on themselves a lot quicker than kids did years ago."

Years and years ago, Johnny Lipon was an American League shortstop with more cunning than talent. Lipon has, with the exception of four seasons as a coach with the Cleveland Indians, managed in the low minors every year since 1959.

On this night, he is sitting on a rolled-up blue tarpaulin off the left-field foul line in Hagerstown's Municipal Stadium. The Prince

William Pirates (of Prince William County, Virginia) are about to engage the Hagerstown Suns of the Baltimore Orioles' system in the third game of a four-game series in the Class A Carolina League.

Tonight, there is a certain scent in the humid air—not cowhide nor tobacco nor hot dogs, but rather more like a concentrated cologne spray, perhaps Scoundrel. As a prelude to the regularly scheduled Carolina League game, there is an appearance by 10 women billed as the Hollywood Covergirls—actresses and models on a coast-to-coast tour in support of the notion that you need not have small breasts to challenge local softball teams to a game. The 2,763 people in attendance are now sure they know what is meant by an exhibition game.

Lipon is moderately incredulous, but it doesn't keep him from talking baseball.

"I consider all my players prospects except maybe for a couple of guys that maybe don't run too well," he says, working his Red Man. "All the rest have a chance because, even though we might not be too impressed with them right now, next year they can arrive. I've seen that happen. When I was in Salem (Virginia) in 1974, (John) Candelaria was there. He started the season not throwing very well at all. Then, all of a sudden, he was throwing a major-league fastball, had good control and a good curveball. Some of the players I've managed and some that have played against us, I wasn't that impressed with them, and now they're in the big leagues.

"The first year I managed, I saw Pete Rose, and he did not stand out that much. He was just an ordinary lookin' kid, with the exception that he looked like he had great desire. He ran everywhere. He had a lot of energy."

No man is more energetic than Lipon. Throughout the 140-game season, he sleeps six hours of every 24 and sneaks a 30-minute nap in the afternoon. When the season is over, he will be 62. Every day for the last 10 seasons, he has conducted a team meeting. He telephones in a report to the parent club after every game, issues a weekly review and prepares midterm and final reports on every player in the league.

"I really want them to have fun," Lipon says, pointing toward the young Bucs limbering in the outfield. "They are all ambitious, of course, and they want to go higher. But if you are a nice relaxed player who has fun when you play, then you are taking advantage of your full potential."

Two and a half hours later, there are nine Pirates on a shadowy field who are not taking advantage of their full potential. They are grim-faced as the Suns threaten to snap a 5-5 tie in the bottom of the ninth.

The inning begins with Pirate reliever Wilfrido Cordoba striking out Hagerstown's Fran Fitzgerald on three pitches, but Angelo Bruno slaps a one-out double inside the third-base line, and Lipon orders Mike Lopez walked. Jeff Jacobsen then beats a potential double-play ball into the grass near third, but third baseman Kim Christenson can't extract it from his glove in time to get anyone.

Cordoba, by this time having no fun at all, misses the strike zone with the next four pitches and forces in the run that beats the Pirates, 6-5.

In the Pirate clubhouse, a 12-foot by 12-foot house of steam, Crash Brown is not happy. Brown, who doubled twice, scored twice and drove in the go-ahead run in the seventh, is not relieved when a visitor tells him that the Pittsburgh Pirates are more likely to be impressed by his performance than depressed by Prince William's.

"It's more important to win than it is for me to get two doubles," the rightfielder says. "It's important to win to develop the right attitude. I'd trade two doubles for the win, but I'd rather have two doubles and the win."

Brown looks like a Pittsburgh Pirate. He has a big-league swing, a muscular back and an easy smile. He's even had knee surgery at Passavant Hospital. But in Class A ball, three giant steps from the bigs, he has tried every perspective.

"You have to love the game to put up with this (expletive)," Brown says. "But if I had to do this for the next 20 years, I would. What other job can you get up at noon, wander out to a baseball field around 4, and do what you enjoy doing? I'd say 20 of the 25 guys here are having fun, but there is a lot of bitching going on.

"My attitude is: Look, you know this is going to (expletive), but it's going to (expletive) even worse if we're going to be getting on each other."

★   ★   ★

Lipon does his best to grease his club's emotional gears with a throw-enough-at-the-wall-and-some-might-stick approach to ego stroking. He refers to second baseman Leon Roberts as "Joe Morgan," calls shortstop Felix Fermin "Luis Aparicio," calls third baseman Christenson "Brooks Robinson."

"Stacey Pettis can run like a deer; I call him Beep Beep," Lipon says. Sam Haro, another outfielder who is a step slower than Pettis, is called Beep Beep Beep. It's all very systematic.

Lipon's Brooks Robinson is the kid who couldn't get the ball out of his glove in the middle of the ninth-inning fire. Kim Christenson is one of 10 players between ages 23 and 27 on Prince William's 25-man roster. It is a thicket of varying talent that constantly questions itself.

"This is my last year at this level," Christenson says, more in resignation than out of confidence. "I'll bust my tail and do what I can do to move up, but I won't play A ball again. If I hung up the game, I'd go home to Louisville, Kentucky, probably. I don't know what I'd do."

Christenson hit .323 in the first half of Prince William's season, but has struggled horribly in the first two weeks of the second half.

"Sometimes I have doubt," he says. "I'm in a slump right now and I keep waiting to come out of it, and I'm not. Sometimes it feels like there is no point to it, like you're just driving yourself crazy.

"But I still love the game and I still believe in myself. I'd like to get to AA so that I can see where I stand among those players. But I'm not going to be a guy that will hang around just to play. If I'm not considered a prospect anymore, then I'm getting out."

Getting out is still considered better form than being shown out. The morning after the 6-5 loss, outfielder John Pavlik, who committed a horrid baserunning gaffe the night before, is released. Righthanded pitcher Brian Buckley is also let go. Pavlik had a .173 batting average in Class A baseball at age 27; Buckley a 4.74 earned-run average at age 25.

At the same time, two players—righthanded pitcher Dave Johnson and reserve catcher Jim Aulenback—are promoted to the AA team at Nashua, New Hampshire.

"This is a league where there are a lot of guys 24 and 25 who, if they can get out of this league, have a chance," says Leon Roberts, the mature 20-year-old second baseman. "Some guys come here from Triple A to get rehabilitated. In this league, a lot of guys go up and down all year to see where they can play. Us younger guys, we come here to get experience from those guys. I learn by watching them."

Roberts has learned well and is fairly bubbling in the mold that hatched Willie Randolph and Dave Cash, emulating their skills while eclipsing their confidence.

"I see myself as a Tim Raines-Joe Morgan type ballplayer," Roberts says. "I'm a switch-hitter with pretty good speed (25 steals) and I'm a pretty adequate second baseman right now with pretty good power.

"But I'm just in A ball. I'm here to have fun. The majors is my dream, but it's still a ways off—two, three more years. That's when I'll really get serious about baseball."

Lipon interrupts Roberts to tell him he'd like to see him loosen up more than his tongue before tonight's game, for which the manager has emerged from the clubhouse with the lineup card taped to his uniform top.

There follows a great moment in trivial dialogue.

Scribe: "Johnny, why do you have the lineup taped to your chest?
Lipon: "It holds better with tape."

It's the kind of stone logic Lipon tried on Nick Casteneda, the lanky first baseman with Prince William's most opulent power statistics to date. Casteneda, who grew up worshipping the Lumber Company Pirates from far-off Los Angeles, has 11 homers and 44 runs batted in.

"Lip pulled me aside the latter part of last year and said if I was going to make it as a first baseman in the big leagues I was going to have to hit 20 or 25 home runs and drive in 100 runs," Casteneda says. "In the past, I've always considered myself a contact hitter. It's kind of a big adjustment for me. I always get frustrated when I strike out and I know it's from taking a bigger swing. But if I get another 10 or 12 homers in the second half I'll finish with 20-some and that's what he thinks it's going to take."

★   ★   ★

On this night, it is not going to take very much to get the Hagerstown crowd involved. The promoters have taken care of that by offering draft beer at half price.

By the seventh inning, when Casteneda argues a called third strike, hundreds of damp voices join in the discussion. In Municipal Stadium, there is no big-league organist. There is, however, a man with a frenzied stare and a fearsome snare drum, with which he tom-toms news of every Suns' rally. On this night, he is beating out a headache in advance of tomorrow morning's regularly scheduled hangover.

As the modest Municipal Stadium grandstand sits outlined in brushstrokes of pink Maryland sunset, the Pirates are sitting on a 4-2 lead that will stand up for their only victory of the series.

This victory, like much of their inspiration and their very grip on reality, is owed to one Joe Charboneau, the 1980 American League Rookie of the Year and the 1984 Prince William Pirate leftfielder.

Charboneau has singled, tripled, walked and thrice scored in four very sturdy at-bats that again raise the question: What is he doing here?

"I think the only way anybody is going to know if I can play in the big leagues again is to put me up there," Charboneau says as he awaits a 6½-hour bus ride to Kinston, North Carolina. "Give me two weeks or a month. I know I could help them. Honestly in my heart I know I can help them right now."

There is a muted desperation in Joe Charboneau's voice that sketches a tragic outline of a once-promising career. He hit .289 with 23 homers and 87 runs batted in for the Indians in 1980 and had put the City of Cleveland in his back pocket. In the spring of 1981, a headfirst slide in spring training sent his legs jack-knifing over his back and triggered the first of a series of back operations that left him pretty much useless to the Indians, who released him last year.

"The Pirates have treated me better than the Indians treated me when I made Rookie of the Year," he says. "I hope they bring me up when they expand the roster to 40 in September because I really think I can help them."

Charboneau is 29, revered by his teammates and almost mourned for by major leaguers, and that as much as anything displays the distance between the bigs and A ball. Yet he insists there is still big-league life in his bat at age 29.

"It would be hard for me to face my teammates every day if I didn't think I could play in the big leagues," says Charboneau, who is hitting .280 with four homers, 12 doubles and 32 RBIs. "If they thought I was just hangin' on, it would be hard to face them. But it's not hard for me to play down here. I don't mind it one bit. But I'll tell you, I'd play that two-week trial in the big leagues for what I'm making here.

"Let's face it, you've gotta have a break in this game. That's all baseball is is a game of breaks. If I get another break and get back to the big leagues, I think they'll see I can play. If I don't get it, I'm not going to go around the rest of my life bitter."

The bus driver honks and the guy they used to call Super Joe excuses himself. It was Springsteen who wailed, "The highway's jammed with broken heroes on a last-chance power drive."

"If you need anything," Charboneau says, "call me in Kinston."

The bus pulled out.

Schnellenberger: He'll Leave Mark on U of L

COLLEGE FOOTBALL

By *JIM TERHUNE*

From the Louisville Times
Copyright © 1984, Louisville Times

Howard Schnellenberger speaks:

"Coaches are in the game for two reasons: One, the impact you have on kids' lives. Two, the records you made, and what they say about you after you're gone.

"You want to leave your mark for posterity.

"What greater thing can be said about a man than that he took a program that never was and made it something that is."

The last sentence was delivered with emphasis, each word forceful and calculating, scattering the wisps of smoke from his pipe as they appeared. It was all so impressive, the sound rumbling out of a throat laced with gravel, rolling into the air from under a thick mustache and frozen in space by eyes of steel.

One had to stop and make sure he wasn't listening to a burning bush.

Some think they are. Talk to Schnellenberger's former players, assistant coaches and the support team at the University of Miami. Talk to writers who have covered him and columnists who have examined him, some of them hardened and skeptical. All will say they found someone who goes beyond the normal human condition—call it a sense of destiny.

Schnellenberger slept on a cot in the football office every night of his first full season at Miami, 1979. Even now, back at home, he never sleeps more than four hours in a row. "Sometimes Howard gets up at 2 or 3 in the morning, goes in, turns on the TV and sits in a chair," said his wife, Beverlee. "And thinks."

So the man who has returned to his hometown roots to coach the University of Louisville football team for 1985 is . . . different—different in a mystical way. These are some examples:

The Penn State game, 1979—Miami is struggling. It's Schnellenberger's first season since leaving the comfort of a top assistant's job with Don Shula's Miami Dolphins.

The Miami Hurricanes are 3-4. They haven't been much of anything the last few years, and this is no exception. "They were talking about Schnellenberger not being the right man for the job," said Miami Herald writer Jim Martz. "Miami was a 40-point underdog."

Schnellenberger suddenly changed quarterbacks, starting an unknown redshirt freshman named Jim Kelly, from Pennsylvania, near State College. Kelly had been recruited by Penn State, but as a linebacker. He had family there, friends there, and he had something to prove. It was 10-0 Miami before Penn State ran a play from the line of scrimmage. Miami won 26-10. Back in south Florida, eyes opened.

"I had to give the team time to develop," said Schnellenberger. "And the good Lord shined on us, too. Penn State's (cornerbacks) were not very good."

The Florida game, 1980—Some rivalries are heated, some are just plain mean. Florida-Miami is mean.

With Miami leading 28-3 and a few seconds left, Schnellenberger sends his offense out to fall on the ball and end it. The game's at Gainesville, and Florida fans are pelting the Miami sidelines with oranges—"and rocks and ice," said Schnellenberger. An orange hits assistant coach Christ Vagotis in the temple. He falls to the ground as if shot.

Schnellenberger recalls his offense. He sends out his field goal team. Miami adds three points on the last play of the game.

The offers, 1981—Schnellenberger has a chance to switch three home games for big bucks after the 9-3 season of 1980. Penn State offers $350,000 to come back to State College for the third year in a row; Notre Dame wants to move its Miami game to the Meadowlands in New Jersey or Pasadena's Rose Bowl, and Florida asks Miami to return to Gainesville.

"I'm not going to prostitute the people of south Florida," says Schnellenberger.

He passes up the money. Is it worth it? He beats Florida before 73,000. He gets a national TV contract for Penn State, ranked No. 1 at the time, and upsets the Nittany Lions. It's national TV again for Notre Dame, and Miami blows the doors off the Irish.

Notre Dame, pre-game, 1981—In its preparation meeting, CBS asks Schnellenberger if it can televise his halftime talk live.

The coach sits in a chair, legs crossed, puffing on his pipe, and says, "I dunno, it may be a blowout by halftime." The CBS guy is sympathetic. He says, "Oh, coach, you're going to do all right." Says Schnellenberger, "I mean they might not be very close." The CBS guy whispers to an associate, "Who is he kidding?" Miami leads 20-0 at the half. It wins 37-15.

Ten days before the Orange Bowl, 1983—Nebraska comes to Miami cocky and conservative. A "media day" is held. Nebraska goes first.

Schnellenberger has scheduled a series of car-show appearances in Miami. If he does them all, he can't get to "media day" in time. Unless he gets a helicopter.

As the Nebraska interviews are ending, with Coach Tom Osborne and Heisman Trophy winner tailback Mike Rozier still on the field, a drone is heard overhead. A helicopter lands.

"Oh my God," says Osborne. "Who's that, the President?" asks Rozier. "It's Coach Schnellenberger," comes the reply. "No it isn't," says Rozier. Schnellenberger gets off. "Oh my God," says Rozier.

TV that night and newspapers the next day are filled with Schnellenberger's drama. Miami then beats unbeaten Nebraska 31-30 and wins the national title.

★　　　★　　　★

A sense of destiny? All right. But all that brings questions, too. Can Schnellenberger teach and coach, or was he simply the captain of a miracle season achieved by a missed two-point conversion after winning for four years with Lou Saban's players?

Gary Stevens coordinates the Bernie Kosar-Downtown Eddie Brown-Alonzo Highsmith offense, the most devastating in the land.

There are many ironies here. Stevens coached four years for Schnellenberger, and is one of the few Miami assistants who apparently won't be joining the rush to Louisville. It would be a sideways move for him, because his next step up is to a head job.

No one believes more strongly in Schnellenberger than Stevens.

"Don't expect miracles," Stevens said. "But this man is a teacher, a fundamentalist, sound and knows how to win through practice and organization.

"He has a plan and he knows how to put it into practice. A lot of guys have a plan but they don't know what to do with it. For Howard it's a game of teach and correct, correct and teach. There won't be any highs and lows. He's all business, a good analyzer, and I can honestly say he's never made a bad decision in four years. In '83 people were saying, 'Now Howard's gotta play with his own people' —and we win it all."

Stevens' eyes widened.

"He's intelligent, a hard worker, loyal, honest. . . . He's a machine! What more do you want?"

Comparisons to Bear Bryant are inevitable—porkpie hat vs. the pipe. Schnellenberger gets as many pipes for presents as Bryant got hats, and he smokes a tobacco blend made especially for him in Miami. There's the low mumbly voices you can't quite understand. And there's the presence, a force of some kind.

"He's like Bryant in the way he gets things done and the respect he demands in ways only Howard can do it," said Vagotis, who played for Bryant and Schnellenberger at Alabama and who will be

Louisville's new offensive line coach.

"But now that Coach Bryant has passed, there is no more awesome a presence than Coach Schnellenberger."

John McVeigh started at linebacker most of this season at Miami. He transferred from Kentucky, finding the first year of Jerry Claiborne's rules and discipline unsuitable. He returned to his home state and came in '83, without a scholarship, to a program that took a backseat to no one in the discipline department.

"The restriction at UK was too much for me, like a prison," said McVeigh. "It's strict here, too, but you knew what he was saying was right."

And scary. "It's remarkable how close to Bear he is," said McVeigh. "How he would sit there and stare at you with those eyes. You felt they were inside of you. And the intensity in his voice, rumbling like a damn volcano. You'd go to his office, and he'd be smoking that pipe, then turn and talk to the wall, then turn around, and you also had the feeling something very remarkable was going to happen."

Alonzo Highsmith went to Miami as probably the nation's top high school defensive end. Schnellenberger watched him return kicks and take handoffs during the week of freshmen orientation in 1983. Subtly, he planted the seed in Highsmith's mind that he might want to make a change. Now he is probably the nation's top college fullback.

Highsmith loved it, believed in it, then he'd go into Schnellenberger's office and break into a cold sweat.

"Terrifying," he said. "I was always nervous. Everybody on the team was nervous. When he spoke, people moved. You'd run through a wall if he asked you to, ask how high if he said jump.

"But he didn't fool you or scheme you to get you to work hard or try hard. He just told you what it's like. . . .

"And he'd be right. He's the only coach in America who could take misfits, guys too small, not fast enough, guys with all left feet, and make 'em believe and win. Only 100 people believed he could beat Nebraska, him and his team."

"He's worshipped," said Ron Steiner, who will join Schnellenberger as one of his publicists. "It's debatable whether he knows it, but it's not debatable whether the kids believe it."

Veteran Miami Herald sports editor Edwin Pope, who has known Schnellenberger for two decades, says Schnellenberger "does radiate power, more than players would like, although they want a leader and not a father or buddy, too. He also has a certain aloofness, and he's a very domineering man in a way that doesn't seem domineering.

"I remember a trip he took to Florida to arrange accomodations for a game. It was 100 degrees in the shade, and Schnellenberger had on this huge suit and tie. He's a nut on dignity. Well, the man simply refused to sweat—he willed himself not to sweat. Never saw anything like it.

"He's sensitive to what's written and can be very hostile, one of those coaches, like Shula, who says he never reads newspapers and then reads every word."

The 1983 beat writer for the Herald, Christine Brennan, knows about hostility. It was her first Miami football assignment, and she made an aggressive early-season play on stories.

But a couple of disagreements during interviews and quote/misquote confrontations set Schnellenberger and Brenann on a nineweek campaign of distrust that took two hotel-room sessions with Pope and Schnellenberger to allow her to continue to try to do her job.

And yet that, too, achieved an upbeat finish. "I couldn't believe it," said Brennan, now with the Washington Post. "It got to where I was constantly getting those 'There-you-go-again' looks.

"But after the Nebraska game, after I finished my story, I wandered into a victory party. I walked up to coach and stuck out my hand. He said, 'Christine Brennan, I'm going to kiss you,' and he did, on the lips. Somehow that didn't seem wrong, it was nice. There've been no problems since."

One other writer worth hearing from is John Underwood of Sports Illustrated, who wrote what some consider the definitive book on Bryant. He also lives in Miami and is a UM grad.

"Too often people who brush next to the Bryant brilliance got the wrong things," he said. "They saw the toughness, but missed the human side.

"Where Schnellenberger approximates is to understand the human equation. He makes no conscious effort to imitate Bryant. He has a gruffness, but not stoicism. He's apart from the crowd. But these came from personality traits long since developed.

"The softer side of Bryant was the most important part. Bryant said, 'I don't coach football, I coach people.' That's what Schnellenberger does."

He has soft sides. . . .

Schnellenberger and Roy Hamlin, his promotions/marketing guy who also will be coming to Louisville, cooked up the idea of taking a train to Gainesville to promote a Florida game one year.

They boarded an Amtrak and picked up press people along the way. The train also picked up a group of kids going to camp. The media was lounging in one of the front cars, talking and eating and whatnot, when someone realized Schnellenberger was missing.

Hamlin went to find him. He was sitting in the midst of the camp kids with a sucker stuck to one arm and wearing a conductor's cap. "I thought he was Captain Kangaroo," Hamlin said.

And he has hard sides. . . .

Defensive tackle Kevin Fagen, a fourth-year junior, got in enough scrapes as a freshman that when he was involved in a fight at a campus party the school was ready to kick him out.

"Coach went to the wire for me and kept me in," Fagen said. "But he also said I was on final probation, and that if I screwed up again, that was it. I had the "Breakfast Club'—running three miles or weight and agility drills at 6 a.m. all during spring ball. He made me do it on my own. I never got in trouble again."

"Once a player learns you're going to do certain things to keep him you've lost it all," said Schnellenberger. "You can't be on his side, but you can't make exceptions. You can't hide things."

Linebacker McVeigh: "He'd push you hard, to an extreme. There was never any water on the field, and in August and September it was unbearable, 100 degrees plus, with humidity.

"We were having three-a-days, two-a-days (practices), Sunday scrimmages. If you'd go down, they'd carry you into the locker room, get some water, rejuvenate and go back out to no water.

"But you knew he'd go to the wall for you. All he ever wanted was the truth."

Two-year starting center Ian Sinclair, a one-time tight end from London, Ontario: "Those three-a-days in August of '83. We'd say, 'Why? We're in shape.' Working the blocking sled after practice. We'd say, 'Why?'

"But there was always a reason. No one could see it but him a lot of the time. But it was like he never seemed to be wrong. We'd get in a tight situation in a game and he'd call the play instead of the coordinator. And it always worked. We asked ourselves, 'Why doesn't he call all the plays?' But we never asked him."

Dave Heffernan, two-year starter at offensive tackle: "Do I believe he can take middle-line players and turn them into something great? I was a skinny 208-pound defensive end in college. Now I'm 253. I'm a living witness. He made you believe in yourself. If he'd tell you a green wall was blue, it was blue."

Sophomore Bernie Kosar, second-team All-America quarterback: "He will get people to go above what they're doing. He's the best guy in the nation to turn around a program, without doubt."

So Louisville's many holdovers from a 2-9 season, and the recruits Schnellenberger can muster, may expect long, tortuous days in the sun. Those who survive may also expect a consistency of performance—"We never lost our mind," said Heffernan. "The boat never rocked. We approached Louisville the same way we approached Nebraska." And they may expect some positive results from this.

"The guys from Louisville will wonder if this guy's for real," said Sinclair. "They'll go through hell. I wondered, too. But we went out and almost never lost."

"He'll work harder and prepare more than anybody else in the country," said Fagen.

"Louisville will win early with him," said Highsmith.

"I'm surprised he took the job," said Gary Stevens. "But he was gonna have a list of things he needed. Then he gets those, and around the country they're saying, 'Hey, Louisville is gonna get it, too.'

"Howard's gonna give you a national championship."

Schnellenberger stretched out in the chair in his living room. He puffed on his pipe and he smiled. Sort of smiled.

"It all has to start sometime," he said. "I guess Notre Dame even started sometime."

Jaeger's Losses Show Something Had to Give

TENNIS

By *GARY NUHN*

From the Dayton Daily News
Copyright © 1984, Dayton Newspapers Inc.

I wonder what it's like not to have had a childhood.

Not to have got up late in the summer, watched a game show on TV, gone swimming in the afternoon, played wiffle ball until dark in the backyard.

Not to have gone to football games on Friday nights in the fall, double-dated at the drive in, sneaked your first beer at the class picnic.

I wonder what it's like to have parents push and prod and pull you as if you're a piece of clay.

I wonder what it's like to be a tennis prodigy.

I wonder what it's like to be Andrea Jaeger.

Not much fun, I fear.

Andrea Jaeger is the No. 3 woman tennis player in the world, according to one of those know-all computers that spit out such data.

Wednesday, she lost in straight sets in a first-round match in a tournament in New York. Afterward, she met the press, as the tour rules say she must. She was matter-of-fact about the loss.

But when she walked out of the interview area, she began to cry; not because she had lost, but because she didn't care that she'd lost.

Andrea Jaeger, a millionaire almost twice over in just four years on the women's tennis tour, is an emotional wreck. She is 18 years old.

★　　　★　　　★

Oh, how we love money in this country.

Oh, how we chase the buck.

It is in our fabric, woven in there, I suppose, when half of us were poor, itinerant men of the soil, living from one crop to the next, while the rest of us were working in factories for just enough wages to get through to next week.

When the pendulum swung, we overdid it, of course, human nature being what it is. Sports didn't invent greed, it merely gave it a convenient forum and refined it to an art.

And so we have Roland Jaeger, Swiss immigrant who boxed as a semi-pro when he came to this country in order to pay the rent. He wasn't very good at it—a ham-and-egger, the boxing people call them.

But Rollie got him a daughter, a precocious little pig-tailed kid who at age 14 could stay on the tennis court with the best in the world and beat most of the others.

And Rollie stood by and smiled. And when the kid would rather have been in an arcade, playing Space Invaders, Rollie had her on a tennis court, hitting backhands. And when she would have rather been on the telephone with her best friend back in Lincolnshire, Illinois, she was in another country, on a tennis court, hitting forehands down the line.

And she made a lot of money.

But they didn't live happily ever after.

★　　　★　　　★

Last year, Andrea Jaeger told the media she wanted to go to college, wanted to try to live a normal life again.

Her father nixed the idea. He told her she was making too much money to give it up and go to school.

Andrea had made sounds this year as if she had accepted her father's counsel. But there were previous incidents that indicated Andrea was wrestling in her own mind.

Earlier in February in Houston, she was playing so poorly that the tournament promoter walked onto the court and asked her to try harder.

Jaeger's best friend, Lisa Bonder, said later Andrea gave away the rest of that match.

Two tour officials were quoted this week in USA Today.

"She's a woman and a girl," said Peggy Gossett. "She has grown up on the circuit, and that is a very difficult thing to do. In some ways she is 40 and in other ways she is 10. She gets in her Mercedes and turns the key and drives like a woman of the world. Then she plays tag with the ball kids under the bleachers."

"She appears to have lost heart in tennis," said Ted Tinling. "Nobody knows what's wrong."

Au contraire, Ted. Everybody knows what's wrong.

★　　　★　　　★

It's a blight on women's tennis, this kiddie parade. At first it was cute. But now all the ballots are coming in, we're hearing from the outlying precincts, and we don't like what we hear.

Chris Evert started it, I guess. She played in a couple of pro tournaments when she was 14. But it was different in those days. There weren't tournaments 52 weeks a year. Chrissie retained her amateur status until her 18th birthday.

The ones who followed didn't wait.

Tracy Austin turned pro at age 14; Pam Shriver at 15; Andrea Jaeger at 14; Kathy Horvath at 15; Kathy Rinaldi at 14; and the latest of the little darlings, Carling Bassett, at 14.

What strikes me as I read these girls' biographies in the Women's Tennis Association yearbooks is the injuries they have sustained.

Evert didn't because she wisely kept her schedule to a minimum as she grew up.

But Austin (back), Shriver (shoulder), Jaeger (shoulder and knees) and Horvath (back) should tell someone something. These girls are being shoved too far and they are being shoved too fast.

And Jaeger is turning out to be the Shakespearean tragedy of them all. Trapped, apparently, by her talent and her family. Crying because she used to care.

This Valley Guy's In the Fast Lane

OLYMPIC SKIING

By *LEIGH MONTVILLE*

From the Boston Globe
Copyright © 1984, the Boston Globe

He came down the mountain, dropping empty and imaginary Coca-Cola cans out of the imaginary car window. The radio in his head was tuned to a Top-40 station, mounds of sounds, blasting all the way. He was chewing gum and singing to the music.

"By God" the dour Austrians asked the determined Swiss. "What kind of creature is this?"

"Can't say for sure," the determined Swiss replied to the dour Austrians. "But it looks as if it's . . . an American?"

An American.

His name is Bill Johnson, and you've probably seen his James Dean face and his Robert Redford exploits only about a dozen times already on the news. Never fear. You'll be seeing 'em again . . . and again . . . and again.

He is the stuff of instant 1984-style legend. He is skiing history.

"How does it feel to be the first American to win an Alpine skiing gold medal?" he was asked yesterday after he chopped down Mount Bjelasnica to capture the men's downhill in the XIV Winter Olympics.

"It feels great," Bill Johnson said. "I guess there's been a dry spell for the past 14 Olympic Games."

His style was as memorable as his substance. He boasted, bragged, flipped the bird to the ski establishment as he blew past in the outside lane. He wasn't only an American winning a first Alpine Olympic gold for his country, he was a certain flamboyant breed of American.

An American wise guy.

"What's the longest you've ever worked?" he was asked.

"I think I once held a job for a month," Bill Johnson replied. "I washed dishes in a restaurant in Wenatchee, Washington."

Fast times at Ridgemont High. Let's party, Bud. That was his style.

He wasn't some sort of brooding perfectionist who had laid out a master plan to attack this sport dominated by the Austrians and Swiss. This was a 24-year-old Valley guy from Van Nuys, California, who rolled onto the scene from underneath a backyard stock car on blocks. A big-mouthed, overgrown kid who wanted to go as fast as possible. Everywhere.

"You have this reputation for speed," a reporter said. "You like fast cars, fast motorcycles . . ."

"Women, too," Bill Johnson said.

"What?"

"Never mind."

He said he'd win the race, said it every day for two weeks to anyone who asked. He pulled a Joe Namath, a Muhammad Ali. Did it even better. At least Namath and Ali knew when they were going to play the game and fight the fight. The downhill kept being postponed for Bill Johnson. The race that was scheduled for February 9 wound up being held February 16, twice postponed when all the competitors were at the mountain.

Bill Johnson never even seemed to notice.

"That's the thing," U.S. Alpine director Bill Marolt said. "He had a hype going for him on that first day that was incredible. He was really hummed up.

"To keep at that level for a week is a real tribute to him. Every day, he went to the course and beat everybody in practice. He finished sixth once, then second twice and first twice. He showed them all he wasn't going to be deterred, which is probably when he won."

"Where'd you spend your time during the extra week?" Johnson was asked.

"Doing this," he said, flicking a set of imaginary flippers. "Video games. There's not much going on around here, anyway."

Let's party, Bud. Let's blow this backwater place and get a good cheeseburger and some music with some real, electric guitars involved. Let's do it.

He tangled daily in the newspapers with Austria's Franz Klammer, the patron saint of the downhill. He did nothing to hide his up-and-down relationship with Marolt and the other U.S. coaches. He told stories about how he had been arrested at 17 for stealing a car in Oregon, about how he had been dumped at 22 from the U.S. team for being out of shape, about how he liked to hit the town about four times a week to look for new women.

"Why do they bother to show up," he asked again and again about his competition. "They're only racing for second."

He knew from the beginning that this course on this mountain was made for him. A drag strip of a downhill, few turns involved. He would tuck himself into an egg, make himself into an aerodynamic bullet, and fly. He would be a candy-striped egg, blowing down the mountain in his own Easter parade.

His mountain. *His* style.

"When I was 7 years old in Idaho, I was bombing the rope tow," Bill Johnson said. "Then I got older and I was bombing the whole chair lift. Luckily, somewhere in there, I learned how to turn."

He called the last stretch of this race "a motorway to the end." He put his head down. He bombed to the end, bombed and bombed.

"What'll this race mean for you?" Bill Johnson was asked in a conference room after the gold Star Spangled Banner had been played in Skendertia Square.

"Millions," he immediately replied.

Around his neck was a piece of orange satin, the medal hanging from the ends. He fingered the medal, looked at it. Stared.

"Can't figure out what's on the front of it," Bill Johnson said. "Looks to me like it's an 'M.' Or maybe a building of some kind. Don't know. There isn't even anything that says 'first place.' Nothing . . . but it's gold."

Let's party, Bud.

Jim Fixx: How He Lived, Why He Died

RUNNING

By *HAL HIGDON*

From The Runner
Copyright © 1984, The Runner Magazine

"Running has not yet been shown to make people live longer."
James F. Fixx,

The Complete Book of Running

Early this past summer, while lunching in New York with Hal
Bowser, a former Science Digest editor, Jim Fixx mentioned that he
wanted to obtain a telescope to use during his upcoming vacation.
One of Bowser's hobbies is optics. Bowser mentioned a friend who
was selling a Celestron, a very expensive telescope.

Fixx purchased the telescope, then midway through July called
Bowser from Cape Cod. "I'm here looking out over Waquoit Bay,"
Fixx began. "The images I get don't seem very bright. It could be
haze, but maybe the telescope needs adjustment. I thought I would
call you and ask, what am I doing wrong?"

Describing the incident later, Bowser thought it typical of his
friend. Despite paying a lot of money for a device that should have
functioned perfectly, he didn't blame the device. Fixx worried that
he was to blame.

Two days after the call, Jim Fixx drove to northern Vermont to
spend a month at Caspian Lake. He planned to relax, work on his
latest book, watch the Olympics on TV and take some 10-milers in
the woods. He arrived Friday, July 20. Late that afternoon, Fixx
decided to run. At 5:30 p.m., a passing motorist discovered a man
lying beside the road clad only in shorts and running shoes. State
police got there quickly, but the man was dead of a heart attack.

It was Jim Fixx, the man who had written the amazingly successful best-seller, The Complete Book of Running. Fixx, one of the

leading disseminators of the fact that running was good for your health. Fixx, who helped launch the running boom and whom the boom launched into a popularity so great that he was featured in an American Express commerical. Fixx, fit and active, a longtime runner, a marathoner even, who looked younger than his 52 years.

Was this man who pinned the blame on himself for things gone wrong somehow to blame for his own death? Had he not followed all the teachings in his writings that explained, step by step, how one could reach a healthy life? What happened to Jim Fixx, and what does it mean for the rest of us?

★   ★   ★

James Fuller Fixx was born in New York City on April 23, 1932. His father, Calvin Fixx, worked as a magazine editor for Time. Young Jim admired his father greatly. When Jim came home bruised from a beating by the school bully one day, his father looked at him and said, "We'll have to do something about this."

Rather than complain to the principal, the elder Fixx marched his son to Stillman's Gym and introduced him to Jack Kearns, a well-known boxing manager. Kearns put his arm around Jim's shoulder. "I'm going to teach you the right cross," Kearns said. He worked with the youngster until Jim could throw a respectable punch.

"Don't I need another punch?" asked Jim.

"To succeed," the manager explained, "you learn one skill. But you learn to do it extremely well."

Back in the schoolyard, when the bully began pushing Fixx again, Jim launched the right cross. The bully never bothered him again.

Jim Fixx was still in high school when his father, at age 35, suffered his first heart attack. During the war, the elder Fixx had been under great stress working long hours at Time. He smoked incessantly. "Until he died eight years later," wrote Fixx, "he lived the life of an invalid. Once—just once—in those eight years I remember seeing him toss a football. The rest of the time he sat quietly, read, listened to music and (as I came to realize much later) put his affairs in order."

Despite that forboding example, Jim Fixx copied the habits that probably hastened his father's death. After graduation from Oberlin College in 1957, Jim worked for a number of magazines, including Saturday Review, McCall's and Life. As New York executives tend to do, he dined elegantly every day, bulking to 220 pounds. He smoked two packs of cigarettes daily. He exercised infrequently, playing a little tennis. He had a wife, four children and the pressure of providing them with a good life.

Later, when he wrote The Complete Book of Running, Fixx listed the risk factors identified by the American Heart Association as contributing to the chance of heart attack. These include heredity, blood pressure, diabetes, smoking, excess weight, cholesterol, exercise, emotional stress, age, sex and build. Readers could rate themselves between one and six for each factor, obtaining a score that identified them as low risk (10-20), moderate risk (21-40) or high risk (41-60). In 1967, Fixx, at 35—the same age at which his father had suffered his first heart attack—unquestionably ranked as "high risk."

Still, had it not been for a tennis injury in 1967, Fixx might never have taken up running. The injury, a pulled calf muscle, caused a slight limp that lasted a few weeks. He did not bother to see a doctor. Nevertheless, the injury disturbed him. "What was striking was the way I felt about the damage. My body had betrayed me, and I was angry," he would write.

To recuperate, Fixx began jogging, gradually increased mileage, stopped smoking, lost weight, entered his first race (five miles long) and finished last. There is no question as to why he would later be able to write such a successful book for beginning runners: He was their prototype.

After moving to Riverside, Connecticut, Fixx developed a favorite 10-mile course along tree-shaded streets through Old Greenwich, past century-old homes and St. Saviour's Church, out to Greenwich Point on Long Island Sound, and back. Like millions after him, he had found a new "right cross" and changed his life—although on the heart attack chart, he probably had reduced his risk only to "moderate."

Fixx had already written two books—Games for the Superintelligent and its sequel. Accepting a modest advance from Random House, he began writing a third, a self-help book about running. When it appeared in 1977, the dust jacket claimed: "Runners feel better, become thinner, probably live longer, have a better sex life, and drink and smoke less than their sedentary companions."

Enough people accepted the dust jacket's promise to keep The Complete Book of Running on the bestseller list for a year. To date, the book has sold 940,000 copies (not including 16 foreign editions). A sequel, Jim Fixx's Second Book of Running, sold 180,000 copies. A third book about Fixx's experiences with sudden fame and riches, Jackpot, sold only 9,000, despite offering his wittiest writing. In Jackpot, Fixx told the following "black joke" on himself:

HUSBAND: A guy was talking about this great book in the elevator today. He got off before I got the title, but everybody dies at the end.

WIFE: It must have been The Complete Book of Running.

Numerous factors contributed to the success of the Complete Book, including the fact that Fixx's second wife, Alice Kasman Fixx, worked as a book publicist. (Fixx had divorced his first wife, Mary, in 1972 and remarried in 1974.) The book was clearly written, elegantly packaged by Random House and appeared at just the right moment, both benefiting from and contributing to the running boom. Another subtle factor may have been the author's almost perfect name: Fixx. He was the "Mr. Goodwrench" of fitness, who was going to help people repair their lifestyles.

Fixx's son John, age 23, says, "After the book hit, he made more money than a writer is supposed to. The nice thing was he never had to do anything he didn't want to. He liked things quiet." Todd Benoit (no relation to Joan), a researcher Fixx hired to help him on later projects, says, "Jim was a very careful craftsman. Editors needed to do little to rewrite his copy. A paragraph written by Jim was a very clean paragraph. He started at 8:00. I'd see him for 10 minutes, 20 minutes again at noon, then at 4:00 we might go out running together."

Visiting Manhattan, Fixx often joined the runners in Central Park—although before his book appeared, there were few to join. Most runners like the southernmost region of the park, the area where the New York City Marathon finishes, or the 1.6-mile cinder path that circles the mid-park reservoir. Only the bravest, those requiring the longest routes for the distance treks, venture into the park's northernmost region bordering Harlem.

One day Fixx so ventured, passing several teenagers who shouted insults. Perhaps foolishly (although he still had his right cross), Fixx stopped, jogging in place and asked, "What did you say?"

The kids seemed flustered that their insults had failed to intimidate the jogger. "Why are you running?" one finally replied.

"Because it's fun," offered Fixx. He beckoned them. "Come on. Why don't you try it?"

For several hundred yards the teenagers trotted behind Fixx as he expounded on the pleasures of running. Afterward, whenever he spotted them in the park, Fixx would ask them to run with him, and usually they would.

★   ★   ★

Although Fixx was always looking out for the welfare of others, it appears he was in one way careless about his own. Despite his family history, he did not seek regular checkups. "He really was negligent in that area and rarely went to a doctor," his second wife, Alice, was quoted saying after his death. First wife Mary recalls him obtaining an obligatory physical examination when joining the staff of McCall's in the early '60s. In the Complete Book, Fixx also mentioned taking at least one physical, in November, 1968.

In November, 1980, Fixx obtained a cholesterol test while attending a meeting of the President's Council on Physical Fitness. His triglycerides ("the bad guys"), he said, were 57, compared to the 160 average for a person his age. High-density lipoproteins ("the good guys") were 87, compared to average 31-60. However, Fixx's total cholesterol count was 253, compared to the average of 150-250, seemingly "moderate risk." Fixx wrote a friend that the person administering the test said such a cholesterol level was common among athletes (because of the HDL factor) and that it was "nothing to worry about."

Considering the apparent risk signaled by his father's early death, it seems strange that Fixx never obtained an exercise stress test, vital for diagnosing coronary heart disease. While researching the Complete Book, he asked one of his regular running companions, Steve Richardson, to take such a test and report what it was like. Fixx wrote: "After an hour of intensive scrutiny, he (Richardson) was told that he was in excellent shape and was in virtually no danger of experiencing difficulties with his heart. As a result, he is enjoying his running more than ever."

As further research, Fixx visited Muncie, Indiana, to interview David Costill and Bud Getschell at Ball State University's Human Performance Laboratory. They asked if he'd like a stress test. Fixx declined. On a subsequent visit, Fixx departed saying, "The next time I return, you're going to have to put me up on that treadmill." He never would.

★   ★   ★

One day around 1980, according to his wife Alice, Fixx staggered inside the house after working out in the yard, face drawn. She claims, "Jim had the classic symptoms of heart trouble. He had to stop, lie down, he couldn't move. He was sweating, short of breath, nauseated, pain in the chest. After it passed, he just went about his work."

About the same time, Fixx visited Phoenix and ran with Dr. Art Mollen, director of the Southwest Health Institute. Fixx experienced chest discomfort and a tired feeling. "He said he had had a cold the week before and wasn't feeling that well," recalls Dr. Mollen.

Either incident could have been symptomatic of a heart attack. In fact, Fixx's autopsy showed a minor scar that might have been the result of an earlier cardiovascular incident.

Because of his medically-related research, Fixx certainly knew that cardiovascular disease is the number one disease in the United States: 1,500,000 people suffer heart attacks annually, 560,000 of them fatal. "Every fifth man you meet on the street will have a heart attack by the time he is 70," says Dr. William Castelli of the National Heart, Lung and Blood Institute. Among those whose fathers suffered a heart attack before 40, one third will do the same.

Runners are susceptible to the same laws of probability, despite promises of immunity from the sports zealots. Dr. Thomas J. Bassler, a California pathologist, has for years espoused a theory of "immunity" against heart attack for people fit enough to have finished a marathon. Dr. Bassler offered no conclusive proof but challenged others to *disprove* his theory by sending him medical reports of heart attack victims who happened to have been runners. As those reports trickled in, Dr. Bassler continued to maintain his theory, attributing death to reasons that did not diminish the powers of the marathon lifestyle in the eyes of the faithful.

Asked whether Fixx's death disproved his theory, Dr. Bassler answered only that eventually he would examine the medical reports. How long would that take? "Two years," suggested Dr. Bassler.

"Maybe ten."

In developing a "marathon lifestyle" Jim Fixx had only *moderated,* not *eliminated,* his risk. Was he distrustful of doctors? Or was he merely afraid of what they might tell him?

His friend Hal Bowser never saw any evidence of either. "If there was any anti-doctor sentiment on his part, I would have sniffed it out," says Bowser. "All I ever heard from Jim was praise of doctors and what they were doing. He was excited by stress tests. He knew doctors who were pioneers in this field. They were on the cutting edge."

Yet a subtle undercurrent of medical distrust does trickle through *The Complete Book of Running.* Fixx quotes one friend as saying, "Running is my doctor." He suggests that most physicians don't know much about running injuries. He supports the views of Dr. George Sheehan, who has said, "I've kind of given up on the medical profession." Fixx was both supporting and reflecting the feeling of invulnerability among the growing legions of committed runners.

Dr. Kenneth H. Cooper, another force behind the running boom, suggests that Fixx was guilty of believing four myths about exercise and health. "One was that he couldn't have heart disease and run as much as he did. Two, even though Jim said he disagreed with Dr. Tom Bassler's theory that if you finish a marathon you're immune to heart attacks; I think subconsciously he did agree. Three, he thought stress testing worthless because of too many 'false positives,' and that the average physician could not interpret stress of an athlete. Four, because running had changed his lifestyle, he felt he didn't need to worry about his family history of heart disease."

In December, 1983, Fixx visited Dr. Cooper's Dallas Aerobics Center to research an article he would write for *The Runner* ("The Test of Time," May, 1984) about tests involving 76-year-old marathoner John A. Kelley. "Jim was here for three or four days," says Dr. Cooper, "and during that time it got to be a joke: Why not take a stress test? He refused for reasons known only to himself."

Despite his success, Fixx recently had undergone severe stress. In 1982, he and Alice went through a difficult divorce. "When it was over," says his son John, "Dad felt like a weight had been lifted from his shoulders."

Through the spring of 1984, Fixx worked on his latest book, *Maximum Sports Performance.* The book was past deadline, and says Todd Benoit, "He was working very hard to get the book right." But John Fixx notes, "He had been under greater pressure finishing his first running book. He had worked 12-14 hours a day to get that done in time."

Another son, Stephen, age 21, spent six months living with his father the previous year. "There were no hints to me that he was under great stress," says Stephen. "He was running every day. I'd run with him four times a week, and weekends we'd race." Stephen's twin sister Betsy also visited. "He seemed fine," she says. "No clues."

The summer of 1984 would be special, not merely for Jim, but for the entire Fixx family. For nearly a year, he and his sister Kitty (who lived in Santa Barbara, California, with husband Jim Bower) had planned to rent a house near Waquoit on Cape Cod. Peggy Palmer, a high school friend of Jim's whom he was seeing again, would join them. Jim's mother, Marlys Fixx, was coming from Sarasota, Florida. Other family members promised visits. Kitty says, "This was a lifelong dream of having our vacation together, all the family."

In June, Fixx delivered the manuscript of his new book to Random House. "The only thing he was complaining about was a sore calf muscle," says Joe Fox, his editor. Todd Benoit recalls: "He was eager to get up to Cape Cod and see everybody. He was planning some work, but mostly vacation." After a month at the Cape, Jim and Peggy would spend a month together in northern Vermont. Jim's son John suspected his father might soon ask her to marry him.

During the month in Cape Cod, Jim ran four races: a pair of five-milers in Sandwich and North Falmouth; a 10-kilometer in New Seabury and a 20-kilometer in Bourne. Kitty's daughter Martha was running her first long race in Bourne and Jim paced her. Kitty ran two of the shorter races. Peggy also ran. Jim played tennis as well, two or three sets a day.

He talked about getting in shape for this year's New York City Marathon. Concerned because of a decline in performance, for the first time Jim Fixx was doing speed work: fartlek and surges in the middle of long runs. In the 10-kilometer, he ran his fastest recent time, about 7:10 pace. In one of the five-milers he broke 35:00, not bad for a man of 52 who never claimed to be more than a middle-of-the-pack runner. "He had a good kick," said son John. "Maybe he was sandbagging." Jim had run eight Boston Marathons, achieving a 3:12 personal record in 1975.

One Sunday morning, everybody attended services in Woods Hole. Kitty suggested they remain for a church brunch. "You stay," said Jim. Smiling, he began removing his trousers, revealing running gear. He began what he thought would be a 10-mile run, covering part of the Falmouth Road Race course, back to Waquoit. It proved to be closer to 15 miles. The day was hot; Jim needed to walk several times.

Later, someone would mention to his mother how tired Jim seemed. "Of course he was tired," said Marlys Fixx. "He was sailing and playing tennis, pitching in and cooking. He took me out in a canoe. Everybody was tired!"

The Bowers were fussy about what they ate. As a girl, Kitty had a heart murmur. Her husband had had triple-bypass surgery, and they followed the low-fat Pritikin diet. Kitty noted that Jim's eating habits did not differ much from hers: "He ate sensibly, almost vegetarian. He like pastas, salads, fruit. He didn't eat sweets. He was careful in the amount he ate, very moderate."

After the North Falmouth race, Jim began mentioning what seemed to be a bad chest cold—"except it's not a chest cold," he said. John recalls, "Dad didn't seem to think it was serious." Jim spoke after that race to one of Peggy's friends, a nurse, Shirley Cullinane. Shirley expressed no concern, although she said later she might have if Jim had fully described his symptoms. He would start a workout and, after five minutes, feel tightness below his throat. Sometimes he would walk before resuming to run. Other times, he would run through it. After several minutes the tightness abated. It didn't bother him playing tennis, only running.

"Maybe it's pollen in the air," he had speculated one evening, "but I don't have allergies."

"I don't either," said Kitty, "but my eyes have been watering." They discussed whether the problem might be due to the warm, heavy air.

Jim stroked his throat, pondering, "It's too high to be the heart."

Eventually, he called a physician friend and described the problem. After hanging up the phone, Jim told Peggy, "He said it could be caused by a number of things, and I shouldn't overreact." Jim nevertheless discussed seeing a doctor in Vermont if the condition continued. Maybe in the fall it might be time for a long overdue medical checkup.

Early Thursday morning, July 19, on the Cape, Jim and Peggy went shopping. Later, Jim played tennis with his sister Kitty, then ran four miles with her and six more with Kitty's daughter Martha. At 3:00 that afternoon, Jim called John A. Kelley, who lived nearby. Jim often kiddingly referred to "Old John" as his "athletic father." Kelley was painting at his easel. He told Fixx about a 10-kilometer race in Hyannis that weekend. "No, I'm tired, very tired," said Jim. "I'm leaving for Vermont tomorrow for a month of doing nothing."

Fixx's dinner that evening consisted of oysters on the half shell, pasta, blueberry pie and wine. "It was a wonderful family dinner," recalls Kitty. Peggy says, "Jim was cheerful. He was always a great storyteller. When he worked, he worked alone, but when he relaxed, he liked having people around."

Each of the vacationers was obligated (by family rules) to clean two rooms before leaving. In the morning, Jim cleaned his two, then loaded his car, remembering a small TV set on which he planned to watch the Olympics. He started to help Peggy in the kitchen, but knowing he had a six-hour drive, she told him, "Get out of here." She would be joining him in a week. He hugged everybody goodbye and set out at about 9:30 a.m. "I'll call you tomorrow," he told Peggy before driving away.

Around 4:30 p.m., he arrived at the Village Motel outside the town of Hardwick, Vermont. The house rented for August on Caspian Lake would not be available for six days. He planned to spend those days before Peggy's arrival on revisions of his new book and also on the 1985 edition of The Complete Runner's Day-by-Day Log and Calendar. Once settled, he left for a run along tree-shaded Route 15.

It was an hour later when the motorcyclist spotted Jim Fixx lying beside the road. His position on the right side of the road suggested Fixx probably was on the return stretch of his run when he was stricken. The autopsy by state medical examiner Eleanor N. McQuillen indicated death by heart attack. Fixx's three main arteries showed 95 percent, 85 percent, and 50 percent blockage. Starved of blood, his heart apparently experienced "ventricular fibrillation," or uncontrolled beating. Under such conditions, the heart fails to pump blood. Oxygen cannot reach the brain. Within a few seconds, the victim loses consciousness; within a few minutes, the victim dies.

According to Dr. McQuillen, the autopsy showed scars on the heart, evidence of prior heart damage. "The majority of tiny scars were either two weeks to a month old," she explained. "One small scar might have been earlier." The scars were in the anterior portion of the heart. When anterior damage occurs, the victim is less likely to experience the so-called classic symptoms that might serve as an alert. Dr. McQuillen refers to this as "silent coronary artery disease."

It is not unusual that Fixx could run for so many years yet show so few symptoms of the disease that killed him. "Atherosclerosis, the gradual clogging of the arteries, begins in childhood and is progressive over many years," says cardiologist Noel Nequin. "The body adapts to insufficiencies. Blockage doesn't happen overnight, but when it builds to a certain point, heart damage can occur within minutes. It's like the straw that finally breaks the camel's back."

Did running, in a way, kill Jim Fixx? The run that he took that day in Vermont did "kill" him, although as Dr. Ernst Jokl of the University of Kentucky Medical School points out, "Exercise does not kill. A pre-existing disease does."

★　　　★　　　★

Tuesday afternoon, July 24, family and friends gathered at St. Saviour's Church in Old Greenwich. It was a hot, sticky day. People fanned themselves with a card saying, "A Service of Thanksgiving for the Life of James Fuller Fixx: 1932-1984." With insufficient seating in the small church, people stood in the side aisles. Several were reporters trying to look inconspicuous. Others attending wore running shoes along with jacket and tie. Midway through the service, Hal Bowser rose and told the story about Jim Fixx's problems with his telescope and how he'd wondered, "What am I doing wrong?"

For an hour after the service, those who once knew Jim Fixx lingered in the parking lot, talking, sharing memories, even laughing about silly incidents involving their lost friend. Several runners passed, working out on Jim Fixx's favorite 10-mile course. They too had lost a friend.

Soon afterwards, Kitty returned home to Santa Barbara, where part of the U.S. Olympic track team was training. Several days before the women's marathon, Kitty met Joan Benoit returning from a run. Benoit commented that Jim Fixx was one of the few experts polled by The Runner who had picked her to win the gold medal. Joan said she appreciated that.

"He was looking forward to watching you on TV," said Kitty.

"Wherever he is," said Joan. "I'm sure he'll be watching."

Starting Over

BASEBALL

By *HAL BODLEY*

From The Sporting News
Copyright © 1984, The Sporting News Publishing Co.

Pete Rose is surrounded by expectations.

There are those who are excited about his twilight chase of Ty Cobb's record of 4,191 career hits. Rose needs 202 to shatter the record.

There are the millions of middle-aged fantasizers who want this 43-year-old man to prove he can still slide on his belly and rip a single through the middle with consistency. He's their champion.

There are those long-starved baseball fanatics in Montreal who are praying he'll give the Expos the inspirational leadership they've so desperately needed, disappointing summer after disappointing summer.

And then there's the proud man himself, Peter Edward Rose. Outwardly, he oozes with the almost cocky confidence that has become a blazing trademark during 21 years in the major leagues. Inwardly, he has something to prove—to himself and to the baseball world.

"When you mess with my pride, when you back me up against the wall with my pride, somebody's going to be in trouble," he said last October 20 when the Philadelphia Phillies released him.

Pete Rose is starting over, for the second time.

After three restless months without a team, Rose signed a one-year contract with Montreal on January 20.

The Expos are asking him to be the same miracle worker he was during 16 years with his beloved hometown Cincinnati Reds and the past five seasons with the Phillies.

Rose led the Reds to two World Series victories, then after being cast away as a free agent following the summer of 1978 went to Philadelphia and led the Phillies to their first world championship. Rose, more than anyone else, put the perennial bridesmaid Phillies over the top when they won the World Series in 1980.

As he says, they learned to play race-horse baseball: They didn't fade at the wire.

But with Rose's hair graying, his bat slowing and his average dipping, the Phillies slammed the door in his face. Thanks for the memories, they said, but adios.

All Rose wants to do is play baseball. All he ever wanted to do was play baseball. So when people told him a .245 average and a 43rd birthday coming up April 14 were signs the end was near, he sneered.

In reality, Rose refuses to realize how perilously close he is to the dreaded end. That is one of the basic reasons even his most severe critics are reluctant to write him off for 1984 and the immortal matter of chasing a record that has stood since 1928.

"For those who think I can't play anymore, Montreal gave me a contract, and they're a pretty good team," Rose said. "There's nothing I can do about the date I was born. I wish people would forget how damned old I am. I don't feel old, I don't act old and medical experts have told me my body isn't old. Two years ago, I led the league in hits at age 40, and nobody said anything about me being washed up. The people of Montreal should hope I get 202 hits because, if I do, I'll produce for this team. I'm going to get the record. I'm not worried about that. If I don't get it this year, I'll get it next year."

Yes, Rose is starting over.

Not only has he come to the Expos as an elder statesman who wants to lead more by example than inspiration, but pieces of his often rocky personal life are falling into place. He recently purchased a lavish but cozy home with sprawling acreage in the exclusive Indian Hill suburb of Cincinnati, and there are hints he will marry his lovely fiancee, Carol Woliung, in the near future.

"I think Peter looks great, and I'll be surprised if he doesn't have a good year," said his mother, Laverne Noeth, while visiting him recently at the Expos' West Palm Beach, Florida, training base. "Don't worry about his age. Remember, his father was playing semi-pro football well into his 40s. Peter reminds me so much of him."

What the Phillies did to Rose last season was unjust.

Five days before spring training ended, they told him to play right field. He agreed, but the day he returned from a closed-door meeting with Pat Corrales, then Philadelphia's manager, he was confused and bitter.

During the early weeks of the season, he shuffled between first base and right field, not knowing where he'd be playing.

Later, when his batting average stayed below .250, Rose became a part-time player. For the first time in his storybook career, he went to the ball park each day not knowing his status. Late one night during a drive from New York's Shea Stadium to Philadelphia, Rose shed his macho shield.

"For the first time in my life I've lost some of my confidence," he said. "You know when *my* confidence is messed up, something's wrong."

For most of September, Rose sat on the bench and watched Len Matuszek, who had a key role in the Phillies' winning the National League East, play first base. Matuszek was ineligible for postseason play. Almost by default, Rose was back and batted .344 in the N.L. Championship Series and World Series.

There was no excuse for his not getting to play September 28 in Chicago when the Phillies clinched their fifth East title in eight years.

But the worst injustice happened in the third game of the 1983 World Series, when somebody made the decision not to start him with the Series tied at a victory apiece.

After that, the Phillies went quietly. As Baltimore celebrated its decisive victory, several of Rose's teammates said the heart went out of the team when his name wasn't in the lineup.

Rose probably could have remained with the Phillies had he agreed to a compromise about his status, but he never has been one to stay where he is not wanted.

Several teams, including the Seattle Mariners, California Angels and Pittsburgh Pirates, expressed interest in him, but Montreal made the strongest pitch and signed him to a one-year contract with a base salary of $500,000.

"We seemed to have lacked some of the qualities Pete has," said Expos President John McHale. "Maybe we can get a last breath from him—well, not a last breath, but a couple of breaths out of him. We told Pete we're not interested in him for attendance. We drew 2.3 million last year without him. We told him we're only interested in him helping us win. We told him if he didn't hit, he wouldn't play. And he told us, 'If you got eight guys who can play ahead of me, you got a helluva ball club.' "

"I'm just happy as heck he is a teammate," said All-Star catcher Gary Carter. "I've looked forward to this moment a long time. To be with a Hall of Famer, and he is a Hall of Famer as far as I'm concerned, that's just a great feeling to have that type of individual. Everybody has said with the talent on our club we should have done better. Right? Well, maybe Pete's what we need. He's been in this situation so many times, six World Series, he may be the guy you can look to down the stretch."

When Rose came to grips with the reality of his release from Philadelphia, he decided he probably should do more during the off-season than play tennis with his attorney, Reuven Katz.

People used to say Rose was 35 going on 12, or 40 going on 16, because he always managed to cheat the calendar. But when he woke up one day last October and faced the sobering fact he was 42 going on 43, he did something.

Michael A. Letis, president of the sports marketing division of Robert Landau Associates, the New York firm that represents Rose, convinced him to try a sophisticated form of offseason conditioning.

"I think Pete realized there were lots of reasons for his having a poor year," said Katz. "The only thing he could do about it was try what had been successful for other players—a well-designed, well-executed program with strength and flexibility training."

Rose asked Reds trainer Larry Starr about such a program, and Starr agreed to help all winter, but only if Pete went to Ohio University for tests by Dr. Frederick (Fritz) Hagerman.

"They told me I had the body of a 25-year-old," said Rose, "but my upper body was weak. That's what I spent most of the off-season trying to work on. You have to be careful, because if you do too much weight work, you lose your flexibility."

"I don't think the quickness was there last year, in his bat," said Montreal Manager Billy Virdon, who has adjusted his outfield to allow Rose to play left, with Tim Raines in center and Andre Dawson in right. "He wasn't driving the ball, but I have seen some encouraging signs this spring. He's generating more bat speed. If anybody can come back, he can."

Rose was only in the Expos' camp a few days when first baseman Al Oliver, a career .305 hitter, was traded to San Francisco. Everyone thought that would make it possible for Rose to return to first base.

"I plan to use Terry Francona at first," said Virdon. "Pete seems to want to play left field. If he's got a freer mind out there and can do the job, that's fine."

"From the first day, I've been in left field, and there's been no talk of going back to first," said Rose. "I don't care where they play me, but I want to be able to prepare for one position."

Rose seldom shows impatience, even when he is flooded with reporters' questions about age, the future and last year.

"They keep asking me what I bring to this team," he said. "The only thing I know of is, it's the same thing I bring wherever I go—a positive attitude, a confident attitude, a love for the game and a burning desire to win. I'm just a player who is going to try to do his job. Montreal has always had a great team—on paper. It's just a matter of understanding what they have to do to win. Leadership can only do so much. Any player can help with his contribution. If I do well, that's where the leadership will come out."

Rose, who has played in more winning games than any other player in the history of baseball, says if he doesn't do the job he doesn't expect to be in the lineup.

"Last year I batted .245 and didn't complain when I wasn't playing," he said. "But if I hit .345, I expect to play. It's that simple. This is a very positive thinking team. I get the feeling it's a team that wants to win, like the Phillies when I went there in 1979 and when I was with Cincinnati."

Rose is already the reason the Expos set an exhibition-game attendance record. And fans will flock to games en masse as he closes in on the 4,000-hit mark. He needs just 10.

"And, hopefully, I'll get the 4,000th hit against either Cincinnati or Philadelphia," said Rose, a twinkle in his eye. "That would be nice, wouldn't it?"

Tongue Out of Cheek

by Eric Lars Bakke of the Denver Post. Cyclist Alexi Grewal, an American Gold Medal winner in the 1984 Summer Olympics in Los Angeles, could not hold back his enthusiasm when he reached the victory stand. Copyright © 1984, the Denver Post.

Programmed Goal

by Bruce Bisping of the Minneapolis Star and Tribune. Edmonton's Jari Kurri scores into an almost empty net during the final game of the Oilers-Minnesota North Stars 1984 National Hockey League playoff series. The goal wrapped up the North Stars' season and a disgusted fan, seeing what was about to happen, hit his mark with a masterful program toss. Copyright © 1984, Minneapolis Star and Tribune.

Georgetown's Pressure Cooks, 84-75

COLLEGE BASKETBALL

By *JOHN FEINSTEIN*

From the Washington Post
Copyright © 1984, Washington Post

Two years later, John Thompson and Fred Brown hugged again. They held onto each other for what seemed like an eternity, both men's eyes welling up with emotion.

Tonight, the hug was a celebration, not a consolation. Because tonight, before 38,471 in the Kingdome, Georgetown firmly established the depth and the brilliance of the program Thompson has built, defeating Houston, 84-75, to win the national collegiate basketball championship.

Two years ago, against North Carolina, an errant pass by Brown left an equally superb Georgetown team one basket short of the title. Tonight there was no denying the Hoyas.

Even with defensive catalyst Gene Smith forced to watch from the bench because of an injury to the arch of his right foot in Saturday's semifinal, Georgetown took the lead for good with more than 32 minutes left in the game and was never in serious trouble after that.

"They do everything a great team should do," said a tearful Akeem Olajuwon, who played most of the second half with four fouls and finished with 15 points and nine rebounds for Houston. "They don't care who scores, who takes the shots. That's the difference. They aren't a selfish team. The unselfish team won tonight."

More specifically, the deepest team won. Even without Smith, nine players contributed to Georgetown's cause. And the key offensive contribution in the second half came from Reggie Williams, the Baltimore freshman who has often struggled this season adjusting to being a reserve.

Tonight, Williams scored 19 points, 13 of them in the second half, when the Cougars gamely fought back to within three points. He also had seven rebounds, three assists and a key tie-up of Olajuwon when Houston still had a chance to get back in the game.

"Coach has always told me that if I take good shots, he doesn't mind me missing," Williams said. "I just kept taking the shots tonight because I had good ones."

The Hoyas (34-3) got 16 points from David Wingate, 14 points and five rebounds from their other freshman, Michael Graham, 11 points and six assists from Michael Jackson, and 10 points and nine rebounds from Patrick Ewing.

Although his statistics were not overwhelming, Ewing was named the tournament's most valuable player, and there was little arguing with the choice. It was Ewing who took control of the inside in the first half when the Hoyas built their lead. And it was Ewing who kept Olajuwon from dominating the way he can, pushing him far enough from the basket that Olajuwon rarely got the shot he wanted.

"This morning when we practiced, I came in the gym and Patrick asked me how I was feeling," said Thompson, who was an elated man on this night. "Usually I tell him it's none of his business. Today I told him, 'I feel terrible.' He told me not to feel terrible because we were going to be national champions tonight.

"When the big fella said that, I figured I'd just let him take care of the rest."

Ewing had help, though, more help than Olajuwon, and that was the difference. Although Houston guard Alvin Franklin almost shot his team back into the game in the second half with a game-high 21 points, the Cougars (32-5 and national runners-up for the second straight year) just could not handle the never-ending wave of Georgetown players.

"They were in control most of the game," Houston Coach Guy Lewis said. "Once they got the lead, they controlled the tempo. We have nothing to apologize for. We got beat by a great basketball team."

For five minutes tonight, Houston was more than great, it was perfect. Faced with a 2-3 Georgetown zone, the Cougars promptly made their first seven shots, including two bombs by Michael Young (18 points) over a lunging Ewing.

But it couldn't last. The Hoyas switched to a man-to-man, the Cougars started missing and Georgetown, after trailing by 14-6 early, methodically took command.

"We didn't want to go to the man-to-man as early as we did," Thompson said. "But the way they came out and shot we had no choice. I was worried."

Thompson is, by nature, a worrier. His players made sure his worries were pointless tonight.

From a 14-6 deficit, they put together a 26-8 run during the next nine minutes and took a 32-22 lead with 6:15 left in the half.

Ewing keyed the surge, not just with three baskets and one love-ly assist on a shovel pass to Graham, but—as always—with his de-fense.

If there was a key moment, it might have come with the score tied 16-16. Olajuwon rebounded a miss by Rickie Winslow and had the ball three feet from the basket, a spot he misses from about once a season.

But Ewing was in his way. Olajuwon faked, Ewing never moved. He went up, Ewing went with him and the little shot rolled off the rim. Something seemed to go out of Olajuwon after that play. He worked hard and played courageously with four fouls most of the second half. But he did not seem eager to challenge Ewing again.

"He's the best player I've ever faced," Ewing said later. "Every-thing was hard work tonight."

But that is as it should be in an ultimate game. That is why Hous-ton must be given credit for coming back after the Hoyas used Ewing's intimidation to spur a 16-6 run that ended with Bill Martin's 15-footer and a 10-point Georgetown lead.

By then, Ewing was on the bench with two fouls and Thompson had spread the team out to pull Houston out of its 2-3 zone. Instead of going man-to-man, Lewis went to "50ZA," his zone trap, putting two men on the ball all over the court.

"We just didn't think we could match up with their quickness in the man," Lewis said. "This was our best chance."

The Cougars' chances would have been helped had they not lost their poise during the last three minutes of the half. With Thompson protecting Ewing and his two fouls, Houston cut into the lead, with help from benchwarmer Benny Anders, whose jump shot and steal helped get the Cougars within 34-30.

But with a chance to slice the lead to two, Young tried a forced, off-balance shot and Jackson promptly made one at the other end. Then Wingate drew Olajuwon's third foul on a driving layup and when he missed the free throw, Brown, playing perhaps his best game in this, his last game, rebounded and dished to Wingate for another layup.

It was 40-30 at intermission. "I knew the last 20 minutes would be the longest of my life," Jackson said. "I was right."

It didn't look that way early, when Olajuwon picked up his fourth foul climbing Graham's back in the first 30 seconds and Wil-liams drove right past him on the next possession for a 12-point lead.

But Franklin would not quit.

During the next nine minutes, Franklin scored 14 points, slowed only when he had to come out for 90 seconds with a slight ankle twist. When he hit two foul shots with 10:29 left, it was 57-54 and it was a contest.

Enter, Williams. Thompson always says a basketball team is built, not hatched. That is why he uses 10 men early in the season even when some of those players are still feeling their way. Tonight, some of those early painful moments paid off.

After Franklin cut the lead to three, Williams drove the middle, missed a short shot, rebounded and put it back in for a 59-54 lead. Moments later, after a Reid Gettys charge, Williams made the same move. Only this time when the defense came to him, he slipped the ball to Graham for a ferocious dunk. It was 61-54 with 9:30 left and the Cougars were running out of gas.

Olajuwon tried to make one final move, but Houston never got within five points again. Its one chance to do so came with 2:30 left after Graham had bricked two free throws with the score 74-68. The Cougars went immediately to Olajuwon, posted up. But before he could turn to make his move, the velvety Williams slipped up on him and put his hands firmly on the ball.

The officials called jump ball, it was Georgetown's turn on alternating possessions. Eight seconds later Wingate hit two free throws and, after 12 years as a coach, John Thompson had taken a tiny Jesuit school to the national championship.

"At times I've been obsessed by the national championship. I've awakened in the middle of the night in the summer saying 'national championship.' " he said. "Now, I have one. I don't want 10 like John Wooden, I just wanted to get one."

32nd Place: A Triumph Of the Olympic Spirit

OLYMPIC TRACK AND FIELD

By *GORDON MORRIS*

From The Los Angeles Times
Copyright © 1984, Gordon Morris

It was nearly 9 o'clock last Friday night, and a damp coolness enveloped a virtually deserted Los Angeles Coliseum. A few people, mostly families and friends of the athletes, huddled in the stands. In the press box a smattering of weary reporters hunkered down over their note pads to watch the final event of the decathlon competition at the U.S. Olympic track and field trials.

As in many decathlons, this would be decided by the final event, the 1500-meter run. And walking onto the field were 13 bone-tired men who had completed nine grueling events in just 18 hours. As they trudged slowly to the starting line, one of them—Orville Peterson from Vero Beach, Fla.—lagged behind. After nine events, he was tied for 13th place. With a superb performance in the 1500 meters, he could possibly edge his way onto the three-man Olympic decathlon team.

Yet something was wrong. As his fellow decathletes stretched and limbered up, Peterson stood off to one side, unmoving, staring up at the Coliseum's bright lights.

Finally the starter called the 13 athletes to the starting line. As Peterson stripped off his warmup uniform, he revealed a massive bandage protecting a badly torn hamstring muscle, wrapped tightly around his left thigh. Nonetheless, he took his mark with the other 12. When the gun sounded, the field took off at a fast gait. Peterson—head down, limping noticeably—began a slow, painful trot.

At the 300-meter mark he was almost 100 meters behind the field. The gap grew with each stride. Still, head down, Peterson slowly limped around the track. Soon the field caught up to him, and one by one passed him. He took no notice. His limp worsening with each stride, he doggedly stayed on the track.

Finally the first finisher, John Crist, crossed the line with a time of 4 minutes 28 seconds. His time was worth 596 points. It made him the winner of the decathlon competition and a member of the Olympic team. The second runner crossed the line in 4:29.28; the third runner followed two seconds later. Finally Gary Kinder, in 12th place, finished his 1500-meter run in 5:01.39.

Peterson still had two laps to go. As Crist and the others celebrated, Peterson, head down, limped around the track. When he came across the line to begin his last lap, a strange silence descended on the Coliseum. At once competitors, fans, officials and reporters realized that they were watching something very special. Applause broke out in every corner of the Coliseum. Peterson's fellow decathletes shouted encouragement as he limped around the track.

When Peterson entered the home stretch for the final time, the decathlon announcer, Frank Zarnowski, a college dean from Maryland, caught the magic of the moment. With Peterson limping toward the finish line, Zarnowski's voice, edged with emotion, filled the Coliseum with lines from an ancient Greek saying: "Ask not for victory, ask only for courage. In your pursuit, you bring honor to yourself. But more important, you bring honor to us all."

More than four minutes behind the 12th-place finisher, Peterson staggered across the line into the arms of his fellow decathletes. It would have been difficult to find a dry eye in the stadium. He received no points for his time of 9:44.80. He dropped into 32nd place in the final standings.

Yet, for 10 stirring minutes, Orville Peterson was a champion—providing shining testimony that, through determined men and women like him, America's long tradition of athletic excellence will never be in jeopardy.

Opponents: Faceless, Necessary Losers

BOXING

By *MICHAEL SHAPIRO*

From The New York Times
Copyright © 1984, Michael Shapiro

The opponent, Obie Garnett, came to Chicago to fight two weeks before Christmas. He took the bus from Cincinnati, where he worked in a mill. He arrived alone, as opponents often do, and that night he boxed in the Aragon Ballroom, a dance hall with stars painted on the ceiling. He did not know the man who taped his hands with gauze and adhesive, nor the man who served as his second. A third stranger was prevailed upon to carry Garnett's water bucket. A white towel was placed over Garnett's shoulders and three strangers followed him to the ring.

He did not last a round. At the opening bell, Garnett, a flabby light heavyweight, danced around the local boxer he was being paid to fight. The local fellow measured Garnett and then reached his face with a stiff jab. Garnett crumpled. He rolled onto his side, facing his corner, but he could not see his seconds because his eyes could not focus. His nose ran. His cornermen rushed to him when he was counted out and revived him as the spectators laughed.

Upstairs, in the communal dressing room, Garnett toweled himself dry. Someone offered to buy him a beer. He drank it at the bar downstairs while another opponent, Sylvester Wilder, who, according to the Ring Record Book once lost 36 fights in a row, took a hook to the belly and was counted out.

Garnett waited for his pay. This was his third professional fight. He had lost the first two, also by knockouts in the first round. He would fight six more times and lose the same way each time. He was paid $175 for this fight. The man who had been his second asked Garnett why he was taking the chance of being hurt for so little money.

Garnett, who was rushing so he would not miss his shift at the mill the next morning, turned and without a smile or hesitation, replied, "Christmastime, man."

★   ★   ★

When boxers are known to lose more often than they win they become useful only as opponents. Often they are called less flattering names; but without them the sport, according to those who understand it best, could not exist. Pragmatic opponents, aware of their roles, see no harm in fighting and losing so long as they are not damaged. The romantics among them are sure that someday their true worth will be recognized and they will fight for championships. Boxing purists lament that their sport is not as it was decades ago when there was a club to watch boxing in most every town they visited. But, they add, there has always been a call for opponents to smooth the ascents of new, attractive prizefighters who have the financial backing opponents never know.

"This is boxing as it has been known since the beginning of time," says Hank Kaplan, a boxing historian. "There have always been opponents. Ever since the dawning somebody discovered that the way to build a fighter up was to get him someone he can beat up."

There are good opponents. "A guy who don't get knocked out but who'll always lose a decision," says Chris Dundee, the Miami Beach promoter. "An opponent is a fella that is always dependable, that can give a good account of himself and lose."

There are bad opponents. "If a guy goes out in the first round the fans know you got a stiff in there," says Ernie Terrell, the former heavyweight champion and now a Chicago club-fight promoter who does not like a hard hitter as an opponent because "a puncher is always dangerous."

There are opponents with many aliases. "In older days guys had 10, 15 different names," Kaplan says of the practice of avoiding identification. "They knew when to get hit and when to fall and when to go into convulsions. They were specialists."

And there have been opponents who, if not necessarily gifted boxers, are still remembered long after they fought. "I'll never forget the Gorilla," says Jerry White, a longtime Miami trainer of his fighter, Gorilla Gould. "They called me up and needed a heavyweight to fight. They were looking for an opponent. The Gorilla owed me a few bucks. I took 4-to-1 odds that the Gorilla would go the limit. I gave him a couple of cloves of garlic and gave him instructions that whenever you get in a clinch, blow in the other guy's face. He blew and the poor guy stepped back like he was punched."

Jose Torres, a member of the New York State athletic commission, says that boxing is entertainment and that is why opponents are necessary. "Promoters get people who can excite the public," he says. "Opponents exist and I'm sure that promoters will try to get them and good managers will always look for them for their fighters —these 'tomato cans' who are just in there to lose."

States with boxing commissions—most have them but some do

not—try to keep boxers from fighting and losing too often. Since 1980 for instance, New York has required boxers to carry "passports," documents in which their victories, losses and suspensions have been printed. Neighboring states like New Jersey and Pennsylvania have a similar system and also supply information to one another on fighters whom they have suspended. New York stores that information in a computer—it regularly receives boxing data from 20 states —that is scanned before a boxer is permitted in the ring. In New Jersey, a fighter who has been knocked out is suspended for 60 days. In New York the suspension is for 90 days. In Pennsylvania the commission has suspended a boxer for 90 days for a "very poor showing."

Still transgressions exist. Although New York State will revoke the license of a fighter who has been knocked out six times, Torres says, enforcement is difficult. "They change their names," he says.

Torres, once the world light-heavyweight champion, recalls how his manager, Cus D'Amato, was judicious in selecting the men he fought. In his first fight he knocked out Gene Hamilton in the first round. Hamilton had lost 10 of his 15 fights.

"If I was a promoter and I had a fighter to bring up I'd do the same thing," says David Conteh, who has lost 15 of his 19 fights. "Look, I've been around. I'm 34 and still pugging. I won't be no champ at my age. If I make a few bucks I'll be lucky. I try to take what I can. A lot of people said I had potential but it never materialized. Everybody wants to use you as an opponent. They say, 'He was a good man when he was younger.' What can you do? What can you say? There's nothing you can do."

Opponents sometimes lose so badly and quickly that it seems as if they lose on purpose. Sometimes they do; often they don't.

"He was supposed to get hit on the chin and he was supposed to fall," says Larry Kent, a Miami trainer for many years, recalling a poorly executed dive he once observed. "Every time he fell he didn't get hit. The referee looked at him and said, 'Get up you bum, you didn't get hit.' In the fifth round he got hit and he looked up and said, 'Don't tell me I didn't get hit. Start counting.'"

But paying boxers to "take dives" is seldom necessary, boxing elders say. "There's enough bad ones out there to make the really bad ones look terrible," says Joe Mooney, a manager and gymnasium operator in Savannah.

Mooney is a purveyor of opponents. He is not alone in his vocation and maintains that his service is much in demand. "The main reason they call me," he says, "is because I'm dependable."

Mooney takes his fighters to Atlantic City and Hartford and sometimes Tokyo and South America.

"We go to Bermuda every two months," he says. For these excursions, as well as those to Northeastern cities, he brings only his "main event quality group." The fortunate ones might make $1,500 for a night's work, which is far more than they could expect to make at home.

Opponents, however, almost always lose on the road; and even a knockout does not assure victory. Terrell tells of one especially unsuccessful opponent—"I never in my life saw him win a fight"—who was shipped to Memphis from Chicago to battle a local hero. The opponent, who was offered few fights because of his thunderous punch, surprised everyone when he quickly knocked the local man senseless with a mighty blow. Then the arena lights went out. They stayed out, Terrell says with a laugh, until the local pug was returned to life. This took perhaps 20 minutes, somewhat longer than the traditional 10-count. Upon his revival, the bout continued to its scheduled conclusion at which point the arm of the victorious local fellow was raised by the referee.

Promoters call managers like Joe Mooney with specifications in mind. They tell him who they have and what they need, Mooney says, and he will tell them which of his fighters might be suitable. Then he tells them, "Take your pick." "Usually," he says, "they don't get beat up."

Mooney might drive 15 hours to bring his boxers to their fights. And if need be, he will step in himself. "Mainly who I fight is the guy no one else will fight," he says. This often means oversized heavyweights against whom Mooney, at 275 pounds, seems a reasonable foe. He has fought 38 fights, he says, and lost 32. But he is never too hard-pressed for boxers. "There's a new guy walking in the gym every day," he says.

Opponents enhance the careers of those who might be champions. Consider the rise of Gerry Cooney, who amassed nothing but victories, 21 of the 25 by knockouts, until Larry Holmes finished him in 13 rounds in 1982. Cooney first knocked out Bill Jackson, who had been knocked out in his first eight fights and never got past the third round. In his fourth he beat Matt Robinson, who had lost 14 of 16. Cooney knocked out Joe Maye in his fifth. That was on November 18, 1977, the beginning of a hectic Thanksgiving-Christmas season for Maye who, in the next 30 days, fought and lost three more times. Maye's entry in the Ring Record Book shows that he lost 18 fights in a row; the streak would have reached 25 but for a draw against Joe Vellmure, who beat him twice before.

Successful opponents are in demand and this sometimes makes their handlers prosperous. "I used to get calls from all over, from Pensacola to Key West, any place you can mention," Jerry White says of his halcyon days. "I used to bring the opponents for half the show. We used to make up the show the week before."

Shrewd opponents know the workings of their sport. "You get in shape, you get a fight and it's canceled," David Conteh says. "Another fight is next week. Do you want to take it or leave it? You need the money." But others do not understand why they are being invited to fight. When Johnny Davis, a New York welterweight, became a professional in 1973 he fought four times between July 18 and August 20 of that year, and five more times between November 5 and

December 17. He lost each time. In his next 22 bouts, Davis won three by knockouts, drew twice, lost a decision and was knocked out 16 times. Twelve of the knockouts were consecutive.

"I know I'm not a bad fighter," says Davis who, at the age of 34, wants to win just a few so that he will not retire a loser. He sits on a couch in Gleason's Gym on 30th Street near Madison Square Garden. He has thick shoulders and arms but there are wisps of gray in his hair. He has sweated through his blue T-shirt. He finished his work-out at the speedbag where he did not sustain a rapid tempo the way most fighters do. "I try so hard at something I like doing," he said. "I love boxing. I dream of being a fighter. I see myself winning the title. I don't know which one. I see myself being picked up, getting carried around, getting my belt. Sometimes I see it in slow motion. I was telling my wife I had a dream last night. I was winning and getting the title. Sometimes she says, 'That's nice.' But she really wants me to quit."

Davis did not think he was an opponent for a long time. He fought a lot and lost most every time but did not question his manager's plan, he says, because he did not think it a fighter's right. He fought the same man twice in Baltimore in his first two fights and, after the second loss, fought in New York three days later and then again, against the same man, two days afterward. "I don't remember," he says. "See, I was fighting every week. I just took them fights. I was new at boxing. I was exhausted. I got knocked out. I tried to get up but I was exhausted."

He paid bills with his first paycheck. Then he bought himself a present. "I think I bought me a suit in a store on 14th street," he says. "I also bought a hat to go with it, a nice big-brimmed, black hat. I felt big. I felt like I was a big fighter, like a big man. I had a few dollars in my pocket. I had a nice suit, a pin-striped suit. I felt like a big gangster. People would say, 'You got on such a nice suit.' Everyone see you looking better. I felt like I was getting somewhere."

He has promised his wife that he will not fight beyond this year. He made the promise once before. He has a job—many opponents do; they run before work and train afterward—as a carpenter but cannot bring himself to stop.

When he boxes, Johnny Davis shows off a part of himself that he can express no other way. "I don't talk too much," he says. "I'm always alone. But when I'm inside the ring I show them something different. People are cheering for me. I feel good about myself, now I can be outside of the ring. I have people stop me in the street, doctors, lawyers, cab drivers and they've seen me fight. They say, 'You didn't get a fair deal.' And I say, 'I'm not such a bad fighter.' "

Sacked, Sorry And Silent

PRO FOOTBALL

By *TOM JACKSON*

From Inside Sports
Copyright © 1984, Inside Sports

"When I was a kid, I didn't want to be president of the United States. I didn't want to be a fireman or a cowboy. I stood behind the center like John Unitas. I wore my face mask like Kenny Stabler. I walked hunched over like Joe Namath. I even limped like Namath. I wanted to be a quarterback."

—Joe Theismann, December 1983

In the life of Joe Theismann, there has never been a moment when it was enough to be "a" anything. A spokesman. A restaurateur. A personality. A humanitarian. A television show host. A quarterback. What's so special, so *exclusive* about that? The connotations are too ordinary. One of the crowd? That's not Joe T. But "the," now there is a word worth aspiring to.

Despite his reputation as the National Football League's leading extrovert, Theismann is more accurately equal parts flamboyance and sensitivity, temerity and discretion—making him ultimately a piece of modern American folklore, driven to be *the* everything. *The* spokesman. *The* restaurateur. *The* personality. *The* humanitarian. *The* television show host.

The quarterback.

On the field, Theismann has, for four seasons, been building toward a crescendo that would make believers—if not admirers—of his staunchest critics. That is, if we can apply the actuarial tables for quarterbacks to Theismann, because at 35, history says he shouldn't be getting much better. And yet, when attempting to predict Joe T's future, it is always a good idea to recall what happened at Notre Dame the fall of Theismann's freshman year.

Ten quarterbacks—so the story goes, and remember that Theismann the Folklorist told the tale originally—10 quarterbacks, most of them high school All-Americas and all of them 6'4", 200 pounds, were members of the freshman class Ara Parseghian recruited to South Bend back in 1967. Theismann, a skinny kid from New Brunswick, N.J.—who was warned in no less than the New York Daily News to pick an Atlantic Coast Conference university because of what was likely to become of his scrawny neck at Notre Dame—studied the daunting array of competition in his class and announced that he, the rail job from north Jersey, would wind up calling Ara's signals.

And he did.

"Joe has always been a sort of self-made team leader," says kicker Mark Moseley, Theismann's closest friend among the Redskins. "He's always bringing himself to the forefront."

Adds Dave Butz, the glowering Pro Bowl defensive tackle: "He's got a lot of moxie, which you want for a quarterback. You don't want somebody who's going to play second fiddle. You want somebody who's cocky, who says he's able to do things and can go out there and do it every time he steps on the field."

Critics? Experts? In a crunch, Theismann listens only to the counsel he respects the most: his own. So, if a thousand statistics indicate that professional quarterbacks begin to lose their speed, arm strength, and decisiveness somewhere near their 35th birthday, we can only expect that Theismann will find a way to become the exception to the slide rule.

Last year, when the Washington Redskins corroborated their Super Bowl success of strike-shortened 1982 by positively dominating the National Football Conference, Theismann painted a Renoir of a season, not simply for himself—as is frequently the case where NFL quarterbacks are concerned—but for his team as well. Unlike our era's other star-encrusted millionaire throwers, getting rich and famous on rules that have opened the airways to anyone who may once have won a Punt, Pass, and Kick regional, Theismann does not live on statistics alone—though he could, and would still feast. In '83, for instance, Theismann launched a flock of Foutsian passing numbers: 60.1% completions (276 of 459 passes), 29 touchdowns (second best in the NFL), and 3,714 yards (second highest total in Redskins history).

The irony is that Theismann toils for a coach at war with himself. On one hand, Joe Gibbs may be the premier offensive innovator of the '80s—what with his single-back set, multimotion, and exotic game plans—but he is also the fellow who has recruited the biggest offensive line since Germany's panzer divisions, to make room for single-purpose runner John Riggins. With that kind of arrangement, Gibbs' heart may cry pass, but his head says run, run, run.

Happily, after some initially rocky times (a hellish 0-5 start in '81), Theismann has matured and flourished dramatically in the

Gibbs system. Not coincidentally, Washington has become the NFL's most successful team: a matchless 36-7 record (entering 1984) since the fifth game of 1981 and consecutive NFC titles, which hasn't happened since the Minnesota Vikings of 1972-73.

Earlier Redskins quarterbacks—the good, the great, and the gritty—were seat-of-the-pants operators who commanded fiercely loyal followings in the nation's capital. Slingin' Sammy Baugh, Silky Sonny Jurgensen, Blanchin' Billy Kilmer. Theismann is beyond so-briquets. Who nicknames technicians? And that, after all, is how Theismann sees himself—the triggerman for Gibbs' pyrotechnics.

Then again, perhaps it's more. Those Redskins heros of yester-year were boots-wearing, hard-swearing, pants-hitching, line-backer-shoving toughs. Alas, for all Theismann has done between the white lines, for all his obvious heroics, leadership, and outright athleticism, critics and peers have rarely been able to pierce the ve-neer of the famous *Theismann Image*, that slick, self-developed, agent-enhanced, made-for-media facade that propelled the quarter-back into national prominence even before he was *The Quarterback.*

Who can hug a magazine cover?

Incredibly, however, just as Theismann arrived at his appoint-ment with destiny, when the force of his numbers and accomplish-ments began to overwhelm the Joe T media package—just when Theismann could stand up and announce, as he had 17 years earlier at Notre Dame, that he was the one, and he'd done it his way, he put a clamp on his media spiel.

The mouth that roared—muzzled.

★   ★   ★

For most of last summer, the only theater in downtown Carlisle, Pa.—a tiny, sleepy university community 30 miles west of Gettys-burg— featured on its aging single screen "Cannonball Run II," star-ring Burt Reynolds and all of his Hollywood buddies. An otherwise forgettable film, Burt's latest was memorable for one reason: It was highlighted by Joe Theismann's second motion picture appearance.

Anywhere Else, U.S.A., that may not have been worth leaving the front porch and lemonade over. But, because for eight summer weeks every year Carlisle goes bonkers while the Redskins hold their training camp there, the name on the marquee wasn't Reynolds, but Joe Theismann, budding matinee idol.

Are you kidding? With those chiseled Grecian features, Theis-mann had the best male profile in the movie. During filming, could anyone have guessed that Theismman's lines in "Cannonball Run II" would be his only public utterances of the summer?

Until recently, Theismann was every bit the match for Washing-ton's other Great Communicator. If Ronald Reagan could make tril-lion-dollar deficits sound like thrilling forays into financial experi-mentation, Theismann made interceptions sound sexy, third-down conversion percentages fascinating.

But that was the old Theismann—the Theismann who talked.

That Theismann, according to the quarterback himself, is no more.

"The public guy doesn't live here anymore," he said last spring before taking himself off the record.

That Theismann, the quarterback, decided in the manner of modern athletes to cut off the media is not significant news. In terms of originality, snubbing the press ranks up there with sunrises. Steve Carlton, Duane Thomas, George Hendrick. Georgetown's national champion basketball team, and Bill Walton didn't talk for the longest time. Gary Matthews, Jeris White, Joe Barry Carroll, Jim Rice, Kareem Abdul-Jabbar—the names go on. On Theismann's own team, enigmatic fullback John Riggins grants only occasional audiences, and silky, sullen wide receiver Art Monk has been known to fall into prolonged silence when his knees act up. Another athlete's not talking? Big deal.

However, that Theismann, the NFL's resident genius of self-promotion, had cut off all his ready-made outlets was worthy of headlines in the astonished Washington Post, and predictions that he'd never make it stick in the adventurous Washington Times.

Reasoned one Redskins beat writer cynically, "He's just building up for press conferences like Riggins has; he likes the idea of all that concentrated attention."

Those who know him more closely suspected otherwise. Since January, Theismann's life had become an unflattering series of upheavals and legal squabbles. There was his marriage of 12 years—kaput. And his negotiations with franchise owner Jack Kent Cooke for a revised contract—stalled. Finally, there was his decision to bear the burden for Washington's miserable showing in Super Bowl XVIII (a shocking 38-9 landslide for the Los Angeles Raiders)—arguable.

"Joe Theismann has talked too much . . . and I think it's time just to start doing things instead of talking about things," he said before signing off. "Maybe the (Super Bowl) week was sort of an eye-opener for me. Maybe it was sort of like: Here it is. I'm going to lay it all out in one week for you and show you the directions you've been going. Maybe it's time you stopped and took a look at it . . . I felt like through the entire week of preparing for the Super Bowl, I had talked my way through a football game. And finally when it came down to playing, I don't feel that I played to the capabilities that I would like to see myself play to."

"If that's the case," marveled center Jeff Bostic, "we all must have done a whole lot of talking that week."

Two weeks into training camp, Theismann derailed speculation that he was building toward any sort of press conference when he issued a communique through the Redskins public relations department that confirmed his vow of silence. "I have been a very public person until now, and my life hasn't changed. If you want to write a story about me, use what I said before."

Not surprisingly, most Redskins are slow to accept that Theismann's public silence, and the reasons behind it, are worth reporting. "It's a non-story," sniffed George Starke, a 12th-season offensive tackle and self-appointed media maven.

"Somebody at Channel 5 (where Starke works as a sort of at-large commentator) asked me what was going on with Joe. It rubs them raw for some reason. I'm really protective of athletes; I'm real touchy about ballplayers and the press. And I think the press, for the most part, has a skewed idea of what obligations ballplayers should have to them.

"Joe has pulled more damn TV shows' fat out of the fire over the years than anybody. You knew if you were a lazy reporter and hadn't done your homework, you could always get something out of Joe. If you had a crew, you could just walk up and stick the mike out and you'd get something the director of news would be happy with, even if you hadn't done crap. So now he decides not to talk and everybody's touchy about it.

"As soon as a person takes a stand, then you have to (bleep) with him. If Joe just avoided you, didn't say anything, never took a stand and said, 'I'm not going to talk,' and didn't, it wouldn't be an issue. *Why* are you not going to talk to the press? And they write stories about why he's not talking to the press. And that's absurd. Joe certainly has talked to the press more than anybody in eight careers."

★   ★   ★

Therein lies the story. Nowhere in the athletes-journalists guide-book is there a mention of quotas. If Theismann had consumed more videotape than "Knots Landing," what can you expect from someone who'd trained himself to talk in 30-second "bites," the building block of TV sportscasts?

Most athletes, when they resign from the world of words-for-the-record, do so because they believe they were mortally wronged by someone in the media, generally someone—or some group—they believe is out to get them. Riggins, for instance, grew weary of reading that he was flakier than Kansas corn. Couldn't they see he was just an excitable boy? Carlton maintains the silence he adopted in the early '70s after he was traded to Philadelphia, then a city with a reputation for hostile media. And Hendrick, like Abdul-Jabbar and Walton before him, simply doesn't want his privacy interrupted. Theismann put a lid on his dissertations simply because he believed he'd said too much already. That, however, is the supreme irony, because it has always seemed that Theismann was just getting started.

Suddenly, Washington's most accessible personality was its most mysterious. Checkout-counter rags printed that Theismann had linked himself romantically with Cathy Lee Crosby, and in the Washington Times' notorious "Ear," gossip columnist Diana McCllelan reported that Theismann was preparing to sell his interest in the Falls Church, Va., restaurant that bears his name.

Obviously, maintaining his previous relationship with the press would have forced him to face those and other chaffing questions concerning the nagging M's in his life: money, marriage, and (Super Bowl) mistakes. But Theismann's teammates saw a few other changes.

"The attitude has changed, but the person hasn't," says offensive guard Mark May, a devoted Theismann admirer. "He's cut a lot of things out of his life. I think he's going to be a better player. He's a lot sharper, he's got his priorities straight."

Gone from the Theismann lifestyle are red meats and alcohol. Initial indications, as the Redskins convened for the first time since the Super Bowl, were that Theismann was also putting distance between himself and his teammates. He'd always maintained a certain noblesse oblige—Theismann has never been "one of the guys" the way Kilmer and Jurgensen were, older Redskins concede—but that sort of space between quarterbacks and their teammates is not unusual in today's high-tech game. But, in training camp, Theismann was reluctant to participate even in those off-duty activities he'd enjoyed before—the nightly poker games, for instance. It took more than a week of coaxing before May was able to get him to ante up.

"His personal life is changing now, and that has to have some effect," says Vernon Grandgeorge, a longtime friend and, for nine years, the manager of Theismann's restaurant. "I think he came to a realization, and I could see him saying, 'Why am I running around like crazy? Why am I doing this to myself?'" Grandgeorge recalls times during previous offseasons when the only sleep Theismann got for days at a time was when he was on airplanes, flying between speaking engagements.

That, if not already history, has been at least tempered. Clearly, though, that sort of lifestyle contributed to the Theismanns' separation. At a Washington fund-raiser last year, one admiring fan sidled up to Cheryl Theismann and gushed about how much she admired her mate. "And what kind of husband is he?"

"Absentee," Cheryl said coldly.

How changed is Theismann? It's difficult to tell. When Gibbs gave his veterans four days off early in training camp, Theismann hopped a Concorde for France: still a jetsetter, after all that heartache. Earlier in that same week, however, he left camp at 5 a.m. to visit his daughter at a nearby Pennsylvania summer camp. Absentee father? Unlikely.

The Redskins—both the front office and the employees—couldn't be blamed if they watched Theismann a little more carefully than usual, however. After all, here was the man most responsible for Washington's highs (an NFL season-record 541 points in '83) and lows (in the Super Bowl, he completed just 16 of 35 passes and uncorked the interception with 12 seconds left in the first half that Raider linebacker Jack Squirek returned for the game's pivotal touchdown). What they saw was not disheartening. Theismann reported to camp alert, sharp, and perceptibly trimmer.

At least one of Theismann's personal hassles seemed resolved. Though Cooke, the tempestuous Redskins owner, refused to confirm it, reliable reports were that he'd extended Theismann's contract two years (through 1987) and made it worth $1 million annually; Theismann's previous deal—he was in the middle of a four-year contract—was worth only $1.25 million overall.

Getting that contract had been an ugly, bloody battle, dragged daily through the Washington media. "We were worried then about how he was going to perform," General Manager Bobby Beathard says, "and he had a great year.

"If this had been the first time that Joe Theismann had ever experienced what you'd call distraction from football," Beathard continues, "we'd certainly have a right to be concerned. You're always concerned about the welfare of your quarterback . . . I don't know what it is inside of Joe, but it never ceases to amaze me that he can do all the things he can do, and he seems to be at the top of his game."

"Joe is what I call a survivor," Moseley says, "a person who can deal with whatever comes up and keep a level head about him. When an emergency arises, he always steps forward and takes charge. I don't worry about Joe; he'll take care of himself."

A survivor. So here is another "a" to subdue. Life—or, more precisely, Joe T, the image guy—has dealt Theismann a difficult set of new rules. Joe T, who sold his name to a camera company, a Washington real estate developer, a chain of health spas, sporting goods equipment, and picnic gear manufacturers, a man who appeared in two movies (the other was "The Man With Bogart's Face"), hosted his own television show, and for a year published a weekly newspaper for Redskins fans, painted Theismann, who really only wanted to be the quarterback, into a corner. Now, to get out of this self-inflicted fix, Theismann has decided it is time to spurn the media, his closest, most enduring ally.

"I can see where he's coming from," says Moseley, himself a chronic grumbler about his treatment in the newspapers. "The situation he's in right now, the press has a very nice way of turning things around and picking sides and doing a lot of things that can change situations that you're in. The best way to avoid that is just not to talk to them, so they don't have the opportunity to quote him on anything."

Said Theismann in a final expansive moment: "I've lived under a disguise for a long time. I think I am a real person and I got away from him. I would like to try to be myself, instead of trying to be what everybody wants and expects me to be."

In other words, now that it has become apparent Joe T's far-flung celebrity had a Neiman-Marcus price tag on it, Theismann is after the media to foot the bill.

Too bad.

Drugs Scar Scurry And Mar Baseball

BASEBALL

By *BRUCE KEIDAN*

From the Pittsburgh Post-Gazette
Copyright © 1984, Pittsburgh Post-Gazette

They kept volunteering testimonials to Rod Scurry yesterday. The Pirates spoke of his talent, of his generosity, of the welcome they would give him when he returns.

"He's a good person," Chuck Tanner kept saying. "He's a fine young man."

They spirited the good person from his hotel room in the dead of night Saturday. They transported the fine young man in cloak-and-dagger secrecy to a drug-rehabilitation center. Cocaine seems not to care whether it is used by the salt or the scum of the earth. It is an equal opportunity destroyer.

There had been no clue, they kept saying. How would they have known? How *could* they have known?

"We were not suspicious of any drug problems," Harding Peterson, the general manager, explained. "When he pitched in San Diego the other day, it was just a matter of wildness . . ."

He had come out of the bullpen with the bases loaded and one out in the fourth inning Thursday and had walked Tony Gwynn and Graig Nettles on eight pitches, never even coming close to the strike zone. The manager and the pitching coach had talked afterward about the fact that Scurry's pitching mechanics were in obvious disarray. "It's like he's forgotten where to release the ball," Harvey Haddix told Tanner. The manager agreed and instructed Haddix to work with the lefthander here the following afternoon.

They did not suspect drugs, although in retrospect, perhaps there were clues. Scurry's earned-run average had soared from 1.74 in 1982 to 5.56 last year. He had lost about 20 pounds last winter. He had shaved off his mustache. And it was not only his appearance that changed. Normally quiet, even aloof around strangers, he seemed

this spring to have become almost puppy friendly. It is easy to piece
the puzzle together, given the gift of hindsight.

"Even if they had suspected, what could they have done?" asks
Bill Madlock, the Pirates' captain. "Rod just would have denied it.
You can't help someone until they're ready to admit they need the
help."

Madlock suspected. He approached Scurry, offering to help. "He
didn't tell me that he was using (cocaine)," Madlock says, "but he
didn't deny it, either."

Madlock wasn't the only one of Scurry's peers who realized what
was happening. The pitcher's closest friends on the team, Don Robinson and Dale Berra, spoke to him in San Diego on Thursday night,
then again in Los Angeles on Friday.

"I could see it was affecting the way he was pitching," Berra
said. "We told him if we heard about it again, if we found out about it
again . . ."

On Saturday morning, Scurry went to Robinson's room at the
Biltmore Hotel and admitted he needed help. Robinson and Berra in
turn informed Tanner, who dispatched trainer Tony Bartirome back
to the hotel to stay with Scurry.

"He was concerned about his parents and his brother," Bartirome recalled. "He was very remorseful, very emotional. I tried to
reassure him that what he did by coming forward probably saved his
career and his life.

"I just wish other players in baseball could have seen him yesterday, so they can see where that road leads."

The truth is, though, nobody knows yet where that road joins the
horizon, let alone where it ends. We know only that Scurry is on baseball's 15-day disabled list, and that treatment is expected to take
perhaps three times that long. We know that the commissioner's office is investigating. But we do not know whether we have witnessed
Rod Scurry's downfall or merely the prelude to his redemption. We
do not even know when it started, let alone how it will end.

The easy assumption is that drug dependency was responsible for
Scurry's sorry 1983 season. But exactly the reverse may be true.

"So much of your life depends on how you do on the field," Madlock points out. "If you don't do well, you begin to doubt yourself.
You ask yourself what happens if you fail, how you could duplicate
the kind of salary you're making in baseball. The answer is that you
couldn't. And once you start dwelling on that, you might be tempted
to use something to get you through the night."

It is Madlock's suspicion that the 1983 season created Scurry's
addiction, rather than the addiction creating his season. "Baseball is
an automatic game," he says. "I can play baseball in my sleep. (St.
Louis') Lonnie Smith was hitting .300 last year when he turned himself in. (Los Angeles') Steve Howe was throwing the heck out of the
ball every time he pitched."

The players fear that the public will begin to assume that every
slump is the byproduct of drug use. That suspicion would complete a

deadly cycle, since it would place a slumping player under even more pressure than he faces already. And the slump is a baseball disease which everyone catches eventually.

"This is a great game," Bill Madlock said. "It's done a lot for me and my family. I love it when I walk down the street and have kids say, 'There's Bill Madlock. I want to be just like him.' I don't want that to change.

"What I'm concerned about is that in the last three weeks, we've had one guy (Lee Lacy) accused of taking drugs and another who turned himself in. You hear people saying there are seven or eight in every big-league clubhouse. I guess people are going to look at us and ask, 'Where are the other six?' "

The suspicion has become as much a sickness as the addiction. Peterson spoke to Scurry on Saturday, but he did not ask him if other Pirates were involved in drug use. "I would not ask a player that," he said. "That would be the last thing I would ask him."

Peterson does not wish to be cast in the role of investigator. His immediate concern, as is Tanner's, is to help a player who has had the courage to admit he needs the help. That is understandable, even laudable. But it fails to recognize the simple truth that there are really two patients—the individual and the game. And what is good for one is not necessarily good for the other.

The *first* question I intend to ask Rod Scurry, when I see him next, is whether other Pirates were involved. Because until that question is asked and answered, the public will presume it knows the answer, and baseball will suffer.

It is time for baseball to realize that nice young men are just as susceptible to drugs as everyone else. It is also time for baseball to train trainers, to teach them how to detect the signs of drug use.

"They had a guy talk to us at the winter meetings last December," Tony Bartirome was saying. "He said it was possible to tell if a player was on drugs. When we asked him how, he said he didn't have time to go into that . . ."

But baseball cannot afford any longer *not* to go into that. And it cannot afford to allow its players to fall under the control of the people who provide the drugs. If it does, then it is only a matter of time until those same people begin attempting to influence the outcome of games.

Perhaps the time has come for organized baseball to draw a line and defend it. Maybe the players and owners should agree to a period of amnesty that would allow any player to do without penalty what Rod Scurry has done, to step forward, ask for help and receive it. After that period of amnesty, however, any player admitting to or convicted of drug use would be banned from the game.

It is fashionable to characterize drug addiction as an illness, and perhaps that is correct. They used to call it a victimless crime. But it is clearly not that. Rod Scurry's teammates are victims. So is the game of baseball.

Life at Camp Meyer

BASKETBALL

By *JOEL BIERIG*

From the Chicago Sun-Times
Copyright © 1984, Chicago Sun-Times

On this morning, the trainer is in business. One player has a broken fingernail. Another has gum in his hair.

"I'll get that out, son, don't worry about it," the trainer says.

Outside, rain is falling.

As the trainer scrapes at the bubblegum, he sings: "It ain't gonna rain no more, no more. It ain't gonna rain no more."

"You keep singing that, son, and maybe it won't."

A visitor tells the trainer the rain won't last. The visitor quotes the weatherman.

"You're in a resort area," the trainer replies. "They're never going to tell you the weather's going to be bad."

Finally, the trainer calls for the peanut butter. After almost 40 years in the business, the trainer knows if there's one thing for sure to loosen gum from hair, it's peanut butter.

Presto.

"You can go wash it out of your hair now," the trainer says.

Besides gum in hair, the trainer sees a lot of sunburn, blisters and sprained ankles. Not to mention homesickness.

He looks out the window. The rain isn't letting up.

The trainer shakes his head. "After a day like this, they'll all have colds," Ray Meyer says.

★　　　★　　　★

Welcome to the North Woods. Welcome to Ray Meyer's Basketball Camp. OK, if you insist on details, you're 330 miles from Chicago. The nearest towns you've heard of—or have you?—are Rhinelander and Eagle River. For the record, you're 28 miles from Michigan.

You say the signs along the road weren't too clear? Made a couple of wrong turns, did you?

No sense putting up too many signs. They just wind up in people's rec rooms. The signs have Coach's name on 'em, and you know how people love to have things with Coach's name.

Well, you made it, didn't you?

Here, have some roast beef. And some mashed potatoes. Great cook we've got this year. Coach brought him in from Chicago. Really puts out a nice spread, considering he's got to cook for 170 kids. Got plenty to drink, too, but you'll have to settle for milk or diet pop. Coach is into diet pop these days.

All right, listen up. Wake-up bell is at 8. Breakfast at 8:30. Drills at 9:15. Warning bell at noon. Lunch at 12:30. Then choose sides and play games. Movin' too fast for you? Don't worry, you'll catch on. Say, we've got movies tonight—"DePaul-Purdue," then "For Your Eyes Only."

Mail call? That comes after lunch. Say, Coach told you about packages, didn't he?

He didn't?

Well, Coach likes to let kids stomp on the packages. Crunch the cookies. Crush the cake. Been doin' it for 38 years.

Joey, Marge and the rest just sit back and cringe.

"We tell the kids we don't want packages," Ray Meyer says. "If a kid doesn't share it with the other kids, he's stingy, he's no good. If he gives it all away, then he's crying.

"Packages are a pain in the butt. Kids write home and say, 'So-and-so got a package. How come you never send me one?' Kids write home for gum and it winds up in other kids' hair."

But kids get hungry at night.

"I get enough to eat here," Ray Meyer says. "So do they."

★   ★   ★

Ray Meyer is on his way to the Rec Hall, haven for foosball, pool, ping pong and video games.

"One mother saw the video games and said, 'Give me $10 worth of quarters,'" Meyer says. "I told her, 'They're free.' She couldn't believe it."

Meyer is on the lookout for homesick kids. "You can always tell a homesick kid; he's walking by himself."

He spots a rotund camper who has been here before.

"Hey, Lardo," Meyer says, smiling. "Nobody at camp can be fatter than I am."

Lardo smiles back.

Camp consists of four two-week sessions, each attended by 170 to 180 boys. They live in cabins called "Bulls, Globetrotters, Lakers, Celtics," etc., depending on their ages (9 to 18). Most are from the Chicago area, although in recent years, Ray Meyer's national TV exposure has helped lure kids from other states. Some campers are sons of former campers.

Bob Pettit slept here. So did Dan Issel. And don't forget Mark Aguirre.

But for every Aguirre, there are 10 "Lardos." And 20 "Professors."

"There's this one kid with glasses," Ray Meyer explains. "They call him Professor. Last year, he couldn't even bounce the ball."

★　　　★　　　★

At some camps, the coach-director gives his name but not his time. He throws up the opening tip, then disappears to the opening tee.

"Coach is always here," says Jim Burns, one of the assistant coaches. "You figure a guy like that, a legend, wouldn't have to be. But he's on that little court every morning, teaching pick-and-rolls.

"He calls games himself. He can't sit still to save his soul. And he coaches in a pick-up game the way he does at DePaul. Sometimes he'll say, 'Jim, I don't know what's wrong with this group. They're not playing the way they can.' "

Ray Meyer tapes ankles and calls fouls. He pulls water-skiers (well, most of the time) and pulls campers' legs (all of the time).

Meyer doesn't live with the "Celtics" or "Globetrotters." He opts for the comfy home he built six years ago for his family ("Seventeen people can sleep here," he says). It is barely a floor-length pass from camp.

Meyer seldom leaves the grounds. "Last year," he says, "I left camp once, to go out to dinner."

None of which surprises a visitor. At DePaul, the visitor watched Meyer lead players from practice to birthday parties. Still in uniform, they would eat cake and ice cream provided by Meyer's wife, Marge, or Joey's wife, Barbara. The celebrant sat in a special chair while his teammates sang "Happy Birthday."

All that's missing here are the "L" tracks.

"Things are looser than at most camps," says Joey Meyer, his father's No. 1 helper. "They do more things than straight basketball."

The staff reflects the philosophy. Aside from Ray and Joey, the coaches bring bigger hearts than names. A favorite is little Jim Burns, whose wife, Patsy, is DePaul's basketball secretary.

Yet, for all the emphasis on just plain fun, this still is a place to hoop it up. There are contests for horse and one-on-one and free throws, awards for Best Defensive Player and Mr. Hustle and Best Dunker. The booty includes 76 trophies.

"You have a pretty good chance to go home with something," Joey Meyer says with a wink.

And if you trip over your shoelaces, you still can win the contest for cleanest cabin.

If nothing else, you remember Coach.

"A kid can say, 'Ray Meyer sat down and talked to me,' " says Joey Meyer, a former camper. "The touch of camp is Coach. The personal touch is the added thing that makes camp camp."

One of the assistants, John Muraski, knows what makes camp

camp. Muraski, newly named head coach at Biscayne (Florida) College, remembers looking for summer work when he was coaching at Three Lakes High. He called on the Meyers in 1979, a few months after they had coached in the Final Four.

"John came over and asked if he could work for us," Joey says. "He couldn't believe what I was doing."

Joey Meyer was painting a toilet.

★   ★   ★

Strange, the way things work.

"I could have been pumping gas as a summer job," says Joey Meyer.

His father almost invested in a service station instead of a boys' camp. Thirty-nine years ago, making $2,500 as a coach, Ray Meyer sought a gainful way to occupy his summers.

A friend approached him about a gas station. Father Charles Williams, a DePaul faculty member, mentioned the need for a boys' camp. "And you've got your summers free," he told Meyer.

Soon, a tradition was born on Little Fork Lake, 10 miles south of Eagle River. After a summer of preparation ("We did all this by hand; it was all forest," says Meyer), camp opened.

Barely.

There was no electricity the first year, says Marge Meyer, although Ray Meyer insists it was longer. At any rate, Ray Meyer couldn't see the forest for the trees.

His camp, in the middle of the Chain O'Lakes area, now covers 66 acres and touches 3,000 feet of shoreline. Camp buildings are 200 yards from the beach.

Campers pay $355 per session, with about 25 boys working instead of paying. Meyer says dairy products cost him $25,000. He estimates his operating expenses at $150,000.

If the camp seems profitable, it also is taxing for a retired, 70-year-old coach who insists on doing everything himself (although he has developed remarkable confidence in his full-time caretaker, Larry Rempert).

Yet, Meyer says, reflecting on his 42-year career, "This is one of the reasons I could stay in coaching so long. It's so relaxing here." Purely a summer tonic for the coach, who has yet to see the camp snow-covered.

"I think he enjoys it more than the kids," Marge Meyer says.

Marge enjoys it less than Coach or the kids, but enough to keep from complaining. When she gets bored, she can pack up her kids and grandkids for a mini shopping expedition.

At night, she can look into her husband's eyes and see the beauty of camp.

"It's good for him," Marge says, and leaves it at that.

★   ★   ★

Joey Meyer is hurting. After aggravating his testy back on a Florida vacation, he has trouble standing for more than a few minutes.

For the first time in 18 years, he can't be on the court for drills. He feels guilty. There are charts to be drawn up, tournaments to be organized, statistics to be kept. And Joey Meyer's back hurts.

So he sits in the mess hall, analyzing last year's films, preparing for his first season as DePaul's head coach.

Ray Meyer's back doesn't hurt. Megaphone in hand, Meyer follows the action up and down the court.

A free throw clangs off the rim. "Must be thinking you're shooting for DePaul," he bellows. "You'll always miss."

Eventually, Meyer vows, he will hand the megaphone to Joey and walk off into the sunset. "I'll gradually withdraw," he says somberly.

In the distance, Joey can only laugh. He has heard that line before.

Lives Overshadowed By a Day in the Sun

HOCKEY

By *JANE LEAVY*

From the Washington Post Magazine
Copyright © 1984, Washington Post Magazine

The corridor echoed with emptiness. At one end, a hockey player in long johns quietly sawed at his stick. At the other, Buddy Kessel unloaded crates and duffels and trunks, all red, white and blue, all marked "USA, USA."

"I expected to see ghosts," said Kessel, the equipment manager for the U.S. Olympic hockey team. He had not been back to Lake Placid since the night of the miracle four years ago. "I could just see them walking down the hallway, the Russian players, their officials."

There were no ghosts. There were New York Rangers in Dressing Room 5 where USA had been. There were fresh-faced kids with new USA sweaters in Dressing Room 2 where the Russians had been. The 1984 U.S. Olympic hockey team had come to Lake Placid to test itself against the memory of 1980 in an exhibition game against 1980 coach Herb Brooks and the Rangers.

For the members of the 1980 team, the challenge of the last four years has been to avoid becoming flesh-and-blood memorabilia. Sometimes, it seems all people want is to put them inside one of those snow globes—with the flag draped over their shoulders and their gold medals around their necks. Then, when things get dreary, they can shake the globe and the snow will fall, emotions will be jostled and they can feel it all over again.

To resist such a pastoral imprisonment is an act of sanity, maturity, necessity.

Brooks, who is firmly committed to the present tense, didn't want to come to Lake Placid, refused to be introduced. He remained aloof, in character, watching from high above the press box. "When you work in the world of professional sports, you don't have time to reminisce," he said. "You're in the now."

Lake Placid is a prisoner to its past. In the shops on Main Street, there are souvenirs from the 1932 Olympics and the 1980 Olympics: T-shirts and ashtrays and pens celebrating the miracle on ice.

"It was one of those moments," Brooks said. "People want to freeze-frame it, put it on ice. I had friends who said I should never coach another game. Walk away. Some nights when we're not playing well, I might agree.

"We're trying to keep our lives in the proper perspective. We never thought we were better than we were. Failures are people who think they are better than they are. When we won in 1980, it was a great moment. We don't think we're better than that moment. We're flattered, respective of the nice treatment, but we know life goes on."

Brooks is the coach of the Rangers now. Craig Patrick, who was his assistant, his buffer, is general manager. Eight of the players, including Dave Christian, who plays for the Washington Capitals, are regulars in the National Hockey League and four others are up and down from the minors. John Harrington and Phil Verchota play for the 1984 Olympic team. They are the conduits to the magic.

There were 20 of them. They have been married and traded; feted and exploited. They have achieved and overachieved. They have survived.

"No matter what you do, you're still from the 1980 Olympic team, whether or not you score a winning goal in the Stanley Cup final at Madison Square Garden," said Dave Silk. "You have to be pretty vain to say, 'Woe is me,' to feel badly about that being your lot in life. There's a lot worse."

"We have things in our lives more important than remembering," said Rob McClanahan, who is with the Rangers. "The time for remembering is when we're done playing hockey. Now we have jobs to try to keep."

The week after the game in Lake Placid, the Rangers traded Silk to the Boston Bruins, who sent him to Hershey.

How to grapple with the plateaus beyond the peak. "You have to find other things to look to in life," McClanahan said.

To do that, it is necessary to put the Olympics aside, which no one wants them to do. Maybe that's why McClanahan put his medal in a safe-deposit box, along with his memories, treasured and internalized but not something to carry around every day. "If you sat back and lived off that, you'd be lost," Christian said.

Jim Craig knows that now. If there is a casualty of the adulation and expectations, it is Craig, the goalie with the vulnerable eyes. He admits to cynicism, but denies the bitterness in his voice. Everywhere he goes, people want to know about the Olympics. "It's something I'm trying to get by," he said. "It's a big roadblock. It's a real pain in the ass."

A week after the Olympics, he played his first game for the Atlanta Flames and shot a Coca-Cola commercial with his father. When the Flames moved to Calgary, he was traded to Boston and found out he couldn't go home again. He was injured and then hurt when the Bruins sent him to the minors. A year later, he was charged with a misdemeanor (driving to endanger) after an accident in which a woman was killed. One month after he was found innocent, the Bruins released him. No one gave him a chance to be a rookie, he says.

"It's been a long four years," he said. "It's just as much of a battle after the Olympics as winning it.

"Once, I felt so sorry for myself, I said, 'I wish this didn't happen.' After I read it, I said, 'What the hell are they doing to me? How can you let them get you so down that you can feel that way about something you worked all your life for?' "

Last year, he played for the USA team that won the Group B world championship. He was signed by the Minnesota North Stars and sent to their Utah farm club. In November, he was brought up for a game against the Capitals when the North Stars needed an emotional lift. He gave up five goals in the first two periods and was given a plane ticket back to Utah.

"He was really down," said Warren Strelow, goalie coach for the 1980 team and now for the Capitals. "He kept saying, 'This is my last shot.' "

"I'm just looking for *a* shot," Craig said. "A shot will tell me whether I can do this for a living . . . Till I know that, I'm not going to give up."

Five days later, he started against the 1984 team and lost, 8-4. It was a setup, a hype. "You can't wait for it to be over," he said.

"I guess the American way was the way we won. What they've done to us all is also the American way. Commercialization. Utilization. Make as much off it as you can and the hell with how the person feels."

He gave his medal to his father. "So somebody can enjoy it, be proud of it, so little kids can hold it and touch it, the way it should be," Craig said. "I sure as hell can't do that. It will come back to me, when I'm old enough. Then it will be something other than something that sits in a dark room and has no value other than its face value. My father enjoys it. Nobody gives him a hard time about it."

He had to go. His team was waiting, the future beckoning. "If you see any of the guys, tell them hello," he said.

The past beckons, too. Harrington says he still gets form letters from fans saying he was the greatest ever and could he please send everything he had from the Olympics. "They send the envelope," he said, "but you have to get the stamps."

When he arrived in Lake Placid, his first time back since the Olympics, "They were showing the tape of the Russian game in a store across the street," he said. "I wasn't going to watch it. I said, 'I can't stop and start watching the thing.' "

But he did. And he remembered: "It was 2-2 in the second. I got a penalty. The player was Kharlamov. There I am hauling down the best player in the world. They scored a power play to go ahead, 3-2. A couple of shifts later Mark Pavelich sent me in on a breakaway. I had a chance to be a hero. I missed the whole net. I dumped it in the corner on a breakaway."

He did get an assist on Mike Eruzione's game-winning goal. "I was forechecking and it came off the Russian's stick and mine at the same time," he said. "It went to Pavelich, who threw it in the slot. Mike had just come on the ice and it came right to him."

And then the score was 4-3 and they were counting down the seconds and screaming, "USA! USA!" Said Strelow: "It was like a 10,000-volt wire was running through our bench.

"I turned to Herb and I gave him a squeeze and he said, "We did it, we did it.' All smiles. Then, bam, he turned it all off and he walked right out."

The distance between Brooks and his team was his loss in that moment of victory. "I really wanted to be very close to those people at that time," he said. "I knew it would be out of character. I knew the players would say, 'Take a hike. Where have you been?'

"I just went in the locker room. I took a deep breath and everything sort of stopped. That might have been my freeze frame. It's not so much you're stunned. It's the moment every athlete and every coach strives for: getting to the point of having the opportunity to pull it off."

And, of course, they did. They beat the Finns, 4-2, in the final game and sang "God Bless America" in the locker room. Brooks told them not to drink too much because the president was sending a plane for them and they were going to the White House. The feelings were so overwhelming that even four years later, Patrick and Christian remember only one undifferentiated glow.

"It made me believe everything was possible," Christian said.

It was a giddy, drunken time. "Jack O'Callahan and I got picked at random for the urine sample," Harrington said. "We each grabbed a bottle of champagne and said, 'What the heck. Let's get hammered.' We came rolling into the press conference with a couple of bottles of champagne."

"And O'Callahan came on the stage and said, 'We won today just like when the Americans won the battle of Bunker Hill,' which they didn't," Christian said. "Everybody just took his word for it. He's from Boston."

They left for Washington thinking they had won a gold medal and arrived to find they had rescued the free world. Four years and one U.S. Olympic boycott later, the Soviets are still in Afghanistan.

They flew home in a presidential jet, sky high, making calls from 30,000 feet. They landed and the circle was broken. "Nobody wanted to admit that the team was over and everyone was going their separate ways," Christian said. "After that final game, that team was history, immediate history."

There was hardly time to say goodbye. "It was shake hands and see you later," he said.

Of course, they don't. "I keep up through the papers," said McClanahan. "I don't go out of my way, it's sad to say."

Someone wanted to know if Brooks had said anything to him about this game, this return to forever. "I haven't talked to Herb in a long time," he said.

High above it all, Brooks watched young men with young legs and USA on their breast outskate his team. Verchota came on the ice and for a moment Brooks relented. "I saw Phil before the game," he said. "I said, 'What are you doing?' He said, 'I'm playing for the team.' I said, 'Oh yeah. I thought you went back to school.' He just looked at me. I had the kid five years and I'm still giving him a bad time. He's a terrific kid. Sometime I'll buy him a beer and tell him that."

Later, as Kessell repacked the team's equipment and his memories, someone told Verchota what the coach had said. He rolled his eyes. He doesn't get caught up in *deja vu*. "The bottom line is making a living," he said. "Memories don't do a very good job of that."

To Louganis, Diving's The Easiest Part

DIVING

By *RICK REILLY*

From The Los Angeles Times
Copyright © 1984, The Los Angeles Times

They lug their cameras and their metaphors to Mission Viejo looking for "The Real Greg Louganis," but they do not find him.

They are the networks and the affiliates and the national magazines and what they usually find is not "The Real Greg Louganis" but Greg Louganis, the Ken doll; the Greg Louganis who will tell them how wonderful it is to be history's greatest diver; to be handsome and hunky; all tan and teeth; to have two Olympic golds waiting on ice.

They don't find the Louganis who says that actually he has spent much of his life without friends, without much family; his adoptive parents have just finalized a divorce; he only recently became reacquainted with his adoptive father after a lifetime of "resentment"; he has had no feeling—good or bad—for his only sister, at least since that day in 1976 when she told his mother that she would not go to the Montreal Olympics because she didn't want to watch Greg "make a fool of himself."

They don't find the Louganis who was born with dyslexia, a reading disorder; who was a stutterer as a child; whose Samoan heritage caused classmates to call him "Nigger."

They don't find the Louganis who says he has spent most of his life without laughter; who has no girlfriends; who, in fact, has never enjoyed the simplest of things—fun.

"Let me tell you something that makes me kind of sad," the real Greg Louganis is saying. "In all my life, I've never really had a good time. Never gone out and had fun; never really let loose. Not once."

For when you are Greg Louganis, perfection is supposed to be a matter of course, and so you wake up every morning with failure grinning back at you in the shaving mirror and Time, Esquire, Sports Illustrated, and ABC in the kitchen.

"Everyone justs wants to meet an image," Louganis says. "They don't want to meet a person. So you keep up the facade."

No, you would rather be anyone in this world than Greg Louganis.

Until one year ago.

★   ★   ★

If you were there, seconds before Soviet diver Sergei Chalibashvili began his fatal dive off the 10-meter platform at the World University Games in Edmonton, Canada, last summer, you might have seen Greg Louganis waiting on the seven-meter platform, his eyes closed, his hands over his ears, his back to the pool.

Louganis knew.

"I had a premonition . . . I was standing there on the platform. I had closed my eyes and plugged my ears and started humming to myself so that I wouldn't hear anything. I didn't want to hear it . . . "

★   ★   ★

You want The Real Greg Louganis? Take a look.

The Real Greg Louganis is a supreme athlete, yes, the most gifted his sport has ever known, and nearly as good a dancer as diver. (He has a drama degree from Cal-Irvine.) World champion Phil Boggs once called him "the most physically gifted person I've ever seen come into the sport of diving."

But Louganis says he also happens to be insecure, underconfident, nervous, intimidated, introverted and, just now, at 23, starting to "figure some things out."

The Real Greg Louganis may well end up the lovable darling of the Olympics, a good bet to win both the platform and springboard and then cash in on his smile, his looks, his killer body. He could be the new Bruce Jenner, everything Mark Spitz wasn't, Eric Heiden with sex appeal. Already, Paramount has talked to him. ("Just a friendly meeting," Paramount says.) Within a year, he could be worth millions.

And never mind the money, just think of the *girls* . . .

Let's face it, what this guy has you can't get. Long eyelashes, a Clark Gable jaw, 28-inch waist and 44-inch chest, graceful like a cat on a fence. Louganis could walk up the side of a window, push off and do a three-and-a-half layout coming down without his shirt coming untucked.

And is this guy built? If you're a man, you try not to stand next to him at a party. It's odd, but for some reason, the muscles that keep a woman's bottom jaw clenched to the top seem to surrender when Louganis walks into a room.

At Southern Methodist University one day, Louganis and Cynthia Potter were putting on a diving exhibition. The pool was in a courtyard surrounded by dormitories. Halfway through it, a coed leaned out her dorm window and screamed: "Greg, I want to have your baby!"

In Caracas, Venezuela, at the Pan-Am Games last year, girls were throwing pieces of paper down from balconies with their phone numbers scrawled on them. A few carried messages, too, but this is a family newspaper, and besides, they were in Spanish.

Once, in the middle of a big meet, this bashful bombshell blonde wearing about 36 cents worth of bathing suit sets up her chaise lounge right in front of the ladder so that Louganis actually has to step around her to get to the diving board. (They both got 10s.)

So why doesn't Louganis have any girlfriends?

Jim Babbitt, a Laguna Beach playwright and Louganis' best friend, has an explanation.

"All these girls think he has all these women, so he has no women," says Babbitt. "You know what I mean? They're intimidated by him. So he doesn't really go out."

And when women *are* nice to him, its worse. Are they nice to him because they think he's a nice guy or because they can get their picture in People Magazine?

"You find yourself trying to second-guess people," Louganis says. "If someone casually comes up and says: 'Oh, you're Greg Louganis, the Olympic diver,' you're like: 'OK, what are they after?'"

Mostly, the trouble with being Greg Louganis is that you can never be anybody else. The world knows it is you, and it makes acting the fool once in a while impossible.

"I've never really gone out and had *fun*," he says. "I guess it's because I'm always too worried about what people will think. You know, if what I'm doing is kosher. Something as ridiculous as that. So I've never really had a time when I've gone out and had fun. I'm always very reserved—never really letting loose . . . Just once, I would love to cut loose and go for it. Have a blast."

As Mission Viejo teammate Wendy Wyland says, "All I can say is, thank God I'm not him."

★   ★   ★

The Soviet diver had been close to the platform all week on the reverse three-and-a-half tuck and his coaches had warned him. Louganis knew, too, since only he, the Soviet diver and four others in the world had ever tried the dive in competition. Still, there was nothing he could say.

And now Chalibashvili stood at the end of the platform, arms stretched out in front of him. He leaps high and forward, then throws his head backward, hard enough so that he can spin three and a half times and pull out in time to "rip" the water—hit it perpendicularly to get a good score from the judges.

But he is too close. The back of his head hits the hard edge of the platform. It shakes the entire diving column, even the platform where Louganis stands, and the diver's body falls limply into the pool.

Within two days, he will die of massive cerebral hemorrhaging.'

★   ★   ★

Until a year ago, the depth of Louganis' personality went no further than the bottom of the diving pool.

When was there time for the real world? Louganis never went to the senior prom. He never registered to vote. "Last year, you could have asked me what I thought about nuclear power and I'd have said: 'Nuclear what?' . . . I was socially retarded."

At the Dallas-Fort Worth airport once, Louganis was approached by a fan.

"Are you Greg Louganis, the Olympic diver?" the man asked.

"Yes."

"Well, I just want to say I'm a big fan of yours," the man said, "and I want to wish you the best of luck in Los Angeles."

"Thank you."

It was no different than any of a thousand fans a year, but this time, Louganis' coach, Ron O'Brien, scurried over.

"Greg, do you know who that was?" O'Brien whispered.

"No. Who?"

"Johnny Mathis!"

"Really?" said Louganis. Pause. "Who's Johnny Mathis?"

The price of an Olympic gold? Louganis has paid with his awareness. His social adolescence. And perhaps his happiness.

Babbitt: "He doesn't have a positive self-image. He hasn't had that many successes in other fields. He's been a machine that's been oiled to do one thing. And because of that, he has a hard time in relationships, he has a hard time in different areas. What he knows how to do is dive. He's been programmed to dive. He hasn't been programmed to do anything else. That's really rough."

The price of perfection? Sometimes Louganis wonders if it was what he really wanted all along.

Adopted at the age of 9 months by the operator of a San Diego tuna-boat fleet and a Texas farm girl—Louganis' natural parents were two 15-year-olds, a native Samoan man and a Swedish-linked woman with blonde hair and blue eyes. Too young to keep the child, they gave him up for adoption and have never surfaced in Louganis' life since, though it is possible they still live in the San Diego area.

Louganis knows little about his genetic parents except that the father was "very athletic . . . They said he was good at all kinds of sports—swimming, basketball, everything."

At 21, adopted children are legally able to seek out their natural parents, but Louganis never did—"I just wasn't curious anymore."

And if one day he turned on his answering machine and he heard his natural father speaking, how would he react?

"That's hard to say. I might call my father, maybe. I'd like to see the similarities—how much I resemble my father. . . . I have a feeling it would be like looking in a mirror of myself. . . . But I'd do it somehow so that he wouldn't know it was me. That's an awful burden on someone. He chose to give me up. That was his choice. He doesn't need for someone to come up after all these years and say: 'Oh, hi. I'm your son.' . . . He's probably got a family of his own now. Why drag out skeletons? It was a mistake that happened when he happened to be 15 years old."

But like a lot of adopted kids, there were times growing up when Louganis must have longed for his real father, for he says he saw his adopted father infrequently. Peter Louganis, who refused to be interviewed for this story, worked hard to keep his business alive. Greg says he was gone before the children awoke in the morning and came home after they were asleep again.

"I always resented my father because of that," Greg says. "He was never around when I was growing up. All the other kids had their fathers. I never got into boy scouts, anything like that. Some kids' fathers were scoutmasters . . . I missed out on that. He didn't have time."

Occasionally, he would go with his father to the fueling docks on Saturday, "but he'd always say, 'Greg, go out and play. I've got business to take care of.' And that was our weekend together."

At home, Greg says: "I was always taught children are to be seen and not heard." So he was reared physically, not emotionally. He says his older sister, Despina (also adopted and not related by blood —she now lives in San Diego), made things harder—"She always spoke for me. She'd finish my sentences for me." Louganis developed a stutter. (He does not stutter today.)

Additionally, Louganis was born with dyslexia—an impairment of the ability to read, which is often the result of a genetic defect or a brain injury. It went untreated until the third grade, and was worsened, he says, by a teacher who was convinced the way to cure him of his stuttering and inability to read was to have him read aloud in class. "She thought she was doing me a favor," Louganis remembers. "Every time we had to read aloud in class, she'd call on me. Every single time."

Schoolyard cruelty made things worse. With his Samoan heritage, Louganis was darker than his classmates. "They called me 'nigger' because of my skin," he says. "I was everybody's nigger.'"

Obsession is often born of other wounds and Louganis' life had those. If he was neglected by his father, embarrassed at school, humiliated by his peers, there were always places he could go where life was easy; where he could lose himself—literally—in something at which he was not just good but excellent—and then some. Dancing and diving.

And that's what he did. Eight hours a day.

"All the times I should have been going to the birthday parties and eating cake and ice cream I was in the studio, or on stage, or in the pool," he says. "I was committed to diving or dancing or gymnastics. I had tunnel vision. I had to. I didn't feel like I was ever going to be accepted for my intellect."

Funny how things work out.

Fifteen years later, he would like nothing better than to have things just the opposite.

★   ★   ★

"I didn't hear anything. I didn't see it until after, but I felt the platform shake and I know that he hit. My first reaction was to run out and dive in after him. But I stopped myself. I ran out to the end of the platform. I heard somebody screaming, 'Don't touch him!' And then the lifeguards went in after him. After that point I couldn't watch anymore. I couldn't watch them sweep all the blood off the pool deck. He was bleeding a lot. It was spurting out real bad. I remember after, that there was blood they hadn't gotten to in some of the strangest places. . ."

When Chalibashvili had been loaded into the ambulance and order was restored, it would be Louganis' turn to do the same dive.

★   ★   ★

"Greg Louganis is the closest thing diving has ever come to perfect," says O'Brien.

Actually, Louganis is so good they had to think of a new perfect.

Once, no one had ever scored more than 700 points in springboard diving. Louganis has gone over it five times. Still, no other diver has done it. The maximum points for the springboard series is 800, but Louganis has made them rethink it. If he can perfect a three-and-a-half reverse tuck off the *springboard,* it would mean a degree of difficulty of 3.5—the highest ever, allowing for a possible total over 800.

International meets have become almost a joke for Louganis. While he usually beats opponents in the tower by a comfortable margin, he usually humiliates them in the springboard, sometimes by 100 points or more. Often, he doesn't have to complete his last dive.

In one meet this year, Louganis' most frequent single score was 9.5. His *second* most frequent was 10.

Like the Great Gretzky in hockey, Louganis makes one think the sport was devised around him. The trinity of power, grace and athletics make him not just the best his sport has ever seen—but one of the most pristine athletes in history.

Louganis' Samoan heritage makes him strong. His arms and legs are thick. His upper torso is more massive than those of most swimmers and divers—but the lines of his chest are clean and defined. Yet Louganis has never lifted weights in his life.

Louganis' power is such that he makes the reverse three-and-a-half tuck (a 3.4, the highest degree of difficulty), look like buttering bread.

Don't tell him that, though. Louganis will snap at you when you suggest that the dive is not an immense amount of hard work packed into a one-and-a-half second fall.

If you sit poolside at the Marguerite Recreation Center in Mission Viejo, you will hear Louganis grunt as he whirls his body through that dive, almost enough to make it seem violent. Yet, from the stands, it is graceful and quiet and beautiful, as though he has nothing better to do as he falls than spin in delightful arcs, then straighten perfectly before splashing cleanly into the water. Doesn't everybody at the club do this dive?

O'Brien: "What is it that Nureyev, the dancer, says? 'We try to create the illusion that we're doing nothing when we're really working.' That's what Greg has been able to take out of dance and put into diving. He can create the illusion."

It is Louganis' 10-meter dance. It is the performance, the old soft shoe. It is effortless effort. And nobody does it better.

Dr. Sammy Lee, an Olympic gold medalist in 1948 and 1952 who was Louganis' first coach, knew it the first time he saw Louganis as a 13-year-old.

"He had the ability to ride the board," says Lee, who lives in Santa Ana. What that means is Louganis can put the fulcrum of the board as far back as possible (allowing more lift, but less control) and still stay on the board the maximum amount of time before exploding off of it. That, coupled with a standing verticle jump of 32 inches (no diver in the world can jump higher), means Louganis gets "serious air" (in the diving vernacular). Louganis jumps higher off both the springboard and platform than anyone in history and that means more time to complete spins and twists before the water comes rushing up.

It is a testament to those God-given abilities that Greg Louganis almost won the gold medal in Montreal at age 16.

He barely missed his last dive in the springboard and lost the gold by a mere 23 points to the Italian, Klaus Dibiasi, the Blond Angel. Afterward, Dibiasi walked over to Louganis and said: "Next Olympics, I watch you."

But the Americans didn't make the next Olympics, in Moscow in 1980. The U.S. boycotted the Games because of the Soviet invasion of Afghanistan. And of all the athletes who lost, perhaps Louganis lost the most. He was then by far the world's best diver in both springboard and platform diving. (Now there are challengers—none quite in his class—but challengers, especially the American Bruce Kimball of the Univesity of Michigan.)

Afghanistan and *boycott* weren't words that fit into Louganis' easy little life and he refused to admit the possibility of a boycott existed. "Some guy tried to tell me about it in a bar in Colorado Springs once," he recalls. "I wouldn't believe him. We got in a fight . . . He almost killed me."

In fact, not until Louganis stood to receive the first-place gold at the Olympic trials did he realize that it would be 1984 before Dibiasi would see him dive for the gold. And as he bent down to receive the trials gold, he cried.

"I finally realized we weren't going. It took that long. I don't know why . . . Finally I'm thinking, 'All this work and we're not going anywhere.' I was crushed."

So there would be four more years of the obsession. And while Louganis' twisting dances would improve further still, his personal growth was getting shoved further behind.

Until last year, when he met Babbitt, whose first words to him were: "If you don't get that cigarette out of my face, I'm going to stick it up your nose."

★   ★   ★

"I was so shaken . . . I thought about it on the end of the platform. I said to myself: 'My God, I'm the only other person in this contest who is doing this dive.' I asked myself, 'Is it worth it?' "

★   ★   ★

Babbitt met Louganis at a party in Miami. Louganis was having a rare smoke (he has since stopped, as with drinking) and Babbitt took offense to the way Louganis was holding it—in his face. That's when Babbitt revealed his plans for that cigarette.

"I think he liked the fact that I didn't treat him like some big jock superstar," Babbitt says. "I didn't. I didn't know who the hell he was."

They became acquaintances, then friends.

But when he asked Louganis to step outside his life and look hard at it, Babbitt became more than a friend.

"Everybody else was telling him he's God—that's a crock of bleep," Babbitt says. "It's all temporal and it's all superficial and it's all going to end."

And one day, Babbitt told him just that, saying something like:

"Everybody makes a big deal about you, but you go home alone and those people aren't there. You look in the mirror and you're still the same. . . . And after you get those two medals, it's over. That's it. You're left with a bunch of newspaper clippings and yourself. And what happens then? There's a vacuum. It's a big buildup for nothing."

The cost of an Olympic gold?

Louganis was paying too much.

"What's important is how you feel about yourself and your self-image," Babbitt told him. "And if it's the cost of two medals, it's not that important; not at the risk of compromising yourself; not at the risk of cheating yourself."

For Louganis, it was confusing. "Everyone had always made life so easy for me." And here came Babbitt to screw everything up.

Talk about degree of difficulty.

★   ★   ★

Louganis had hit the platform once himself—in Tibilsi in the Soviet Union at an international meet. The dive was not a reverse three and a half. It was a simple one-and-a-half twist. That he did not have to "throw" his body hard to complete the spins may have saved his life.

"I kept thinking about me watching myself in Tibilsi. I remem-

ber jumping off the platform—reaching up and touching my toes and seeing the sun through my feet. I remember hearing my head hit, but I don't remember feeling it. I don't remember hitting the water. And so I was standing up there hoping Sergei wouldn't remember anything.

"I calmed myself down and said, 'Hey, what is this? I can do it. I've been doing this dive all year.' So I started counting. I always count. I went 1, 2, 3 . . .'"

★   ★   ★

The change in The Real Greg Louganis first manifested itself in, of course, a female.

He had never had a serious relationship except one. Her name was Maile. It's Polynesian. Maile and Louganis had a special thing going for years. Louganis loved Maile more than any woman in this world. Then he made the ultimate sacrifice. He gave her away. Maile was a dog.

"It wasn't fair to her," Louganis said. "I'm never home. She was always cooped up in my house."

So Louganis found a home for her on a one-acre ranch near Las Vegas. Babbitt and Greg drove to Las Vegas for a sentimental goodbye. Louganis brought all her papers. Her favorite food. Her special bone. The toy that made squeaks when she bit it.

"All the way back Greg cried and cried," Babbitt remembers. "He'd say: "That's my dog.' I said, 'Cheez, how sad. Like they're filming "A Boy and His Dog" or something.' That made him laugh. Then he cried some more. He laughed and cried all the way home. Here was this nationally prominent athlete with tears coming down his eyes. I looked around and said to myself: "God, I wish the media were here.' "

Insignificant, perhaps. But for a kid who never had to take any responsibility for himself except to show up at the pool twice a day for 15 years, it was a big sacrifice, and Louganis is proud of it. "He lived up to his responsibility," Babbitt says, like the surrogate father he has become.

Maybe it was Maile or Babbitt or the tragedy in Edmonton or something else, but something happened to Louganis in the last year to make him a man.

"I guess I'm growing up," Louganis likes to say.

He made the first moves to become friends with his father. "He called him and put the question to him: 'Dad, why weren't you there?' " Babbitt says.

"We were both guilty," Greg says. "I was so wrapped up in myself, he in his business. I was trying to please him through my diving. I knew he enjoyed it. He was trying to provide the best he knew how for Despina and me. It's a shame we missed out on so much time, but we're getting there."

Louganis is taking himself less seriously, too.

At the McDonald's meet this summer, the grand-opening event

for the official Olympic pool on the USC campus, the world's best divers were all to get glowing introductions followed by each diver doing a dive off the high tower.

Divers were doing their best dives to the oohs of the crowd. Kimball did a back three and a half. And this was just *warm-ups*. And now it was Louganis' turn. Long, longer, longest introductions. Twenty-four national championships, the most in history. Four world championships. A silver medal in the '76 games. And here he is (drum roll) Greg Louganis.

Louganis walked to the end of the board, held his nose and jumped off feet first, kicking a kick to make 10-year-olds at YMCAs all over the country grin.

"Of all the dives I've done, I got the most response out of that one," Louganis says. "One guy wrote in and said: "That was my favorite. That's one, at least, I can do.' "

But it is not just taking things less seriously that has made Louganis less machine, more human. It is taking them more seriously, too.

"I know I want a private life now," he says. "The lights of the stage are not going to keep you warm at night. A silver or a gold medal is not going to keep you warm at night. It's something that I'm realizing now. It used to be so important. Now I'm realizing that it's less and less.

"I'm trying to get it together and build relationships so that I don't have to do it alone. I don't want to do it alone. I want somebody in my corner. If I need to be held, I want to be held. I want to have somebody there. And not superficial. Someone, who is really there, intellectually, emotionally and physically."

At the end of these Olympics, he will retire from diving. "And you know what? I'm looking forward to it."

The price of an Olympic gold?

There is no limit to what Louganis will pay.

"Greg is finally changing," Babbitt says. "Diving isn't his priority anymore. He is."

★   ★   ★

. . . 1, 2, 3 . . . Jump! Louganis jumped. And then jumped some more. And then he laughed.

"I was laughing at myself. Right in the middle of it. I realized I had jumped so far out that I was probably going to be lucky if I stayed in the pool."

Louganis received 9.5s on the dive, enough to come from behind and win.

A City in Flames Mars World Series

BASEBALL

By *RICK BOZICH*

From the Louisville Times
Copyright © 1984, the Louisville Times

It is two hours after Larry Herndon clutched the final out of the 1984 World Series. All the champagne has flowed, all the excuses have been offered and all the congratulations have been accepted. Even President Reagan's.

The San Diego Padres have run out of bad-hop singles, no-pop hitters and middle-inning relievers. The Detroit Tigers have proven what they established from the first day of the season: Nobody plays baseball better. Detroit 8, San Diego 4.

Bless you, boys, is the message flashed upon the scoreboard, repeating the battle cry a local TV man originated.

Burn you, boys, describes the situation around the stadium.

Never before have I seen flames dance through the streets of a city. Instead of counting the number of runs Kirk Gibson batted in, I am counting the number of stripped and flaming police cars on Michigan Avenue. Running along the east side of the stadium, Michigan is overrun with celebrating fans.

Champagne dripping through my hair, I left the clubhouse of the world champions long ago. But somehow I do not believe this is a night to write about Kirk Gibson's two long homers or Rusty Kuntz's short sacrifice fly or Alan Trammell's Most Valuable Player award.

I have listened to Gibson say he knew thunder would erupt from his bat, and have shaken my head as Kuntz apologized for driving in the winning run with the strangest play of the Series—a sacrifice fly to the second baseman.

But flames are dancing around the ball park, and the police have requested that nobody—press, security, club officials—attempt to leave.

The situation on Michigan Avenue has turned from celebration to desperation. The behavior is as primitive as I have seen anywhere outside the Louisville Zoo.

The time has come—1984—to play the World Series at neutral sites, away from the hometown crowds who believe that root, root, rooting for the home team is an invitation to destroy property, threaten lives and maim authorities.

Beam the clubhouse scene and interviews into my room and I will remain in my hotel. My job does not include combat pay.

I am standing on the roof outside the third deck on the right-field foul line, and I have never been more frightened in my life. Tiger Stadium is the only place in this city where I feel safe, and I am trapped here.

An American League spokesman has announced, "We are investigating all avenues of escape." Nobody attempts to leave.

It is now three hours after Herndon caught the final out, and the police have asked the press to assemble in the empty Padres clubhouse. I wonder how the losing team escaped.

In time, maybe 30 minutes, a bus will leave for our downtown hotel at the Renaissance Center. But a major league spokesman announces that he cannot guarantee its safety.

Nobody laughs.

A city is burning before me.

Smoke is swirling from a flaming cab and dozens have gathered to urinate on the flames. A knot of crazies hoists a motorcycle into the flames. A cheer—as loud as any Gibson heard as he circled the bases—ripples through the crowd. It is a police motorcycle.

The crowd swarmed upon that spot after jumping off the glowing frame of a police car they overturned and burned an hour earlier. A fire engine doused that flame and then doused the crowd. But resiliency motivates this mob. They will not go home. They return and begin rocking another car.

In the middle of Michigan Avenue, three other police cars have been permanently disabled, doors torn away, windows kicked out, tires slashed. The mob moves in at points all along the avenue until a charge from mounted policemen forces a retreat.

It is three hours since Herndon clutched the last out of the 1984 World Series, and a man is lying in Michigan Avenue. He has not moved for 45 minutes.

Hundreds of bottles have flown from the crowd into tight circles of policemen. Incensed, the cops charge one of the offenders, flashing clubs longer than Kirk Gibson's home run bat.

One cop selects a man he had seen throw something and slams his club into the man's temple. The offender drops faster than anybody Muhammad Ali ever put down.

Friends surround the fallen man, propping his head up. They cry for immediate assistance. From the urgency of their cries, I assume the man needs medical help.

The police move away, trying to repel the crowd—maybe 5,000, maybe more—that has collected at Michigan and Trumbull avenues, just outside the right-field corner of the stadium.

I will not be surprised to discover the man has died. The police refuse to help him. And no emergency personnel could possibly push through the crowd.

This is more violence than I have seen since television captured the scenes from the riot at the 1968 Democratic convention in Chicago. That was political protest. This is sport. This is·entertainment. This is a dangerous situation on the fringe of chaos.

A Domino's Pizza helicopter is flying in and out of Tiger Stadium, airlifting pizzas in and removing some of the winning players. Fumes from the burning vehicles burn inside my nostrils, and I do not feel like eating.

It is a crowd that feels extremely macho, and behaves extremely sicko. This is worse than any scene staged by Alfred Hitchcock or Rod Serling. This is the one step beyond what we have always feared from the infield crowd on Derby Day.

Sirens wail, helicopters flashing floodlights zoom in, and the crowd ebbs and flows along the loose spots in the police line.

These people are determined to hurt somebody, throwing everything they can find—bottles, cans, street barriers, seat cushions.

The one reason the city is not on fire is most of the property around the ball park burned to the ground in the riots of 1968. Somebody demonstrated incredible foresight by not building it back.

It is four hours after Herndon clutched the last out of the 1984 World Series, and the first press bus has returned—safely—from downtown Detroit. An announcement is made that one final bus will make the trip.

The rush begins.

A persistent, driving rain has dispersed much of the crowd, and the threat of arrest has been announced to others. The two overturned, torched cars, burned to the frame, sit on Michigan Avenue. Somebody has finally removed the clubbed man.

Nobody is urinating in the streets as I move into the last bus, which suffers only one broken window on the trip downtown. We need 15 minutes to make the five-minute journey, but we arrive safely at our destination.

A Tigers spokesman announces the team's victory parade will wind through the downtown street tomorrow.

I will leave for home today.

Even if I have to walk.

Homeward Bound

by Mary Schroeder of the Detroit Free Press. Their dreams gone awry, three would-be Detroit Lions football players wait outside the Lions' offices for rides to the airport after getting their notices on the final day of training camp cuts. Copyright © 1984, Mary Schroeder, Detroit Free Press.

In Your Face

by Louis DeLuca of the Dallas Times Herald. Michael Black of
Napa, Calif., reacts to a punch thrown by St. Louis boxer Arthur
Johnson during the Olympic boxing trials in Fort Worth, Tex.
Copyright © 1984, Dallas Times Herald.

Woody: The Private Wars of an Old Soldier

COLLEGE FOOTBALL

By *JOHN ED BRADLEY*

From the Washington Post
Copyright © 1984, the Washington Post

Woody Hayes once said, "Without winners there wouldn't even be any goddamned civilization."

Now he was saying, *"What?* What on earth do you mean?" to a parking garage attendant, a huge specimen of authority in tight blue coveralls, here at the Hyatt Regency.

Hayes had just taken a little pink ticket from a woman in a glass booth, asked where to park and, upon hearing that he could park his El Camino anywhere, had turned into the first queue available. But now this giant, built like the company store, had come off his bar stool and was shouting, "You can't leave your machine there, Chief! That ain't no place!" and sending an echo across the continent like an ugly mule song.

"But this is a place," Hayes protested, pointing at the two yellow lines that created the parking space, and ignoring the day-glo bright cones with little signs hanging by chains that read, "Reserved."

"No, it ain't, Chief. That ain't no place. Get back in your car and move on down the road."

"It looks like a place to me," Hayes said finally, and the attendant cocked his head back the way hardtimers do when prepared to deliver the Word, and gave the former Ohio State University football coach a pair of eyes that said, "Don't get sassy with me, old man."

Hayes grabbed the door handle and shook his head in plain disgust while I waited for him to thrust a toe of his snow boots into the whitewall of the front tire. He mumbled something under his breath, the voice of suppressed rage, of a hard heart clanking against a busy pair of lungs. But I knew that when he got back behind the wheel and headed up the ramp, passing a dozen open spaces without the least bit of outcry, climbing higher and higher until there was enough room to parallel park a caravan of 18-wheelers, that this was what hot-tempered fools considered the stuff of "minor victories."

Woody Hayes, 71 and dead-set in his ways, had not allowed stubbornness to defeat his goodwill. He had come to tell members of the Ohio Agro Expo what it meant, exactly, to be good and decent and rightly American. And maybe that was why he said, *"Aaaahhhh,"* when he finally parked his El Camino and stepped outside. We were standing in an open concrete forest of parking queues, all alone on the sixth floor. Ohio was a storm around us, a white nightmare of snow falling in hard, horizontal sheets, as if on its way south to West Virginia. And still, the old coach found cause to run his hands over his belly and suck in new life. "Damn man called me Chief," he said and pocketed his keys, while I led the way to civilization.

★   ★   ★

On a cold day early this month, I met him before noon at his office in the Military Science Building, Room 201, on the OSU campus, where he is a professor emeritus in the Department of Health, Physical Education and Recreation. Outside his door and a short walk down the hall, there was a bulletin board with pictures of soldiers dressed in combat gear and of tanks and all the mighty machines of war, and these words in stencil type: "Do You Have What it Takes?"

His secretary was typing up notes of preliminary chapter sketches on a book he's writing called, "Football, History and Woody Hayes." The blackboard on the wall directly across from his desk listed each chapter—*The Starting Eleven, Specialty Teams,* etc.—and it was so messy it looked as though a yard bird had stepped in a mess of chalk and walked right across it. There was an old-time phonograph on the table next to him and a stack of albums by folks like Tony Bennett and Glenn Miller. The one on top was an oldie, "Nice 'n Easy," by Frank Sinatra.

And there was his vast collection of history books, most of them pertaining to war and the great leaders of war. They crowded his desk and the bookshelves behind him. Two entire shelves contained books on Gen. George S. Patton.

"The thing about Patton," he would say on the drive to the Ohio Center, "is that his casualties amounted to about one-third of those of the other generals. You had to fight for him, but you didn't have to die."

Woody Hayes wears eyeglasses with frames the color of his hair, the kind punk rockers wear nowadays to look mad with things. And he still has a particular look of dignity about him, a certain stillness that belongs only to those removed of the vicious, old grind. He may well be, as his secretary suggested, the most recognized man in Ohio, for he looks no different now than he did the last time you saw him— the last time everybody saw him—either live and in a rage on the sidelines of the Gator Bowl, slugging a Clemson player for intercepting a pass and killing a last-chance Buckeye drive, or on the 5 o'clock news doing the same.

That all came down on December 30, 1978, the year of injury and ignominy and insult. Now, as folks passed him on their way out of the Ohio Center and offered a word of greeting, he never failed to say, "Men," to the men, tapping the brim of his fancy suede hat, and "Ladies," to the ladies.

Inside the giant convention center, a group of agribusiness sponsors gave him a tour of the tractors and trucks and fertilizer spreaders that crowded the showroom floor, and he had a way of saying, *"Izzat-so?"* in such a way as to make them believe they were showing a retired military leader the awesome machines of the Third World War. He stopped before a mammoth Field Gymmy truck and asked, "How much does one of those big tires cost?"

A guide replied with pride, "These babies go for $3,100 a pair, Coach." And Woody Hayes stood incredulous, scratching his scalp in disbelief. "Thirty-one, you say?" he asked.

"Yes, sir," the man said. "Thirty-one for these babies."

"Well, I'll be doggone," he said and muffed up his lips. "I'll just be doggone."

Then the man said, "Now you wanta talk combines, I'll talk combines with you, Coach. You talkin' combines, you talkin' big money."

Hayes said, "Combines, huh?"

★   ★   ★

Banquet food will give you heartburn, Woody Hayes learned long ago. But he eats it anyway. Sometimes that and the price of gas is all a gathering of two or more needs to offer to get him to talk about right and wrong in America and about the game he sorely misses. On occasion he has drawn as much as $3,000 for a speaking engagement, but the run over the past two weeks has been to small Catholic schools and groups of fraternity and sorority kids and most anybody who'd lend him an ear. He doesn't do it for money. "You can't pay the people back for being good to you," he says. "But you can always pay forward."

After the Agro Expo speech, which drew a standing ovation and a chorus of bird whistles, he said we would take turns driving the three-hour haul to South Point, which was off Highway 52, just below Ironton. At first it was so cold in the cab of the El Camino that you could bite your arm and feel nothing. Then Coach Hayes turned on the heater and it got so hot so quickly that I was struck suddenly with a rush of vertigo and thought I might faint. Coach Hayes said, "Too warm for ya?" and I lied. I said no, it wasn't. He was smiling and squinting into the spinning white face of the road, as George Washington had in the famous painting, "Crossing the Delaware."

His teeth were bared and his brow buckled, and there was an obvious sense of mission in the way he gripped the wheel. He looked perfectly at war with the elements, but perfectly at peace. I tapped him on the knee and said, "I feel fine, Coach. Just fine."

Visibility was poor, but if you squinted and looked hard enough, you could see the open boxcars in the train yards and the simple white farmhouses in the hills, smoke rising from chimney stacks and cows and sheep huddled under dilapidated tin sheds, and all the cars that were stranded in the ditches and in the median. A grader had scraped the road half-clean, and boulder-like chunks of snow and ice were pushed onto the shoulder of the road. Everybody drove with their lights and windshield wipers on, everybody except Hayes, of course, who was well aware of the difference between day and night and would be hardpressed to compromise at 3 in the afternoon.

"I've noticed something about cars," he said. "Your real big cars and your real little cars are the ones that get stuck in the snow. Your medium-sized cars always keep moseying along."

He had owned two Cadillacs for a day back in 1979, gifts from friends of the university in appreciation of 28 years as the head football coach. He refused one entirely and cashed the other in and set up a scholarship fund with the money. The fanciest car he ever drove was a Buick Riviera and it was so fancy it was assuming, pretentious. It wasn't Woody. He had been driving the El Camino pickup for about 29,000 miles and liked it except for the matter of its light rear end.

"I got stuck trying to get up a hill the other day," he said. "I had to get out and walk for it. It was hard. I don't walk so well anymore, not like I used to."

He hated to think or talk about it, but his eyes weren't what they used to be, either. His great love of books had been stifled of late by his inability to call the words from the pages and to hold them in his mind. Even his level of comprehension was not what it had once been. A lady in England had mailed him a book on world history she considered well worth his study time, but he was having the damndest struggle getting through it.

Former President Richard Nixon, whom Hayes has considered a "close, personal friend" ever since their meeting in 1958, when Nixon was vice president and in attendance at a game in Ohio Stadium, had sent him a copy of his work-in-progress, "Real Peace," and Hayes had read it through but with no small degree of difficulty. He memorized entire passages from the book, lines about the future of "this wonderful land," and he could deliver them in such a way as to make you want to stop whatever it was you're doing and run down to your local recruiting office and enlist in the United States Marine Corps.

"Sometimes now," Hayes said in a broken voice, "I get a little bored with myself. I might watch a game on TV, and I worry about it a little. I worry about the game getting out of hand. I do. I really do. The money involved. The overcommercialization of it. Even average football players are making as much as $700,000 a year, *Seven hundred thousand dollars a year to play football!* Do we even know what is happening? Do we really?"

Outside of Circleville, we passed a graveyard on a hill, with its white expanse of stone tablets and angels and obelisks barely visible in the deep white cover of snow. "Why are so many of the men I loved dead now?" he wondered aloud. "Doggone, I miss 'em." And he named a score of them, told stories about them that had somehow remained as bright and burning in his mind as the vision of the road in front of him. He called them all "great Americans."

He talked about the living, too. About his wife Anne, who was once informed by an irate fan that she was married to a fathead. "Of course he is," she had replied quite agreeably. "All husbands are."

And he talked about his sister Mary, who, in 1929, was the headliner in a Broadway play and shared the backside of a marquee with another Hayes of enormous fame, Helen Hayes. Mary had won the part mainly because she could play the piano with the skill of a virtuoso. Hayes remembered that Thomas Wolfe was her favorite writer, and there was a line he knew: "Oh, lost and by the wind grieved, ghost, come back again," from *Look Homeward, Angel*. But Hayes had never read him. "Mary says he's dandy, just dandy," he said. "He died young, you know. He wasn't yet 40. And he's gone from us. A young man, Thomas Wolfe."

Mary lived in New Jersey now. She was 78. He said he regretted having never seen her play the piano on Broadway. And he regretted the matter of Wolfe's early passing.

We reached the River Cities Inn almost two hours before the banquet was scheduled to begin and the management said there was a room waiting, in case we might want to wash up. I gave the key to Coach Hayes, but he suggested we go in the bar for a while, to wind down over a glass of juice. "Don't be afraid of drinking the hard stuff," he said. I ordered a Coke.

We sat at the bar with our backs to the crowd of eyes that fell powerfully upon him and before long a skinny, rawboned woman in high heels tapped Coach Hayes on the shoulder and asked him to please sign a couple of pictures for "little babies back home." The photographs were both black-and-white 8x10s, and depicted Hayes wearing an OSU baseball cap and the same suit he wore this day, a navy coat and slacks and a striped tie that reached way short of his belt buckle. "Make one out to Terry," the woman said, and Hayes wrote best wishes to Terry, then his name. He added a flare to his last name, whipping out a couple of loops that extended across the bottom of the picture. "How old is little Terry?" he asked. And the woman said, without shame, "He's 47."

Hayes put the cap back on his pen, and before he could turn to thank the woman, she had reached for a napkin on the bar and was wiping a greasy run of mascara from her cheek. "The day you dotted the i," she said, referring to an Ohio State tradition in which a celebrated alumnus stands in with the band during the pregame performance, "I never cried so much in my life. Ohio is not Ohio with you gone, Coach. And football isn't football either."

★   ★   ★

There were women of property crying in the audience—here at the banquet for the Boys' and Girls' Club of Ironton-Lawrence County—women with diamonds on their ears and fancy designs stitched onto their black lace stockings. And their husbands, good-looking farm boys in three-piece suits and store-bought neckties, coughed into clinched fists as if trying to unclog all the pain and thunder the old man had just shoved down their throats. They had come in their Sunday best to pick clean a buffet of sliced turkey and pork, roast beef and spaghetti salad, and to hear a voice they worshipped shout in defense of truth, beauty, love and honor, democracy and above all else, the American Way.

And they had come simply to gaze upon the man the master of ceremonies had called "one of the greatest leaders in the history of Ohio." But when he was done, they followed him out to the car and stood in the breezeway and waved goodby, as if they were certain never to see him again. I started the car and made way to the highway, trying to beat the storm of traffic on the trip north to Ironton. He started to hum when we were just five miles out of town, then he sang a verse or two. The snow had stopped, and it was so dark outside that it seemed as though this journey held no real destination. "What's that you're singing," I asked, and he shrugged his shoulders. "Just a song," he said. "But a pretty song."

I was getting sleepy long before he suggested we pull over and get some gas. He got out and stood with his hands in his pockets and his legs wide apart, facing the cold night. He was still standing that way—his eyes blurred by the distance, his tie pushed over his shoulder and flapping in the wind—when I noticed the station attendant staring at him in both awe and wonder, as if gazing into the face of an apparition. "You who I think you are?" the man asked.

Hayes, unmoving except to raise big eyebrows, said, "I have no idea who you think I am, young man."

"Are you Woody Hayes?" the man asked. "Are you *Coach* Woody Hayes?"

Hayes let the sound of his name sink in, and by the sour expression that gripped his countenance I wondered how pleased he was with what he heard. "I might be," he said. "I might be him."

"You like football?" I asked the man.

"I used to," he said. "I hate to say this, but the last football game I ever saw was in Jacksonville, at the Gator Bowl. I was there when you hit that feller, Coach."

★   ★   ★

Five years ago, when Woody Hayes slammed his clenched fist into the neck of Clemson nose guard Charlie Bauman, he proved that some generals do lead by rolling up their sleeves and charging into battle. But he took on more than an army that day. He took on the world. I know now that his fury was not directed at Bauman so much as it was a day of defeated dreams and of a failure to grasp the final victory that would forever elude him. His war was hopeless and probably stupid, but damn if he didn't fight. He had offered no half-cocked explanations of the matter later and thus spared himself the impossible task of explaining how it feels to be a man at war with something like time.

We were coming on Columbus when I asked him why, why he had ever hit Charlie Bauman, and he said he didn't know why. "But you know what (Michigan Coach) Bo Schembechler said about all that? He asked me if I had any intention of hurting that young man and I said no, I didn't. I didn't hit him to hurt him. It hurt only me. You see, it hurt only *me*. But you can't always explain everything. Some things are beyond you."

We pushed on through the snow, and he said he wanted to show me a "place I know of" before I turned in for the night at my hotel. He gave me directions, saying only "left here," and "quick right here," but soon we came upon an intersection with a great white sign burning in the blaze of our headlights. The sign said: *Woody Hayes Road.*

It was almost 1 in the morning and the snow began to fall harder and harder. I waited out the red light, then turned left and worked through the Ohio State campus until we crossed the mushy snow that covered the road between the assembly center and the great gray ghost of Ohio Stadium, *his* stadium. I stopped the car for a moment, and he started to sing again, a song I didn't know. A pretty song. Then he told me to move on. "You must be proud," I said, "to have a road named after you."

He looked out the window and up into the heavens. Then he looked at me. "It's only a road," he said. "But it's a good road."

Decker's Fall Stirs The Great Debate

OLYMPIC TRACK

By *RANDY HARVEY*

From The Los Angeles Times
Copyright © 1984, The Los Angeles Times

Mary Decker was on top of the world for a year, but Friday night came the fall. It was swift and decisive and painful, although her tears were for soothing emotional instead of physical wounds.

Just into the second half of the 3,000 meters at the Coliseum, Decker and South African Zola Budd, the two central characters in this continuing saga, got their feet tangled.

While Budd, who runs for Britain, retained her balance and extended her lead, Decker, who was in second place, grasped at the early-evening air, looking for something, anything, to hold on to.

All she got was the number off Budd's back.

Decker tumbled into the infield, struggling for a moment to regain her footing and continue the fight, then collapsing, in tears, onto her back.

"It was like I was tied to the ground," said Decker, whose injury later was diagnosed as a pulled left hip muscle. The chief medical officer of the Los Angeles Olympic Organizing Committee, Dr. Tony Daly, said Decker could begin running again today.

Today is too late for Decker, who won the world championship last year in the 1,500 and the 3,000 but chose to compete at the longer distance in the Olympics because she felt a gold medal would be waiting for her at the end of it.

Instead, it belonged to Romania's Maricica Puica, who had a time of 8:35.96. Even if Decker had not met with her untimely finish, she was no cinch to beat Puica, who has the best time in the world this year in the 3,000.

Britain's Wendy Sly, who overcame a hamstring injury to be here, finished second in 8:39.47, while Canada's Lynn Williams was third in 8:42.14. Cindy Bremser of Madison, Wis., was fourth in 8:42.78.

Budd faded badly on the final lap, finishing seventh in 8:48.80. That is more than 11 seconds behind her best time, her poor result coming perhaps as a result of the cut she received on her left heel when spiked by Decker just prior to her fall. As usual, Budd did not wear shoes.

An umpire for the International Amateur Athletic Federation, which governs track and field and supplies the officials for most major international competitions, disqualified Budd for obstructing Decker's path.

British officials protested the decision. After viewing films of the incident from six different angles, the IAAF appeals jury ruled that Budd was not at fault and reinstated her to seventh place.

As for whether the contact was caused by Budd or Decker or by both, the debate is likely to continue for years. Track and field experts are still arguing over the cause of American Jim Ryun's fall during the qualifying for the 1,500 meters in the 1972 Munich Olympics.

Decker had the lead for the first three laps, running at a world-record pace for the first two before slowing to allow someone else to take charge. She will be second-guessing that decision for some time to come.

Coming off the final turn on the fourth lap, about 1,300 meters from the finish, Budd moved around Decker and into the lead. They appeared to trade elbows as Budd went past. No harm, no foul. Then, as Budd moved to the inside lane, she cut off Decker, forcing her to shorten her stride.

About 10 meters later, Decker seemed to be ready to pass Budd on the inside. Budd, running on the outside of Lane 1, swayed ever so slightly to her left.

Decker spiked her on the left heel. Budd's left leg shot out from under her, leaving her almost bowlegged for a split second. It was that quick. Decker's right foot and Budd's left crossed. Decker's left foot went over the curb and onto the infield. The rest of her soon followed.

The other runners said Decker screamed something at Budd, although no one could make out exactly what it was.

"I didn't see Mary fall, but I heard her fall," Sly said.

As Dr. Daly and Decker's fiance, British discus thrower Richard Slaney, ran to her side, the race continued. But at every turn, the crowd booed Budd. As a South African whose move to Britain six months ago so that she could compete in the Olympics was not unanimously approved by the British, the sound was not unfamiliar to her.

Obviously distraught, Budd ran the rest of the race in tears.

Afterward, Budd, her eyes red, approached Decker in the tunnel leading away from the track and tried to apologize.

"Don't bother," Decker said. "I don't want to talk to you."

Budd was whisked away by British officials before she could give her explanation to the media. But after returning from the hospital, Decker appeared at a press conference and left no doubt that she blames the bare feet of Budd for her catastrophe.

"Well, Zola Budd tried to cut in without being, basically, ahead," Decker said. "Her foot upset me. To avoid pushing her, I fell.

"Looking back, I should have pushed her. But the headlines to-morrow would have read, 'Mary Decker Pushes Zola.'

"I don't think there's any question she was in the wrong. Maybe it was inexperience on her part, but she was not in front. You have to be a full stride ahead in front before you cut in on anyone. I do hold her responsible."

The interview ended moments later, when Decker broke into tears and was carried away from the media tent by Slaney.

As soon as Decker hit the ground, the U.S. women's coach, Brooks Johnson, was off and running from his seat in the Coliseum to find an official. "Where do I go to protest?" he said.

Not everyone thought a protest was in order. Switzerland's Cornelia Buerki, who finished fifth in the race, did not think Decker was being fair in blaming Budd.

"If it was anybody's fault, it was Mary's," said Buerki, who, like Budd, was born in South Africa. "She tried to get inside of Zola. She hit Zola in the Achilles tendon. It was not Zola's fault. She was in front.

"I wouldn't say it was anybody's fault. But if you had to give somebody blame, it was Mary. She tried to get around Zola, and she hit her."

Detatched observers felt that the incident occurred as a result of the inexperience of both runners.

Running for most of her 18 years in South Africa, whose track and field athletes are not allowed to compete internationally because of the government's apartheid policies, Budd did not have experience against world-class fields until she moved to Britain in March.

She ran a road race in May against Norwegians Grete Waitz and Ingrid Kristiansen but had not faced international competition on the track until she ran here.

Her strategy always has been to charge into the lead from the gun and run alone, perhaps because so few of her competitors have been able to stay with her. But there were questions about how she would react when running with a pack.

"She looked like she didn't know how to run with a lead," said American middle-distance runner Craig Masback, who now works for the International Olympic Committee. He meant that she did not know how to run with a small lead.

As soon as Budd took the lead coming off the curve, Masback said, she should have moved over as far as she could in lane one, not tempting Decker with the sliver of daylight to the inside.

At the same time, Decker, even though she is eight years older than Budd, also is unaccustomed to running in traffic. Like Budd, Decker prefers to set a fast pace and dare everyone else to follow.

"Mary seemed indecisive," Masback said. "She made a half-hearted attempt to take back the lead. If this had been a men's race, a man would have given the leader a little push to let him know that he was coming through. Steve Ovett would have shoved somebody. But the women aren't as experienced at these kind of distances."

This was the first women's 3,000 in the history of the Olympics.

In tears, her left heel bleeding, the crowd booing her, Budd remained in the lead for another lap and a half. But with 600 meters remaining, Sly took over. With one lap remaining, Budd began to fade.

One hundred meters into the final lap, Puica started her kick. Sly tried to stay with her, but she did not have the strength.

Canada's Williams passed Budd, then Bremser, then Buerki, then Portugal's Aurora Cunha.

"I hope nobody blames Zola," British team manager Nick Whitehead said. "She's emotionally drained after her first big race."

The last laugh could have been Puica's, but, like everyone else, she was not in the mood. "I regret what happened," she said. "I feel sorry for Mary."

Slaughter Learns Bias Exists Off the Field

BASEBALL

By *STAN HOCHMAN*

From the Philadelphia Daily News
Copyright © 1984, Philadelphia Newspapers Inc.

Bill Rigney has the scars, evidence of the way Enos (Country) Slaughter played the game, a clutter of white welts in the fleshy space between his right thumb and index finger.

"Twenty-four bleeping stitches," Rigney said last night, before managing the American Leaguers in the Cracker Jack Old-Timers Baseball Classic.

"I'm with the Giants. Johnny Mize is playing first. Slaughter hits a ball that gets by Mize. The ball doesn't go 15 feet.

"But Slaughter, the way he played, he's going for two. Mize gives me a big, lollipop throw. The ball gets there, Slaughter gets there. Spikes flying. Cuts me open like a chicken.

"I'm out 10 days. Next series in New York I'm still a little hissed. I'm hoping he gets to first, so I can turn a double play, low-bridge him.

"We go the whole series and I never get a shot at him. They're going to Boston to end the season, and as we leave the field I hear him behind me, saying, 'Well, Specs, you'll have to wait till next year.'

"Amazing thing is, they go to Boston. He's on first, 3-2 count on Stan Musial, Slaughter is running, Musial hits a line drive, he turns his head to look, pow, ball hits him in the face, puts his nose under his right ear.

"I sent him a wire. Told him I didn't have to wait till next year after all, and I was glad that they found his nose.

"Thing is, that's the way he played the game. We try to teach our young kids to play the game that way. Talk about Pete Rose if you want to, but nobody played harder than Country Slaughter."

Played hard for 21 years. Has a lifetime average of .300, knocked in 1,304 runs. Scored from first on Harry Walker's base hit to win the 1946 World Series for St. Louis against the Red Sox.

Slaughter's got scars that go deeper than Rigney's. Of the 55 old-timers gathered here, he is the only .300 lifetime hitter who is not in the Hall of Fame.

Why not?

"You'd have to ask the writers," Slaughter said earlier in the day. "It makes me feel bad to talk about it. Because of what I gave to baseball it makes me feel kind of downhearted.

"I never snubbed a writer. I gave honest answers. Probably not the answers they wanted to hear. I am outspoken.

"I gave the game my life. I don't think anybody played harder. Look at my statistics. And remember that I missed three of my greatest years, 27, 28, 29. Gave them to my country.

"I don't begrudge that. I came back in good health, resumed my career."

The writers did not vote for Slaughter at a time when they were voting a one-dimensional player like Ralph Kiner into the Hall of Fame.

After 15 years, they removed Slaughter's name from the ballot. After five more years he was eligible for election by the veterans committee. They chose Pee Wee Reese and Rick Ferrell. Rick Ferrell?

"I don't know how the vote came out," Slaughter said glumly. "A lot of the members I played ball with or played against."

Maybe that's it, maybe Slaughter slid with his spikes too high. Maybe the answer to why he's not in the Hall of Fame is spelled in the blood he spilled on the basepaths.

"I played the game the way it should be played," Slaughter said. "I asked no odds and gave none. Pitcher knocked me down, or hit me in the back, I went to first base. Someone blocked a base, I went in, spikes flying.

"If someone got spiked, I couldn't help that. I was playing for my bread and butter. I spiked a lot of guys, but never intentionally."

He spiked Jackie Robinson the first time the Cardinals played the Dodgers. And that is why he is not in the Hall of Fame. A phantom has slashed him, deep inside, and he cannot get even. He is 68, and it hurts more every year.

"I never had a problem with nobody as long as I played," Slaughter said, his voice raspy with anger. "I put on that uniform, I gave 120 percent of my life to baseball.

"I see Red Barber has written a book on the '47 Dodgers. In the book he says I intentionally spiked Jackie Robinson, and for that reason the writers in New York didn't ever vote for me.

"Robinson had moved from second to first. A throw came, he reached for it. He came back to the bag, and that's when I stepped on him.

"I was a Southern boy. The writers made a big issue of it. I didn't care who played. Red, green, black.

"But the writers tried to make an issue of it because I was a Southern boy. Ask any teammates who played with me. I never, at no time, spoke against a race.

"Once, we played the Phillies, then moved on to Brooklyn. Stan Musial had appendicitis. Had ice on constantly.

"We get to New York and one writer writes a story that Musial and I got in a fight over the race issue and I had punched Musial in the stomach.

"I never opened my mouth about Jackie Robinson and (Roy) Campanella joining the Dodgers. When the ball game started, I was just out there to win.

"In my hometown (Roxboro, N.C.) I haven't got a white person within a mile of me. Maybe 75 or 100 of my neighbors are black. And they're some of the best neighbors I've had."

It shouldn't have to come to that. Some of his best neighbors are black. But he is 68, growing tobacco, showing up at old-timers' games with the scars in his belly, raising hell.

He was a Southerner playing in St. Louis, and historians insist that the Cardinals threatened to strike rather than play the integrated Dodgers.

"I never heard anybody on the Cardinals ball club talk about going on strike against the Dodgers. All I knew, I read in the papers.

"They say (Commissioner) Ford Frick got involved, went to the Cardinals owner (Sam Breadon). Nobody talked to me. I was one of the veterans on that club. They might have gone to Musial or Marty Marion. But I was the oldest.

"And never, at no time, did I hear anybody say anything about going on strike. Dixie Walker, on Robinson's own club, he was upset. And that's probably why they traded him afterward.

"I know every player would like to get in the Hall of Fame, but I'm not going to change my way of living for nobody. I've lived this way this long."

If they culled every bigot, every drunk, every wife-beater out of the Hall of Fame, you could tour Cooperstown in 18 minutes.

You are not supposed to vote for guys who have become famous for one game or one historic swing of the bat. That keeps the Bobo Hollomans and Don Larsens out of the sacred precincts.

Perhaps there's a backlash toward Slaughter's famous sprint from first base in 1946, when Johnny Pesky hung onto the relay throw a moment too long.

"If Dom DiMaggio had been out there, in center field, I'd never have tried to score," Slaughter said, describing the play for the 18,036th time.

"I studied outfielders. I knew who had good arms. They'd put Leon Culbertson out there.

"I led off with a base hit. (Whitey) Kurowski tried to sacrifice and popped up. (Del) Rice flied out to left. Two strikes on Harry

Walker, I was running.

"He hit the ball to center, and when I got to second I said, 'I can score.' I guess the scorer gave him a double, but he really went to second on the throw home.

"And I don't blame Pesky. I blame his other infielders, Bobby Doerr and Pinky Higgins, for not letting Pesky know I was running.

"You have to know that in an earlier game, (third base coach) Mike Gonzales had stopped me at third. There was a bad relay throw and I could have scored.

"Manager (Eddie Dyer) came to me and said, 'If you have a chance again, go ahead and gamble, I'll stand up for you.' So, next time, I took the gamble. It's the way I played."

He can name every man on the veterans committee, and if you listen carefully you can tell how he thinks the guy voted. He hears whispers that Ernie Lombardi and Arky Vaughn will get in before he does.

"I played more years, more games, had more singles, more doubles, more runs batted in," Slaughter said glumly. "Why would they keep throwing me behind?"

Why indeed?

"He belongs in the Hall of Fame," broadcaster Bill White said. "I don't know why he's not in there. I heard that stuff about the Cardinals and Dodgers, but what does it mean?

"It doesn't matter whether you like a guy or dislike him, if he belongs, he belongs."

"I never heard that stuff," said Larry Doby, who was Robinson's pioneer counterpart in the American League. "And even if it's so, so what? It's a guy's stats that count, not what you thought of him as a person."

"It's a joke, him not being in the Hall of Fame," said Hall of Famer Robin Roberts. "He belongs."

But, maybe, it was suggested to Roberts, Slaughter had angered too many ball players with the belligerent way he played the game.

Roberts laughed, and through the laughter, he summed up Slaughter's career. "I know," Roberts said, "he made a lot of pitchers mad."

For Cremins, It's Been Wild Ride from Bronx

COLLEGE BASKETBALL

By *THOMAS M. STINSON*

From The Atlanta Journal-Constitution
Copyright © 1984, The Atlanta Journal-Constitution

In December of 1964, while the rest of the All Hallows High School basketball team of New York City went to a tournament in upstate Schenectady, Bobby Çremins, age 17 and the best player in school, stayed home in the Bronx with a dislocated shoulder. And, well, home was a good place for him.

He was good, but he was trouble. He'd already flunked out of school once, and done enough to make a new coach dislike him, and cared so little about making amends that he spent most of his free time playing semi-pro football with a block team from his neighborhood in the Highbridge section. He'd hurt the shoulder there. He didn't care.

"So on that trip to Schenectady, all the players go out drinkin'," Cremins says. He's behind his own desk on Georgia Tech's campus now and, as almost always, he's grinning. Buster Brown nearing middle age. "'They went to a bar, what, about seven of 'em, and they get caught, and the principal threw 'em off the team.

"So I get a phone call, and they ask me if I can play. Because if not, they're gonna cancel the season. I was startin' to heal, so I told 'em I could play. So I came back, and there were six of us on the team, and obviously I had to play. And I had a great year."

This wasn't the first time, nor would it be the last, that something happened to save Bobby Cremins from himself. But it was the most important salvation; for it finally started him off on his long, strange trip that has led through a military school, several colleges, Ecuador, the front door of the Waldorf-Astoria Hotel, a collection of city jails and many other states of despair. But it also delivered him to Tech, where he strives to establish a top-flight basketball program, where he is making a *real* name for himself, where—though he's reluctant to admit it—he's having the time of his life.

"He'll capture that city," says Frank McGuire, his old coach at South Carolina. And he has made inroads. He's a popular public speaker. Tech home tickets have become precious. Single women approach him, even as he stands beside his wife. He walks into local saloons and men cheer.

But does anyone here really know where Bobby Cremins came from? He played over his head at South Carolina. He talks with a New York City accent. And just where is Appalachian State? There are also things they don't talk about at Tech cocktail parties. He was disciplined, but he was also wild; and when he hears stories about trouble and talent, about waste and youth, he simply shakes his gray head.

"My life is so confusing," he says.

One other thing about Bobby Cremins. He doesn't lie.

★   ★   ★

The third of four children of Irish immigrants, he was born the Fourth of July, 1947. He first lived at 149th and Southern, in the heart of the South Bronx in New York City. It was rough then. Now the old neighborhood is burned-out brick. Cremins played a respectable game of stickball and could catch a football but soon found basketball was not just a sport but a vehicle. He started to concentrate on it at St. Ignatius, his grade school, and soon it consumed him. He didn't care for books, but as a teen he'd spend 10 to 12 hours a day on weekends on the neighborhood asphalt courts.

"I had little respect," Cremins says. "There weren't many guys I could beat up. I didn't have a good arm in stickball. I was OK in football. But now, in basketball, I started to beat everyone one-on-one. And it gave me a sense of power. Pretty soon, no one could beat me. I became known as 'The Basketball Kid of Southern Boulevard.'

In the meantime, Southern Boulevard crumbled. By 1962, drugs started showing up on the streets and crime, never a stranger, picked up. Soon the family retreated 40 blocks north, to the Highbridge section of the Bronx, right behind Yankee Stadium. Cremins enrolled in All Hallows High, a local parochial school, and took his game to the new streets. Some games were interrupted by gang fights. Other times Cremins was beaten, often for no reason. A street kid, he sought safety in numbers. He found The Gladiators. He bought a leather jacket.

"I joined that gang because I was always getting beaten up," Cremins says. "They were predominantly black. Some Puerto Rican. I joined for protection."

And soon he was a criminal. There were arrests. The Gladiators met on the corner after dinner and, bored by 8 p.m., they'd go looking for kicks. Car thefts. Muggings. Terrorizing subway cars. Robberies. By 1962, at age 15, Cremins was a street thug. He does not discuss it easily.

"I've been involved in car thefts," he says. "We were robbing grocery stores. I can't tell you this. One night, I got lowered down from the roof inside a grocery store and was going to get the cash register. They were lowering me down, and one of those big dogs, you know, like Rin Tin Tin, came running out barking at me. I started screaming, and they pulled me up, and we ran."

Although he tried to keep the truth from his parents, Bobby Sr. soon caught on to the miscreant son, and there was discipline, old Irish style. The father beat his kid. There was some relief when a brother got Cremins a night job at an A&P to keep him off the streets. But Cremins flunked out of All Hallows his junior year. And there was more discipline.

"My father grabbed me by the arm, beat me up and then dragged me back to the school, threw me on the floor and asked the brothers to take me back."

Eventually All Hallows did, but Cremins was gloomy and was forced to repeat his junior year. But then the basketball team went off to Schenectady without him, and he rediscovered the game.

There's no telling where a life without basketball would have led. A strong season led to a scholarship to Fredrick Military Academy outside Portsmouth, Va.

Frank McGuire, working on his second legend in his first year at South Carolina, saw him play one day when he was scouting another kid.

"Anybody we recruited, we knew they all had possibilities; and he exceeded anything anybody could think of him," McGuire says. "He was a nice, skinny, little kid, you know?"

That spring, Iona offered Cremins a partial scholarship. South Carolina offered him a full ride. Cremins chose USC. Saved again.

Back home, the Gladiators dwindled. "A lot of them went to reform school," he says. "A couple of them became genuine gangsters. Several of them are in jail. Several of them got shot. I have not seen very many guys from the old neighborhood. Every once in a while, I might come upon a survivor, and we'll talk."

His mother bought her son his first suit to send him off to college. It was a three-piece wool suit, and Cremins wore it on the plane to Columbia, S.C., where it was around 100 degrees when he landed. He was so hot he broke out in a rash. His roommate, Corky Carnevale, checked out the suit, the military overnight bag and the long sheathed implement he carried and figured, 'Wonderful, the soldier brought his sword.' But Cremins pulled a pool cue out of the sheath.

Two nights later, after Cremins hopped on the back bumper of a Columbia bus for a ride to his dorm—"That's automatic in the city," he explained—he was chased by city police, surrounded and arrested.

Carnevale strolled into the station shortly thereafter and announced, "How much do you want for Cremins?" It cost just $25, and a great friendship was born.

Says McGuire, "If Bobby was in trouble, Corky usually got in trouble trying to help him."

Cremins excelled in the game. He played forward his sophomore year at just 6-foot-2 and was captain and point guard his junior and senior years. All of USC's games were televised around the state; and Cremins, always ready to spend time with a fan, became one of the most popular figures in all of South Carolina. During the season he was straight, all basketball. In the offseason he was still the hellion.

Cremins and Carnevale did much of the on-campus recruiting entertainment for McGuire. They became experts at spending just half of the allotted $100 on a recruit and keeping the rest. One such night, when they thought they had signed Henry Wilmore, who later became an All-America at Michigan, Cremins almost wiped out the team. Driving an alum's loaned station wagon, he inadvertently piloted the car into the first floor of a Columbia home. Among the passengers were the starters on the team that began the 1969-70 season ranked No. 1 in the nation.

"Not only did it total the car, but it totalled the house," says Carnevale. "The house sat there for six months. You could just look into the living room and bedrooms from the street. It was amazing no one was hurt. The car was about three feet tall. They eventually had to bulldoze the house."

Cremins tried to impress women as well, but, at least before he was a star, it was difficult. Carnevale did what he could, but Cremins was no rose with his big ears, shiny black hair, dose of acne and the Bronx accent no one could crack.

"His freshman year, I'd try to dress him," says Carnevale. "He had these stove-pipe pants that looked horrible with anything he'd wear. And he had these Elvis shirts with big zippers up the front and stuff like 12-inch collars. I started dating the girl who became my wife my freshman year, and I'd ask her to get him a date. You know how a lot of times guys would run, you know, when they had a bad blind date? Well, his date ran. She thought she was going to get stabbed."

In 1970 his senior season came to an ill-fated end with the Atlantic Coast Conference tournament. USC was upset in the finals by North Carolina State and lost its shot at the NCAA tournament. Cremins, so stricken by the loss, pulled a disappearing act. For three weeks he hid out in a friend's house near Asheville, N.C., and when he finally returned to school, something was different. College would be over. He was 12 hours short of graduation.

In Columbia he was all. "Columbia was a great time," he says. "They were good to us."

But elsewhere he was a curio.

Marty Blake, now the NBA scout but then general manager of the ABA's Pittsburgh Condors, called and said to come up. Maybe that saved Cremins again.

★   ★   ★

But Bobby Cremins still wanted to play basketball.

It was then that Carnevale, also back in Columbia, told a scout from a league in Ecuador that Cremins was 6-10 and just the gringo his league needed. Cremins left for a tryout in New York in a heartbeat, but had to get the scout, depressed by the short, ugly American, out to a street court to show him he could shoot. He also dunked a couple times. That did it. Within a few days he was on a plane to South America.

After an eight-month season, he was back with his hair curling down over his shoulders, wearing beads and sandals. He tried out for the 1972 Olympic team but was cut, and there it ended. He'd promised himself the Olympics would close out his playing time. He was 24 and "I just decided to keep my word, and it was time to move on in my life. Basketball had kind of exhausted me."

So he saved himself. Now, he said, he would coach. McGuire got him his first assistant's job at Point Park College in Pittsburgh. After one season he went back to South Carolina for two seasons. He watched and learned. Along the way, he met a woman at a mixed-doubles tennis tournament at his apartment complex. She had two daughters, was divorced from a political science professor at the university, and she and Cremins teamed up to win the tournament.

"I didn't know he was supposed to be anyone famous," says Carolyn Cremins. One year later, on Cremins' 27th birthday, they were married. Cremins danced with a champagne bucket on his head at a party. Two days later, they moved to Boone, N.C.

Appalachian State had taken a McGuire suggestion and hired Cremins as its head coach. He was going to be the youngest Division I coach in the country.

Nowhere, at any age, do head coaches dance with champagne buckets on their heads.

★   ★   ★

His first year was disastrous. Unaccustomed to smaller budgets, Cremins unknowingly spent his entire recruiting budget in just more than a month. He paid to fly in one recruit from California, only to check his grade transcript and find he couldn't get into any college anywhere. He went to the Bahamas with $25 in his pocket to recruit another kid, and the school had to wire money and accreditation to get him back into the country. His players were not top-drawer. Neither was the coaching.

"None of us knew what was going on," says Kevin Cantwell, an Appalachian assistant and now the school's head coach. "Bobby would make up plays in the middle of games, and it was unbelievable. . . . But that goes back to Bobby's luck. He's the luckiest person I've ever been around."

Cremins realized he knew nothing about his craft and started studying and going to clinics. Still, without enough money, without the finest players, he sagged and wondered that first winter if he'd made a career mistake. His first team was 13-14. He fumed at the players, and the young ones started to understand. Within two years

Appalachian State dominated the Southern Conference. He earned three coach-of-the-year awards. He had a son, Bobby III, in 1977. And he got cocky. He wanted to go big-time.

Says Carolyn Cremins, "He wanted the Tech job bad." He'd been recommended for openings at Duke, North Carolina State and at Tennessee, but none of them even called. Tech frittered away 42 days after asking Dwane Morrison to quit in 1981 and then chose him. Without skipping a beat, Cremins spent $40,000 recruiting in his first six months. He has yet to come in under budget at Tech. It's nice when you've got it. Luckily, they're winning.

He originally signed a four-year contract at $40,000 a season. Last year they gave him a raise. And an extension.

★   ★   ★

Sometimes it's hard to tell who's coaching whom. Cremins shoots craps with his team sometimes. But there are other times. Like one day at practice when Cremins screamed at the team, tore off his sweatshirt, and forward John Salley thought, "He was going to fight all of us."

He borrows plays from high school teams and draws diagrams on paper while watching cable television at night. One can't help but wonder if Cremins is dispensing advice or asking for it when he calls Mark Price to the sidelines during a game.

About his speech: It's terrible. At South Carolina, he told friends he had to go read some "Buff." He meant Beowulf. He dated a girl who drove a "Kugah." She owned a Cougar. At Appalachian State he told players to use their "peruvial vision."

About the yellow ties: He calls them "lawyer ties." He owns two or three. He wears one of them at almost every game. Carnevale, who comes to games often, is proud. Says Salley, "He doesn't know he's big-time yet. He'll see someone wearing something and ask how much it costs. Dean Smith doesn't care how much it costs."

Bobby Cremins on Bobby Cremins: "I don't recognize these times as the happiest times or whatever you want to call them. Sometimes I do. I mean, like right now, I don't think I've ever been happier in my life before. My family's growing. My two stepdaughters and I have become much closer. My son's growing up. I got a nice house. I got a good job. I'm very happy in that respect. But I'm not happy, because I haven't accomplished what I want to accomplish."

Just understand that The Basketball Kid of Southern Boulevard still wants to beat everyone on the block.

For Colleges, the Need is Integrity

COLLEGE SPORTS

By *KEN DENLINGER*

From the Washington Post
Copyright © 1984, Washington Post

Walter Byers saying that 30 percent of all big-bucks college sports factories probably cheat, as he did over the weekend, is like the president of United Airlines admitting his skies aren't always friendly. Or a used-car salesman suggesting he just might have a clunker or two on the lot. Or the Ivory man confessing his soap is only 71 and 57/100ths percent pure.

That all prominent football and basketball coaches are not purely pure hardly will nudge innocent, high-minded Republicans and Democrats off the front page; that the executive director of the National Collegiate Athletic Association fingered such a high percentage of criminals in his own lodge is startling.

"There seems to be a growing number of coaches and administrators who look upon NCAA penalties as the price of doing business —if you get punished, that's unfortunate, but that's part of the cost of getting along," he said. "In basketball, there may be one or two athletes involved in questionable transactions. I've reluctantly come to the conclusion there are volume violations in football."

Byers has been 34 years getting to those conclusions, but he's right. In basketball, it takes only one or two players every couple of years to make a dormant program dominant. Thieves can be a bit more selective. With football, you buy bulk in bulk. That's because O.J. might have been a deejay without blocking.

For scores of years, nearly everybody who has looked beyond the pompons and scoreboards has realized that the major leagues of major-college sports are a sham, just a javelin throw short of the Olympics when it comes to hypocrisy.

So clearly professional are these alleged amateurs that the presi-

dent of Stanford called for open payments to college football players.
In 1905.

Comes the man who saw very little harm and fewer fouls for
ever so long, Mr. Simon Squeaky Clean himself, with the revelation
that three of every 10 programs at the highest level of collegiate
sport cheat. Most of us figured no more than 18 percent tops.

What prompted Byers to bare his soul, to the Associated Press, is
as uncertain as the block/charge in hoops. Maybe his conscience
mandated it; maybe he's finally realized the NCAA actually is what
Joe Paterno suggests, a dinosaur about to be destroyed by a 20th
century predator called the College Football Association; maybe he's
telling a concerned Congress that, bad as it is, the NCAA still is the
best way for the colleges to police themselves.

It is.

If they care.

If the college presidents give a damn, their sports programs can
take a 180-degree turn toward integrity in a hurry. Sometime soon,
they must:

• Cut the number of football scholarships in half. No way does a
college need 95 hired hands to impress the alumni. Common sense
shouts that a Maryland team that plays no more than 12 games
should not have twice as many players as a Redskins team that plays
at least 16. Make it 52 players per college team. That allows the
coach to field 11 on offense, 11 on defense and 11 to run under kicks; it
also gives him 17 extras, to hold dummies, or whatever, until somebody gets hurt or ineligible. That means admitting 13 players a year
instead of 30.

• With the significant savings from such a drastic cut in scholarship money, pay the players. Not enough for a Porsche or a vacation
on Maui, but enough to finance something second-hand, if they
choose, and a trip home now and then. A free education simply is not
enough in terms of what players generate for a school.

• Allocate scholarships based on graduation rates. For every
three players who failed to graduate, say, take away one scholarship.
Because lots of ordinary students also do not stay in school four
years, the one-to-one ratio suggested by Bobby Knight seems overly
harsh.

• Be up-front about money and pay a coach what he's worth,
from university funds. Accept the fact that most tunnel-vision football coaches are four times more valuable than most award-winning
research professors and pay them four times as much. Then demand
that they accept no money for anything that might smell of compromise. Such as shoes. An athlete who sees a coach getting $50,000 or so
a year to convince him to wear a particular sneaker can easily assume it's OK for him to grab whatever an alum, or known gambler,
might offer. He's already being used. Also, give that coach a contract
based more on the usual university priorities than a won-lost record.
Give him more security, perhaps a 10-year contract instead of the

usual four-year deal, and sue him for everything up to and including his daughter's record collection if he so much as winks at a school with a better offer.

• Do not hire known cheaters. This means anybody the NCAA has found guilty of significant crimes. Charley Pell slips into the mind about here, to illustrate two points. Like so many others, he skipped town (Clemson) unharmed before the sheriff (the NCAA) made any arrests. By prostituting itself the day Pell was hired, Florida deserves every bit of mud slung toward Gainesville.

The instant solution for Pell-like problems is not play schools who hire known cheaters. If Pell gets another job and Florida gets convicted by the NCAA, anybody who plays him is contributing to the delinquency of college football. Colorado had no business hiring Chuck Fairbanks; same with West Virginia and Gale Catlett. Except both schools would have had immense lawsuits to fight, Jerry Tarkanian having shown how long a coach can keep the NCAA tangled in an all-court press.

Each school determines its degree of honesty. The NCAA, CFA or any other arrangement of the alphabet can no more legislate morality at Maryland than the Democrats can in every Senate seat. One step forward is to come to terms with what most of us already know: The basketball and football programs are professional; treat them that way.

Be honest.

Be realistic.

Be cost efficient.

Be quick about it.

Now Crenshaw Stands Second to None

GOLF

By *GARY VAN SICKLE*

From the Milwaukee Journal
Copyright © 1984, Milwaukee Journal

The setting sun shined golden through the broken clouds long across the 18th fairway. The tall, majestic pines in every direction wavered only slightly, perhaps less from a spring breeze than from thousands of hands clapping in front of cheering faces.

Ben Crenshaw did not waver at all. And no sun was ever as golden as his putter was on the magical Sunday when he won the 48th Masters tournament.

No pine tree ever reigned as majestic as the high, floating, utterly perfect 6-iron shot that he hit at No. 12, the heart of Amen Corner, where prayers are so often heard and so seldom answered.

And surely no shadows ever danced as long as the unforgettable, elegant putt he holed for an unexpected birdie on the 10th green. Was it 60 feet, or 75? Or was it from another planet, entirely? No matter. It was an ocean liner of a putt. It was the Titanic. It was unsinkable. But Ben Crenshaw sank it.

"Gosh, I want to see that again," Crenshaw said later, smoothing the collar of the Green Jacket he'd just been awarded as the Masters champion. "I couldn't do that again if I had a thousand balls."

A golden sun. A golden moment. A golden time.

"This is really a sweet, sweet win," he said. "There may never be a sweeter moment."

★　　　★　　　★

Imagine walking to the 18th green with a two-stroke lead over Tom Watson, 25 feet from a major championship.

"I honestly didn't know where I was," Crenshaw said, unable to quell a grin. "I thought about that this week. I woke up at three in the morning and was awake an hour. I was thinking everything. But

I just kept a hold on myself. Today was my day.

"I haven't been through this before. There's a feeling of relief, more than anything. No question, I've put a lot of pressure on myself to win. I was determined."

The heartbreak of coming close finally ended for him. He's finished second in the Masters twice, including last year. He's finished second in the British Open. He hit a ball into the water on the 71st hole of the U.S. Open and missed getting into the playoff by one stroke. He's been in five playoffs and lost all five, including one to David Graham in the PGA Championship.

The heartbreak was felt by others this day, particularly Tom Kite, who grew up with Crenshaw in Austin, Tex., attended the University of Texas with him and is among Crenshaw's close friends. Kite, after finishing the seven holes left by Saturday's rain delay, began the final round with a one-stroke lead over Mark Lye, two over Crenshaw, Nick Faldo and David Graham.

        ★   ★   ★

But Crenshaw assumed the lead with birdies at eight, nine and 10, and assumed command when Kite hit a poor 7-iron into Rae's Creek at No. 12 and made a triple bogey to fall six strokes back.

"I made one bad swing and it absolutely nailed me," said Kite, whose face was flushed and whose voice was empty and almost cracking. "As good as Ben was on the greens, I was that bad."

Asked if he could imagine what was going through Crenshaw's mind, Kite said, "No, but I can guarantee you he knows what's going through mine. And it's sure not jubilation, fellas."

Kite and Lye played in the final group, behind Crenshaw and Faldo. Kite was standing in the 10th fairway, watching as Crenshaw holed that putt, that unsinkable one.

"Uh huh," Kite said. "And I saw the putt he made at nine, and at eight, and at 12. . . ."

Lye said: "When we saw the putt at 10, it was turn the lights out. Tom had a 4-wood in his hand, and I had a 4-iron. You could see it. It virtually hurt Tom."

        ★   ★   ★

Crenshaw, 32, was aware of his friend's feelings. "Gol, I know, he's got to feel sick," he said. "I'm not gonna say I know how he feels. Believe me, he's hurting.

"He came to Austin when he was about 10 and I was eight. We've played a lot of golf against each other. We played at the same club, had the same teacher. All he did then was play golf. It was a heck of a rivalry. Now we have a professional, friendly rivalry."

There were many rivals on this day for Crenshaw. He emerged from the pack. It looked like the whole Augusta phone book on the leader board.

There was Lye, who led after two rounds. Many expected him to imitate a blasting cap and explode under the final-round pressure. He didn't, but he succumbed to a double bogey on the fifth hole, an overlooked par 4 that played the toughest of any hole at Augusta National Golf Club this week.

Faldo, the Englishman, lost pars the way the British have lost colonies the last two centuries, taking four bogeys on the first seven holes.

Larry Nelson, last year's U.S. Open winner, got within a shot of the lead. His hopes, too, drowned in Rae's Creek when he hit an awful-looking, slicing shot that led to a double bogey.

★   ★   ★

Graham bogeyed the first hole and never got any momentum going. The same happened to Tom Watson, who thought he was about to make a move after a birdie at No. 4. "And bang. I bogey No. 5," he said.

Crenshaw coasted in, holing a 15-foot birdie at 15 that gave him a four-shot edge, and the luxury of bogeying No. 17.

"I was waiting for him to make some mistakes because that was the only way I could catch him—unless I made a couple of holes-in-one," Watson said.

It was the end of a roller coaster week for Crenshaw, who opened with a 67, struggled a bit with rounds of 72 and 70, then finished strong with a 68 for a 277 total, 11 under par.

Watson made birdies on 16 and 18 to finish second with a 69 for 279. Gil Morgan and David Edwards shot 67s, too little too late, to tie for third at 280. Nelson was one shot back, followed by Graham, Kite, Lye and Ronnie Black.

★   ★   ★

"After I made the par at 16, I knew I couldn't throw away three shots the last two holes," Crenshaw said. "I just tried to hit fairways and greens, and I did a darn good job of it.

"A year-and-a-half ago, after my bad golf, Harvey Penick, my teacher, and my father said, 'You've got to believe in yourself and your game again.' Since then, I haven't thought about my swing. All I've thought about are timing, ball position and aiming. I used all kinds of swings in 1982, and it took me nine months to figure out none of 'em worked.

"Golf is the hardest game in the world. I know it. When I came up 18, for some reason I was thinking of high school golf. I thought of all the people who meant so much to my career. I won this tournament for my friends. I'm so lucky to have so many."

After he tapped in his final two-footer on 18, he slumped, momentarily, as the weight and pressure of a major championship slipped away into the Georgia red clay. Then he straightened, hugged his caddie, raised an arm and strode off the green proudly. Watson came out of the scorer's tent to shake his hand and say, "Welcome to the majors club."

Ben Crenshaw smiled a forever smile. And the sun shined golden upon him.

Cubs Lore No Longer So Poor

BASEBALL

By *RON RAPOPORT*

From the Chicago Sun-Times
Copyright © 1984, Chicago Sun-Times

These are the gladdest of possible words:
*   "The Cubs have finally won."*
Shout from the rooftops and sing with the birds:
*   "The Cubs have finally won."*
Wondrously swelling our gonfalon bubble,
Pushing the Metsies down into the rubble—
Words that have banished our hearts from all trouble:
*   "The Cubs have finally won."*

Rick Sutcliffe struck out the last batter, was escorted off the mound by a phalanx of his teammates and the longest night, the longest season, the longest wait was over.

In years to come, they will say the game in which the Cubs clinched the 1984 National League East Division championship took 2 hours and 14 minutes to play, but that is patently false.

This game took 39 years to complete, longer than anyone on the Cub roster has been alive, longer than any faithful Cub fan has wish to remember.

It was a title the team hungered for and fought for and richly deserved. And if it was nailed down before only a few thousand people in a plasticized multi-purpose stadium, instead of before an SRO crowd hunkered in amidst the red brick and ivy, that did not detract from the moment. There will be time enough for homecomings.

★   ★   ★

But we do not need them in our midst to reflect on what has been done and who, besides the doers of the deeds, this championship might have been for.

It was for the players with attendance clauses in their contracts and the fans with attendance clauses in their lives.

It was for Ernie and Billy and Fergie and Randy and Ron and Don and Glenn and Leo and the rest of the class of '69. You can come out now, gentlemen. The long civic nightmare is over. From this moment on, the definitive moment in latter-day Cub history will be not that great collapse but this great triumph.

It was for Rita on the roof of the building behind the left-field wall. She liked to hurry home for the last few innings, finding them a perfect relaxant after a day of trying to keep a public-school classroom under control.

It was for the nuns selling parking spaces at the convent a block from the ballpark and for Decker placing bets on the next pitch in the grandstand. "The Bleacher Bums," that wonderful play in which the 1977 season was flash-frozen in time forever, pretended Decker was a fictional character. All true Cubs fans knew better.

It was for Herman and Preston and Joey and Lee and all the managers who lost their sleep and their hair and their tempers trying to do what seemed so impossible then and seems so easy now.

It was for Roger and Keith and the rest of the boys on the ground crew, who kept the grass high and slow and the basepaths hard and fast.

It was for Arlene and Mary Beth and the rest of the girls in the office, who looked good no matter what they wore.

It was for Dick Selma who led the cheers from the bullpen in 1969 and for Gary Matthews who leads them from left field now.

It was for you, too, Dave Kingman, you big goof.

★   ★   ★

It was for Dallas Green, the best general manager who ever lived, though he doesn't need us to tell him that.

It was for Bill Buckner, who gave the Cubs seven good years, but whose greatest contribution to the team was leaving it.

It was for Bill Wrigley in the building with his name on it and for Bill Veeck sitting with his shirt off in the center-field bleachers underneath the scoreboard he helped build.

It was for all those faceless millions who bought all those tickets for all those years and now won't be able to get any closer to the playoffs than their television sets.

It was for Harry and Steve and Milo and Vince and Lou and, come on, Jack, move into this picture, will you? Say, Harry, pass some of that good Italian sausage from the place on Taylor Street and some of those Swedish meatballs from the place on Clark Street and, just a second, the cake that little old lady just brought in *does* look good, doesn't it?

It was for Bob Kennedy, who didn't really do all that badly considering his budget. Jody Davis was his, you know, and Leon Durham and Lee Smith, and Kennedy didn't even have to go to Philadelphia for them.

Speaking of which, it has to be for Phillies president Bill Giles, too. Thanks a bunch, old pal. A guy recently asked if there was a list of the trades Dallas Green has made since coming to Chicago. Was it mean of me to tell him he should call the Phillies?

It was for the old guard, for Lew Fonseca and Vedie Himsl and Emil Verban before he became famous and all the former players who still feel that they are Cubs. It was for Dutch Reagan, making up amiable lies about what was going on at Wrigley Field when the ticker connecting the ballpark to his radio studio out in darkest Iowa failed. Whatever happened to him, anyway?

★   ★   ★

It was for Jim Finks who in less than a year got in on something that eluded him for almost a decade in the game he knows something about.

It was for Charlie Grimm, who died less than a year too soon, and for Steve Goodman, who died less than a week too soon.

It was for Jim Frey, who would have been the nicest guy to manage championship teams in his first year in both the American and National leagues, even if he weren't the first.

★   ★   ★

It was for the homer in the gloamin' and Brock for Broglio and the Friendly Confines and Charlie Root's pitch to the Babe and Don Young dropping the fly and Franklin P. Adams up there in doggerel heaven with Tinker and Evers and Chance and for all the rest of us, too.

We ain't trash no more, baby. Not for at least another 39 years.

Oh, That Old College Spirit

COLLEGE FOOTBALL

By *FRANZ LIDZ*

From Sports Illustrated
The following article, "Oh, That Old College Spirit" by Franz Lidz is reprinted courtesy of Sports Illustrated © Time Inc., September 5, 1984.

Like vintage wine, these lifetime loyalists grow more intriguing with age. Refusing to wither on the vine, they have put together amazing attendance streaks that date back as far as 1911. What keeps these diehards going? For Giles Pellerin, who calls the USC players his "children," the Trojans are like family. Lourene Wishart hasn't missed a Nebraska home game in 61 years because she likes a "winner." Wes Schulmerich, an 83-year-old Oregon State fan, says he refuses to die until the Beavers win three games in a season. Indeed, it can be said that all of these devotees live for their teams.

LOURENE WISHART
Nebraska

"Lourene, quitcher bitchin'!"

That's Virginia Hadley talking. She and her friend Lourene Wishart are having lunch at the Cornhusker, as swank an eatery as you can find in Lincoln, Neb. Lourene's been bitchin' about the food, the service and the color of the tablecloth. Being 91 years old and all and having accumulated a certain amount of wisdom in those years, she figures she has a right to speak her mind. She asks a young waiter what he thinks of the Big Red's chances for the coming season. "Pretty good," he says, a little timidly.

Lourene smiles a big, round, toothy smile and lets him shuffle off. When he's almost out of earshot, she hollers, "That pansy! What the hell does he know about Nebraska football?"

Certainly not nearly as much as Lourene. She hasn't missed a home game in 61 years. "I go because I like a winner," she says. "I've always been a winner."

She's also a woman of immense vitality. She ambles around her colonial-style cottage in glasses with rhinestone frames, a lace blouse and skirt, and a pendant strung with big plastic elephants. "The fella who gave it to me said they were ivory," she says with some indignation. Evidently, she doesn't know ivory as well as Cornhuskers. Lourene wears elephants mostly because she's a lifelong Republican. Her late husband, Joseph, ran for governor as a Republican in 1946. Her other passions are raising prize Manchester terriers, the country music of Red Foley and lilacs. Lourene was born on Lilac Farm in nearby Bennet. She sold the homestead 10 years ago, but plenty of hybrid lilacs surround her house: pink lace, woodland, Carolyn Mae and snow shower.

Lourene is small and frail, and takes your arm as she walks down the wooden steps to the Go-Big-Red Room in her basement. She pokes around the shrine, shoving Husker artifacts at you: Big Red beer mugs, Big Red pennants, Big Red deck chairs. She has a crocheted doll of Mike Rozier and a gold statuette of Johnny Rodgers filled with 100-proof Kentucky bourbon. Her collection of Big Eight swizzle sticks is perhaps unrivaled in the Western Hemisphere. In the far corner stands her hangin' tree, a willow branch painted red that's modeled after the one in Boot Hill cemetery in Tombstone, Ariz. After Nebraska victories she holds mock hangings of the loser. She has strung up stuffed Kansas jayhawks, Army mules and LSU tigers.

The game she cherishes most is the 1973 Orange Bowl. "Our quarterback, Dave Humm, licked the pants off Notre Dame," she says. "Oh boy, they were mad. I got in the Irish players' bus after the game and Otto couldn't find me." Otto, her chauffeur, used to drive her to games in a lilac-colored Cadillac. "Wow!" she says. "You better not tell how much those fellas swore. I don't suppose Parseghian knows that."

Her favorite player? "Dave Humm," she says without hesitation. "He was the handsomest thing I ever laid eyes on. He used to come over here and just sit and talk. Drove the women crazy."

Lourene will never forgive Miami for stealing the national championship from her Huskers last season. "My feelings about that wouldn't be fit to write," she says. "It was the worst thing that happened in my life." But she thinks her friend Virginia is wrong in saying the '83 squad was Nebraska's best ever.

"Well, how come they won all those awards then, Lourene?"

"Yes, Virginia, they did win lots of awards, some of which nobody ever heard of."

Lourene says she prefers the '71 team that won the national title.

"Well, Lourene," says Virginia, "they didn't win the awards."

"Yes, Virginia. But they didn't lose the championship, either."

THE HOWELLS
North Carolina A&T

When President Truman's telegram arrived, Mary Howell was out on the front porch, gazing at the crowd headed for World War Memorial Stadium. Her husband, Clifton, was already at the game, cheering on his alma mater, North Carolina A&T. The telegram said that their oldest son, Clifton II, had been killed in action in Korea. Mary sent a friend to the stadium to tell her husband, and the sad news was broadcast over the loudspeaker. "That was the only Homecoming I've missed in the 62 years we've been married," she says. "I guess God was in it somehow so we could get the message."

But Mary went back the next season and every one of the 32 since. For seven decades porch-sitting and Aggie Homecoming games have been autumn constants in the Howells' lives. And except for the time somebody snatched Mary's purse—"I really only had but two or three dollars in it," she says—the Homecomings have been a lot happier. In fact, Mary's and Clifton's Homecoming Day bashes have become legendary. "We just love the fellowship," she says. "We have chicken, ham, potato salad, candied yams—everybody loves candied yams—pickles and icebox rolls."

Both Howells are in their 80s. Their faces have the burnished look of old leather covering fine and learned books. Mary is a warm, comfortable woman in a cherry floral dress. The number "50" glitters on a gold chain around her neck. A dentist friend made it for her 50th wedding anniversary. On the wall of the Howell home in Greensboro, she proudly displays her diploma from the Academy of Millinery Design and a citation for "excellence and creative achievement in the subject of the bridal veil." Clifton is a happily mismatched kind of guy who'll wear a powder-blue shirt, bright yellow pants held up by red suspenders and Converse low tops he keeps loosely tied because of bunions. He walks with a metal cane, and when he's not walking, he's rocking and chewing Juicy Fruit gum at the same pace.

When Mary and Clifton met, she was just a local girl and he was an Aggie football hero and president of the student body. He'd seen her drive across campus in a red Chevy, and said, "Now that girl is for me." He asked her to be his guest on the next hayride. "From then on we became friends," she recalls. They eloped in Clifton's senior year, but they didn't live together. "We still courted like we always had," Mary says. "We knew Clifton's daddy would pull him out of colllege if he knew we'd married."

A touch of rheumatism has cramped Clifton's style a bit on Homecoming Day, but he gets riled up all the same. "Clifton is still a wild man," says Mary. "He gets too nervous, and I have to calm him down. He'll scream, 'Play 'em off the field! Hold 'em! Get 'em below the knees! That's not the way to tackle!' "

Clifton became an expert in tackling in 1922. That was the year his crucial hit helped the Aggies beat Virginia Union, a victory that earned them football respectability. Dr. Albert Spruill, the historian of A&T football, wrote in Great Recollections from Aggieland, "He (Howell) caught up with his adversary and made him the victim."

The truth, Clifton says, was somewhat less heroic: "Coach was shouting at me from the sidelines, 'Big man, if you don't get that guy, I'll kill you.'"

WALTER MAY
Clemson

If you ever find yourself in Columbia, S.C., cruise up Main Street past the Takin' Five 41-item salad bar, past Taco Cid, past Wigs 'n Things and the Duck-In restaurant ("Quackin' Good Food"), past the Seoul Restaurant & Lounge and the sign that says SWAMP WIGGLER'S, RED WORMS, NITE-CRAWLERS, MINNOWS, PRODUCE AND CRICKETS and turn right after the Krispy Kreme Doughnut shop. At the bend in the road you'll come to a brick bungalow. That's where a retired bookkeeper named Walter May has lived for 61 years. "There's nothing fine about it," he says, "but it's comfortable and paid for."

Which is about how South Carolina fans regard May at Williams-Brice Stadium in Columbia: not exactly interesting, but modestly monumental. He has attended every Clemson-South Carolina game since 1911, the year he dropped out of Clemson. All May remembers about that first game is the score. "We beat them 27-0," he says. He doesn't know why he left school. "To tell you the truth," he says, "I never have been able to figure it out."

May is a homebred Southern boy, born in Columbia, where he learned to love country music, go to church on Sunday and ignore the University of South Carolina, his hometown team. His one year at Clemson made him a lifelong Tiger fan. His devotion to the university 140 miles to the northwest earned him the nickname Clemson.

May is thin and wiry, and his hands are strong and embossed with veins. He's 92 and he talks slow and easy, like a courthouse whittler. If you've got a minute or two he'll remind you that a couple of Heisman Trophy winners, George Rogers and Herschel Walker, failed to cross the Clemson goal line. He'll also tell you how Banks McFadden, a Tiger quarterback in the '30s, flummoxed South Carolina with a quick kick on first down.

The closest May ever came to missing a Clemson-South Carolina game was in 1942, when an inner-ear infection nearly felled him at the gate. "My head started spinning and people thought I was drunk," he recalls. In those days, South Carolina was always the home team, because the big game was played at the state fairgrounds in Columbia, and highway patrolmen used to prowl the bleachers for bootleg liquor and take-out rowdies. "I got inside and the thing hit me like that," says May, snapping his fingers. "It kinda

—heh-heh—held me up. So I set down on a Coca-Cola crate for 10, 15 minutes and it passed off." May has many down-homey anecdotes like that, in fact exactly like that.

He loves Clemson, but he has never worked up much of a distaste for South Carolina. "I'm not the type of guy that hates the Game-cocks," he says. "But Lord knows, I sure don't pull for them."

GILES PELLERIN
Southern California

Then there's the story of the game that almost got away from Giles Pellerin. He was pledging allegiance to the flag at a Rotary Club meeting in Burbank four days before USC's big game with Stanford in 1949. One of the Rotarians told Pellerin he looked as white as a polar ice cap. "It was appendicitis," says Pellerin. "The first question that entered my mind was how long I'd be in the hospital."

He didn't want to mess up his streak. The doctor at Queen of Angels Hospital said he didn't think Pellerin would make the game, but Pellerin had other ideas. Clad in his hospital gown, Pellerin had his brother Oliver walk him up and down the corridors so he could regain his strength. And when the physician didn't show that Saturday, Pellerin slipped on his street clothes, snuck out of the hospital and rode to the game with Oliver.

When Pellerin returned to the hospital later that afternoon, his face was a little sunburnt. "Where have you been?" asked a nurse. "Oh," answered Pellerin, "I've been getting a little exercise."

He has been getting a little exercise now for 58 years. Neither rain nor snow nor appendectomy can keep Perpetual Pellerin away from a USC game. The Trojans haven't played without him since 1926. At his first game he watched them innundate Whittier 74-0. That's 618 games in a row and counting.

Pellerin graduated from USC with an engineering degree in 1923 and spent the next 45 years working at Pacific Telephone. He has traveled more than 750,000 miles to see the Trojans play. He's dapper and goal-post slim, and looks a good deal younger than his 77 years. During the season he watches the Trojans practice two or three times a week, and on the road he hangs out in the team's hotel lobby, talking to the boys and meeting their parents. "We've played in cities like Austin, Little Rock and Ann Arbor," he says, "and each gives me the opportunity to see college campuses and go to pep rallies and make hundreds of friends throughout the United States and correspond with them." At Christmas he sends out about 150 cards to people he has met in his Pellerin peregrinations.

All his old ticket stubs are held together by rubber bands in a shoebox in his San Marino home. He used to have all the programs, too, but he lost most of them in a garage fire. He still has the gold watch USC gave him to commemorate his 500th straight game, the

1973 Rose Bowl. "Sure, I could sit in my rocking chair and grow old," he says. "But I don't intend to do that. You've got to have something to look forward to."

Oliver had a streak going himself, but he took a break for World War II. He hasn't missed a USC game since 1947. Pellerin's youngest brother, Max, had his streaks interrupted by the Korean War and an assignment with Northrup Aircraft in Saudi Arabia. Max is now working on a modest 50-gamer. And then there's Pellerin's wife, Jessie, who has accompanied him to games since 1935. They courted at USC games for almost two years. "When we die," Pellerin says, "We will bequeath $750,000 to the team. We consider them our children."

His extended football family includes such favorite sons as Anthony Davis, Gary Jeter, Lynn Swann, Pat Haden, Mike Garrett, Marcus Allen and Frank Gifford. Gifford's 1951 squad gave Pellerin his quintessential football experience, a quasi-mystical event that began at halftime when USC was trailing Cal 14-0. "At the start of the third quarter," he says, "off in the distance you could hear drumbeats. They got louder and louder. Suddenly, in marched the Trojan band, which had been waylaid by a train wreck. With the beating of those drums you could almost see the momentum building." The Trojans scored the next three touchdowns and won 21-14.

"Every year I tell myself I'm not going back," Pellerin says halfheartedly. "Then I look ahead to something like this season's Arizona State game, in Tempe. We've never won in Tempe, and, I just *have* to be there with 'em." He can hardly wait until 1992 when, he reckons, he'll see his 700th straight game. "That is," he says, "unless USC goes to the Rose Bowl two or three times before then."

ROGER CONNERS
Lafayette

In that misty era before brittle quarterbacks and 300-page playbooks, a rugged brand of football was played between the Lafayette Leopards and the Lehigh Engineers in the rolling hills of Eastern Pennsylvania. Legend has it that the colossal Leopard linebackers could strip an Engineer halfback naked with a single sweep of their paws and pull off his toes as if they were daisy petals. It's said that the officials in those days were usually prison wardens, and instead of meting out yardage as penalties, they decreed sentences varying from two days to 25 years.

Of course, not many people think of Lehigh and Lafayette as football schools anymore, but a few relics survive from that time. The Lehigh-Lafayette series, which dates from 1884, can claim the all-time greatest fan anywhere in Howard Foering, who had seen 99 games in a row before he died nine years ago at 106. (The teams played twice a season through 1901, and in 1943 and '44.) Lehigh has a dozen alumni who have witnessed at least 50 Double-L games. Heading the list is a retired steel-mill superintendent named Albert

Chenoweth, 91, who saw his first Big Game in 1912, the year he was a backup quarterback as a freshman. He missed the 1918 game because he was in France serving with the U.S. Army. Since then he has been to 67 consecutive Double-Ls.

Chenoweth, however, lags behind Roger Conners of Lafayette. Conners, who attended Lafayette but never graduated, has seen *every* game in the series since 1912. "There doesn't seem to be the enthusiasm there used to be," he says. "But because of this record, it's hard to miss. Besides, by going to college football games, you meet a nice class of people."

Conners, 82, lives in Easton, the Leopards' den. He spends much of his time between games hanging out at the insurance company he founded, which is now run by his son and grandson. Conners remembers that he went to his first Lehigh-Lafayette game with his father and Dr. Arthur Fox. He treasures a souvenir ticket that he keeps in his wallet. Unfortunately, it's from his second game, in 1913. Conners almost didn't make that game because Dr. Fox's Model T lost the plug in its oil pan. Dr. Fox jammed a corncob into the hole, and they made it to Taylor Field in time for the kickoff. Chenoweth threw a touchdown pass to give Lehigh a 7-0 win.

Conners remembers the old players best. Like Joe DuMoe. "Joe was sort of a tramp athlete from Syracuse and Fordham," he recalls. "They found out he was a professional hockey player and tossed him out of school." And Doc Elliott, a freshman who took over as fullback midway through the 1921 season and scored every Leopard touchdown in a 28-6 rout of the Engineers. "After the season Doc got mixed up with a bad crowd," says Conners. "He and some guys cleaned out the York Restaurant and threw a safe out the window. Doc was thrown out of college, too."

The one game Conners didn't particularly care for was the Engineers' 78-0 win in 1917. "We always claimed all our boys went to war," he says, "and theirs stayed home and went to Lehigh."

The Leopards have won only three times in the past 13 years, but they still hold a 65-49-5 edge. "We're so far ahead that they'll never catch up while I'm alive," Conners says. "At least I have that satisfaction."

WES SCHULMERICH AND CHARLES THARP
Oregon State

Wes Schulmerich seems as tall as a Douglas fir and has a booming laugh that sounds like an eruption at Mount St. Helens. He's 83 and his face has a crisp ruggedness to it. Charles Tharp, who is 79, is a rotund, short-legged former Chrysler dealer with steel-frame glasses that make his ears bug out. His hair has thinned considerably, and his face has some well-earned lines.

Schulmerich and Tharp share a love for gin rummy, trout fishing and Oregon State football. They've been to every Beaver home

game for 62 years. They've sat in row 34 at Parker Stadium in Cor-
vallis for the last 35 years, though not necessarily together. They
argue too much. Usually Schulmerich's wife, Cecile, sits between
them as a buffer. Schulmerich tends to yell his head off, and Tharp
looks on with plump-cheeked amusement.

Schulmerich might say he thinks Terry Baker was the greatest
Beaver of them all. "I wouldn't go for Baker," says Tharp. "Never
did like him personally."

"That's isn't the object, Charlie."

"He wasn't any better at his position than Leonard Younce was
at guard."

"Well, that's your opinion."

They have such a boyish camaraderie that you half expect one of
them to burst out singing, "Here's to good friends, tonight is kinda
special." Their friendship has endured moose hunting trips to Alaska, the 1968 Olympics in Mexico City and a trek across the Outback
of Australia. "It keeps us young," says Tharp, who lives a block from
campus with his 15-year-old apricot-colored poodle, Beethoven. His
wife, Jane, died in 1979. "After the games we all came to my house
for a big feed and to tip a few," Tharp says.

Schulmerich and Tharp both went to Oregon State in the '20s.
When Tharp got out of college he sold Chryslers and eventually
opened his own agency. He got out of the car business six years ago.
Schulmerich still drives to games in the Dodge Charger his best
friend sold him in 1978. "That s.o.b. has kept me broke since 1945,"
says Schulmerich.

"Are you kidding?" says Tharp. "That s.o.b. kept *me* broke every
time I traded with him."

In 1927 Schulmerich turned down a $100-a-game contract to
play football for the Frankford, Pa., Yellowjackets of the NFL. He
kicked around bush-league baseball for a while and even played in
the majors for four seasons with the Braves, Phillies and Reds. In
1933 he started in the same Philadelphia outfield with Chuck Klein.
Batted .318, too, fifth best in the National League.

By then, he and Tharp were well into their string. They only go to
home games, and they never go to Eugene to see the rival Oregon
Ducks. "Wes and I don't like them, and they don't like us," says
Tharp. "Walk down the street and they'll throw mud at ya."

Tharp says the "meanest, nastiest thing" he ever did was after a
game in 1924 with Oregon. The Ducks had just beaten the Beavers,
and a couple of Oregon fans had stolen Tharp's rooter lid, which is
what he called his hat. "I stood behind a tree and waited until their
car came around the corner," says Tharp. "Then I threw an oak
branch through their windshield and ran off."

"You see what a disposition he's got," says Schulmerich.

If the Beavers win when Schulmerich has his letter sweater on,
he'll keep wearing it to games until they lose. He hasn't worn his
sweater three games in a row since 1978. Still, he and Tharp remain

loyal. "They need you more when they're losing than when they're winning," says Tharp. "Everybody comes to see a winner. We've never quit 'em."

Schulmerich, a retired fishing-resort guide, has beaten cancer. He says he refuses to die until the Beavers win three games in one season. "Every year they don't do it," he says, "and I say I'll be back for the next campaign. My ambition is to live long enough to see it, but I don't think I'm gonna make it."

"I think this year's team is good enough to win two games," Tharp says.

"I'll bet you right now that we don't win two games."

"A bottle of booze?"

"A bottle of booze."

PAUL RIDINGS
Texas Christian

Paul Ridings is spinning his Yard-O-Matic punting wheel—a cardboard contraption that measures the lengths of punts—in the press box at Amon G. Carter Stadium and is wearing these clothes: lilac pants, mulberry blazer, violet shirt with fuchsia cuff links, prune-colored tie, lavender cowboy hat and magenta cowboy boots. A TCU pinkie ring adorns his right hand. He looks great.

Ridings loves the Horned Frogs with a purple passion. In the bedroom of his Fort Worth home he keeps more than 50 purple shirts, 15 pairs of purple socks, four purple jackets and one purple suit. And those are just his lounging clothes. On road trips he takes along his purple pj's and purple smoking jacket and purple-and-white bedroom slippers. Guess what color his underwear is.

Ridings has attended 381 straight Horned Frog home-and-away games. He hasn't missed one since a 13-9 loss to Ole Miss in the 1948 Delta Bowl. He has traveled as far as Seattle and Miami, paying his own way, to keep the string intact. He figures he has seen 521 TCU games all told. That's 63% of the games the school has played since its first one, in 1896, against Toby's Business College. "We won 8-6," he says, consulting his voluminous library of statistics. Ridings was TCU's statistician for 35 years.

"I'm infamous now," he says. "My wife, Freddie, wishes I'd quit, but it's some idiot thing I can't stop." Ridings likes action. He's 67 and he doesn't want to sit around waiting for an opening in a retirement village. He runs a public relations agency, and he's there every workday from 9 to 5:30. He has been an action guy since 1929 when, at age 12, he was the Horned Frogs' mascot during their first Southwest Conference championship season. Young Paul sat on the bench and wore a little Frog uniform. Naturally, he went to TCU. He had a 100-game spectator streak going that ended in 1937 when he left Fort Worth to attend Missouri's school of journalism.

His current skein started when he returned to become chairman of the journalism department at TCU. The string was nearly broken 13 years ago against Penn State. Ridings and several cronies chartered a private jet to fly them to the game in University Park. Fog grounded the plane in Wheeling, West Virginia. They had to take a commercial airliner to Pittsburgh, rent a car and race the 124 miles to Penn State.

"We didn't get to the stadium until halfway through the first quarter," says Ridings. "By that time Raymond Rhodes had scored TCU's first touchdown. Then Penn State ran it up in a barnburner." Rhodes' TD is the only Horned Frog score in 36 years that Ridings hasn't seen.

Ridings has preserved his streak despite a cataract operation and a heart attack. "Paul always manages to arrange all his problems in the spring," says Freddie. The Ridingses were married one autumn night in 1939 after a TCU-Texas A & M game. They flew home from their 25th wedding anniversary in Acapulco in time to see the Horned Frogs beat Clemson 14-10. They cut short their 30th anniversary in Honolulu to catch the night owl to Dallas and make a connection for Florida only to see TCU lose 14-9 to Miami.

Ridings admits the decline of the Froggies in the last decade has taxed his loyalty. His record for the past 10 seasons is 15-90-5. Very few people know this, but TCU has never lost to Texas when Ridings delivered the pep-rally speech. He always ends his call to arms by saying, "Frogs, go give 'em hell—but do it in the Christian spirit!"

BOBBI HOVIS AND TWEEDIE SEARCY
Navy

Claiming to be Navy's greatest fan is more slippery than dredging oysters from an icy Chesapeake Bay skipjack in mid-winter. But one Middie follower is more dogged than any other. She's Teako Taco, a 6-year-old miniature dachshund the color of a football and the shape of a bratwurst. She lives in Annapolis and goes to Navy home games with a couple of other ladies named Bobbi Hovis and Tweedie Searcy, who are retired U.S. Navy nurses.

They take Teako to the games in a personalized duffel bag. She wears a tiny Navy bridge coat to pep rallies, a dinky sailor cap to tailgate parties and a wollen GO NAVY sweater to the games. She eats subs and drinks navy-bean soup poured from her own thermos. She even has her own gate pass. The only other animal that regularly attends Middie home games is the Navy goat.

Teako has been going to Middie home games since she was a pup. Six seasons may not sound like much in human terms, but in dog years it's 42. Bobbi, 58, and Tweedie, 61, have missed only a handful of games at Navy-Marine Corps Stadium since 1968. The ladies used to take another dachshund named Snoopy, but she died in 1978 after 11 campaigns, which may be all the Navy football a dachsie can stand.

Bobbi is the more adventurous of Teako's companions. She owned a plane before she owned a car, and was the first woman to fly a Navy jet, an F3D Skyknight. She was also the first Navy nurse to volunteer for Vietnam duty and the first woman elected to the Naval Academy Sailing Squadron. She keeps a 22-foot Catalina moored to the dock behind the house where she and Tweedie live.

These two Navy hellcats met 33 years ago while stationed in California. Bobbi was making medical evacuation runs between Hawaii and the Alameda Naval Air station during the Korean War. Tweedie was a nurse anesthetist at the submarine base on Mare Island.

Bobbi is the bigger football fan. She bicycles to practice two or three times a week, often with Teako bundled up in the basket. She grew up in Edinboro, Pa., wanting to be a flight nurse and listening to Navy games on the radio. She was particularly inspired by the movie Navy Blue and Gold, in which halfback Truck Cross (Jimmy Stewart) radiates the All-America virtues of decency, optimism, idealism and wholesome naiveté.

Tweedie didn't care for football all that much. She saw her first game in 1949, but she doesn't remember a lot about it, except that the opponent was Army. Tweedie got her name from a parakeet named Toby. Toby pronounced Owedia, Searcy's given name, "Tweedie." Tweedie joined the Navy to see the world. And she has. Her tours of duty have ranged from Cuba to Alaska to Southeast Asia. She has attended cooking school in Dieppe, France and written a cookbook called Tweedie's Treats. Included in it are recipes for Parfait Peggy Sue, Mocha Mambo and Warm Clyde. Her game-day party meatballs are enlivened by grape jelly.

If every dog has its day, then surely Teako's was the 1979 Oyster Bowl in Norfolk, Va. Navy trailed William and Mary at the half by a TD. "We changed her from her little blue-and-gold T shirt to her blue-and-gold sweater with the anchor," says Bobbi. "The kids came out steaming, and we won handily." Now, whenever Navy is behind at intermission, Teako does a quick change.

Teako hasn't disclosed which of the 48 games she has seen she liked best. It probably wasn't when she came snout-to-snout with the Yale bulldog. She also appeared somewhat chagrined during her lone encounter with Navy's human mascot, a Middie in goat's clothing. "Teako barked and barked at him," says Tweedie. "She's not used to goats who wear boxing gloves."

Teako's favorite player is Joe DiRenzo, '82, a second-string placekicker. "When she sees Joe," says Bobbi, "she just wags and wags and wags and slurpy-slurpies." In fact, Middie players seem to look forward to Teako's visits. As Tweedie points out, Teako smells a lot better than the goat.

Ceremony is Much More Than a Show

THE OLYMPICS

By *MIKE LITTWIN*

From The Los Angeles Times
Copyright © 1984, The Los Angeles Times

We saw America at its best at the Coliseum Saturday afternoon. The America we all believe in. The America we're so proud of. The America we love.

The Opening Ceremonies were guaranteed to produce several large lumps in the throats of anyone breathing. No one who saw it will soon forget the reception given the U.S. team, Ed Burke proudly carrying the flag with one strong arm. Or Gina Hemphill, the granddaughter of Jesse Owens—the man who helped teach America that a black man can be a hero—carrying the Olympic torch around the Coliseum track. Or Rafer Johnson, 24 years ago the Olympic-champion decathlete, who as a child once lived in a boxcar in the San Joaquin Valley, lighting the Olympic flame.

The show was vintage Hollywood, an old-fashioned, flag-waving musical tribute to America as we want it to be. In one part of the show, there was an old-west town, straight from a studio back lot, constructed on the Coliseum floor, recalling pioneer days, invoking the American spirit that made this country great.

It was an enjoyable afternoon, a moving afternoon, a cry for international peace as athletes from around the world joined in hand and in spirit. It almost made you believe that peace could be achieved as easily as the releasing of so many pigeons.

Just as the Olympic spirit has been torn by consecutive boycotts, however—first America's, then the Soviet Union's—the American spirit may also be in need of some repair.

In the Munich Olympics 12 years ago, 11 Israelis were murdered and the world was shocked by the senseless carnage.

In Westwood on the night before the Opening Ceremonies, a man drove his car onto a crowded sidewalk, killing one person and wounding scores.

In San Ysidro only days earlier, a man, after telling his wife he was going out to hunt humans, massacred 21 men, women and children, using a pistol, a rifle and a semi-automatic weapon.

★   ★   ★

I wonder what our thousands of foreign visitors must think of this country where such random violence is all too common.

Those acts were the work of madmen, isolated incidents, we tell them. They don't represent America, we tell them.

Of course they don't represent America. But what of the story of Paul Gonzales, an Olympic boxer out of Aliso Village in East Los Angeles, 10 minutes from downtown? In a recent interview, he recalled that as a youngster he was involved in a gang fight in which somebody might have been killed; he couldn't be sure. He told of young people in the barrio, young people not yet teenagers, who carry guns and knives.

Which is the real America?

We are the richest, the freest, the most powerful and arguably the best country in the world. But in the swell of patriotism that swept the Coliseum and the nation Saturday, we should remember, too, the other America.

Some of our best athletes have seen firsthand the underside of this great land. Some of our best athletes have escaped the drug-filled, crime-ridden ghettos where survival is considered success.

★   ★   ★

Often, we hear these Olympic athletes called our nation's best hope. They persevered, they overcame, they proved the value of hard work, they proved that anyone in America can climb to the top.

I was touched by the sight of Jesse Owens' granddaughter carrying the torch, glad that he was remembered. But I have read that Jesse Owens once had to race horses to put food on his table.

I was touched by Rafer Johnson. My memory of the great athlete is not of him on the athletic field, however, but at the Ambassador Hotel alongside Robert Kennedy on the night the presidential candidate was assassinated.

President Reagan said in an interview after the ceremonies that if international problems were given to the young people on the Coliseum floor, the problems would be solved by the next day. Reagan, who was once shot by a would-be assassin, spoke those words from behind a bullet-proof window high above the Coliseum floor.

Watching the ceremonies, it is easy to get caught up in them, in their splendor, in their breathless patriotism. I recall my own good fortune—living in a land where I can earn an excellent living, where I can vote and speak freely, where I can write this column without fear, saying that America, while often great, is not perfect.

I have a 10-year-old daughter who lives in comfort and safety, whose room is lined with cuddly stuffed animals, who has Michael

Jackson's latest album and a stereo to play it on, who has never faced any danger greater than crossing the street or taking a math test.

She watched the Olympic celebration at home on television, along with hundreds of millions around the world, and believed with all her young heart that what she saw is America.

I want to believe it, too.

Punchy

by Mary Butkus for United Press International. The camera was ready when Philadelphia catcher Ozzie Virgil charged the mound and started swinging at St. Louis pitcher Joaquin Andujar in a 1984 National League game in St. Louis. Virgil, who was ejected from the game, was reacting to a high, inside pitch from Andujar. Copyright © 1984, Mary Butkus.

Touchdown!

by Art Phillips of United Press International. Chicago Bears receiver Willie Gault was in the mood for a celebration after catching a touchdown pass in a 1984 National Football League game against St. Louis. The two Cardinals were in a different frame of mind. Copyright © 1984, United Press International.

Bird: a Flawless Gem In Solitaire Setting

PRO BASKETBALL

By *DAVID REMNICK*

From the Washington Post
Copyright © 1984, Washington Post

Much of the time, Larry Joe Bird played basketball alone, dawn to dark, in the schoolyards and driveways of his tiny hometown in southwest Indiana. "Larry'd play anywhere he could find a hoop in French Lick," said his mother, Georgia Bird. "He felt he had to be perfect, and a lot of people say that's the way it turned out."

It was never easy to find a real full-court game in French Lick or, for that matter, in Loogootee, Paoli, Santa Claus and all the other towns off State Highway 56.

"French Lick's only got about 2,000 people, so you can figure out the numbers," Bird said. "You ran out of kids to play with after a while and you ended up playing by yourself. There just weren't that many people around."

If you walk through the streets of Boston these days on a spring afternoon, be it in the tiny sections like the Back Bay or Beacon Hill or in low-income areas like Roxbury, you can hear school kids on the basketball court assigning themselves Celtic identities. The lankier ones will assume the role of Kevin McHale or Robert Parish. The guards will be Dennis Johnson (if they like to shoot) or Quinn Buckner (if they can't). Only the local braggart or genuine prodigy will dare say, "I'm Bird."

But whether he was playing with friends or by himself, Bird never assumed a mask. When he was shooting a desperate jumper as the scoreboard clock in his mind ran down to the final buzzer in some far-off championship final, he was never John Havlicek or Elgin Baylor.

"I was just myself," Bird said. "I didn't need none of that to keep me in the game. I always knew I wasn't very quick. I knew I couldn't jump too high. The only way I could succeed was on know-how. So I didn't watch anybody else, really. I watched myself."

Teammate Kevin McHale comes from Hibbing, Minn., a small town that was also the home of Bob Dylan. "I have this theory," McHale said of himself and Bird. "Us country boys who didn't have a city playground to grow up on learned there's not much else you can do. You can get some pick-up games, but you're always playing the same guys. Sometimes they can challenge you because they've learned all your moves, but after a while you learn on your own. You spend hours and hours out there by yourself."

It's hard to hit fly balls without someone around to shag them. It's not much of a challenge to play football with trees as tacklers. Of all the major American sports, basketball is the one that adapts best to solitude and imagination.

Bill Bradley, who grew up the son of a prosperous banking family in Missouri and went on to play for Princeton and the New York Knicks, used to put slivers of lead in the soles of his sneakers and play hundreds of games of 'round-the-world against himself. He would drill himself on shooting with the opposite hand, dribbling blindfolded, following up missed shots.

Bird does not possess Bradley's intellectual ambitions. Instead of a career in the Senate, Bird's immediate retirement plans run more toward "going back home" to fish in Lake Potocha and be with old high school buddies like John (Beezer) Carnes. And yet Bird's ability to teach himself the game so thoroughly and properly that the extraordinary becomes instinctual is reminiscent of Bradley. The difference is that Bird, now 27, is four inches taller and a world more gifted.

"People said I was from a small town and wouldn't be able to play college ball, but I knew I could," Bird said. "People said the same thing about the pros, but I knew I could play in this league. I taught myself things like a fadeaway shot because I knew I wouldn't be jumping over too many people. I just worked at it, that's all.

"Sometimes, though, I wonder how much better I might have been if I'd grown up playin' in the city. Hard to tell, I guess."

★   ★   ★

Until the game begins, Larry Bird is not exactly anyone's athletic ideal. True, he is 6-foot-9. That does distinguish him from most mortals, but beyond his height, Bird has the musculature of a weekend racquetball player. He hardly leaves his feet on jump shots or rebounds.

"I don't care what you say about his athletic ability," said Celtics Coach K.C. Jones. "He's the best all-around player I've ever seen. He can do it all and he makes everybody around him better. He's a winner. I can't imagine this team without him."

"The best ever," said Bob Cousy. "I used to think it was Elgin. Then when Doctor J became really consistent I thought it was him. But no one in all my years in this foolish game has ever been able to do so many things so well."

Bird operates in a time warp. He is the science fiction character who sees everything around him in slow motion while he, and only he, has the chance to make just the right move that changes the course of events. Like a rock garden in the middle of Tokyo, Bird provides a certain stillness, a tranquility to the furious traffic around him.

While everyone else is racing up and down the court and from sideline to sideline, Bird has the presence of mind to thread a pass, make a steal or just take a little step that makes all the difference.

That is why Bird is so dangerous when he is holding the ball. The opposition seems almost nervous waiting to see what he will do because he can do everything. You can let Magic Johnson shoot from long range. You can guess that George Gervin won't pass. Oscar Robertson may be one of the few players to compare with Bird, yet Bird's height gives him an advantage even there.

In the current playoff series against the Milwaukee Bucks, Bird has attracted double and triple coverage as if he were a dominant center on a mediocre team. But since Bird plays with excellent players and is about as selfish as Mahatma Gandhi, the Milwaukee defense has failed.

Bird's tricks are manifold. When he is guarded one on one, he will hold the ball above his shoulders with his right side facing the basket. From that position, Bird can throw in a jumper, pass or make a head fake and drive to the basket. From the sideline, Bird's fakes look as obvious as something out of an Adolph Rupp instruction manual, and yet Bernard King found himself chasing Chimeras for two weeks.

"He's the best forward in the game," said King, Bird's principal competition for the Most Valuable Player award.

Because of his relatively slow feet, Bird is not as good a one-on-one defender as Los Angeles' Michael Cooper, for instance. Instead, he usually lets Cedric Maxwell play the opposition's big scorer and assumes a middle-linebacker role on defense. Of all the league's glamourous forwards, including Julius Erving, King and Marques Johnson, Bird is the best defender.

This year Bird averaged 24.2 points, 10.1 rebounds, 1.7 steals, 6.6 assists and 38.3 minutes per game. He hit 49.2 percent of his field goals and 88.8 percent of his free throws, tops in the league.

In the 1981 playoffs, the Celtics overcame a 3-1 deficit to beat the 76ers on Bird's winning jump shot in the seventh game.

"There was no other place in the world I wanted that ball except in my hands," he said then, and the ball has been with him ever since.

"The first time I negotiated with Red (Auerbach) for Larry it was a 100-day war," said Bird's agent, neighbor and close friend, Bob Woolf. "Nobody has to tell you how tough Red can be in negotiations. But the second time, it was easy because I never had to sell Red on the worth and value of Larry Bird. I felt he should be the highest paid player in the game. Every Hall of Famer and former coach you talk to will tell you that he's the best all-around player ever. Red didn't need much coaxing."

"Larry still surprises me," Auerbach said. "He makes the extraordinary play all the time. I always loved Bird's competitiveness, his passing and his shooting, but I never thought he'd be the rebounder or the leader he is. It was like (Bill) Russell. No one, not even me, thought the guy would ever be that good. Guys like that you don't mind paying."

According to Woolf, the seven-year contract Bird signed last year is worth $14 million, while Moses Malone's $13-million, six-year pact depends on performance bonuses.

"The money," Bird said, "that don't mean anything. I don't even think about it. It hasn't changed me or the way I play."

Asked what he thought was the most amazing thing he'd ever seen Bird do, M.L. Carr said, "I once saw him pick up the check."

★   ★   ★

It was Bird himself who came up with the tag "just a hick from French Lick."

The town got its name from the critters who used to come out of the local spring and lick the minerals off their fur and from the old French fort that used to stand in the area.

Bird's father worked as a piano finisher for the town's primary employer, the Kimball Piano & Organ Co., while his mother raised six children.

"I met Larry when he was a freshman. He was 14 years old," said Gary Holland, Bird's coach at Springs Valley High School. "He was no more than an average player at first. It's hard to say what happened. He just got better is all. Better all the time."

One of the transformations that helped turn Bird from an ordinary high school player into a potential pro was a serious injury.

"I broke my ankle and had to sit out almost an entire season when I was a sophomore," he said. "When I came back, I began to throw these fantastic passes I had never thrown before. I have no idea where it came from, but there I was, throwing all kinds of passes. I remember being in the locker room after the first day back and guys asking, 'God, Larry, where did you learn to pass like that?' Suddenly, I had a whole new way to play.

"It was great, because when you pass the ball like that, everybody likes you, and it was also great because when you pass the ball well it makes it easier to shoot. It just gave me a whole new dimension to my game."

Holland speaks with a certain reverence of his time with Bird.

"Larry was like he is now. He made everyone around him seem better than they were. He's just able to foresee everything that's going to happen. I was 25 when I had him, my first coaching job. It was a once-in-a-lifetime thing for me. I'm almost sorry it happened so soon."

That dimension and some added inches and strength drew Bob Knight's attention at Indiana. But Bird was intimidated by a school with 33,000 students and he dropped out after a month.

Bird's parents had been divorced for a few years by then and soon after Bird left school, his father shot himself to death. Bird also had a brief, unhappy marriage to a girl who had been a cheerleader and friend at Springs Valley. Their child lives with Bird's former wife in Indiana.

After five years in the league, reporters know better than to ask Bird about these two events in his life. Even a close friend, like Woolf or former teammate Rick Robey, say they have never heard him talk much about it.

"Larry handled it very well," Georgia Bird said. "I don't want to dwell on this, but he learned a lot and grew up a lot."

While waiting for a second shot at college, Bird held a job with the city highway department painting white lines on roads and collecting garbage. After a redshirt year at Indiana State, Bird had an extraordinary career there that culminated in a loss to Magic Johnson's Michigan State team in the 1979 NCAA final. The redshirt year allowed Auerbach to draft Bird while he was still a junior.

The Celtics were 29-53 the year before Bird's arrival. With only Bird added to the starting lineup, they went 61-21.

"What more do you say when a team improves like that?" asked Bucks Coach Don Nelson. "What more can you say about Larry Bird?"

★   ★   ★

When Bird came into the league, some suspected he was little more than the hick he claimed to be. He still drives a Ford Bronco, chews tobacco, favors bib overalls or warmup suits to Saville Row suits, has a collection of 600 trucker caps, talks in fractured backwoods syntax and treats interviews like an appointment for root canal surgery.

"But he ain't dumb," Auerbach said. "He's dumb like a fox."

In the offseason, Bird spends his time in French Lick fishing on the lake or on Cape Cod in a house next door to one owned by Woolf. When the Celtics are at work, he allows no reporters—be they from the local penny-saver or CBS—near his split-level house in Brookline.

"I'll tell you how much he's changed," Woolf said. "He still loves to do his lawn more than anything. There isn't a day I go over to his house and there isn't somebody there from Indiana, some teammate or school friends. He isn't impressed by celebrities or by himself. And the guy still calls me Mr. Woolf."

While Magic Johnson thrives on an emotional relationship with the crowd and radiates the pleasure of mastery and play, Bird creates a quiet aura on the court. It's the slow-motion world he can control, a replica, perhaps, of the game he played in his mind as he practiced by himself in French Lick.

"People here in French Lick—this is a real small town—they don't get impressed by much," Holland said. "Larry just likes to be left alone and play basketball. He's always been that way. I don't expect that'll change much. It hasn't so far."

Marathoner Benoit: The Reign in Maine

RUNNING

By *JANE LEAVY*

From the Washington Post
Copyright © 1984, Washington Post

Her eyes are slate blue, the color of the steely winter ocean outside her window. Joan Benoit's house sits on an icy inlet just down the road from L.L. Bean, where there are no locks on the doors and you can buy long underwear 24 hours a day.

Every morning, Benoit puts on her woolen longjohns and runs. Icicles cling to her face. She runs on, circling the same snowy loops day after day. The only thing that wanders is her mind. She thinks about her wedding next September, about knitting, cooking, the renovation of her 150-year-old house. And she picks up the pace because she realizes how much she has to do. But never does she think about stopping.

Here, in rugged isolation, away from the running communities where mileage is a form of currency, Benoit, the world record-holder in the marathon, has chosen to prepare for the 1984 Olympics. This strikes just about everyone but her as strange. "People think I'm an oddity training up here," she said. "I consider myself a perfectly normal Maine person."

The smile was wry. "The reason I'm in Maine is that it's where I grew up," she said. "I'm very comfortable around the ocean. I find the ocean is very much like my own personality. I can be so calm and soothing. Other times, I'm so turbulent and riled up. People get the impression I'm a hermit up here. I'm not. I'm surrounded by friends who accept me for who I am and not what I've accomplished in running."

Last spring, she won the Boston marathon in 2 hours 22 minutes 42 seconds, not just breaking the world record but obliterating it by almost three minutes. Her time was 25 seconds slower than the men's winning time in 1968.

She has not run a marathon since, eschewing the first world championship last summer in Helsinki and a confrontation with Grete Waitz, and won't run another until the Olympic trials in May. There are only so many marathons in her 5-foot-3, 105-pound body, she says.

That morning last April, when she stepped to the starting line, she brazenly handed her split watch to her trainer, Bob Severny. "She didn't want any barriers," Severny said. "If you got a watch, you've got barriers. If you look down and you see 32 minutes at 10 kilometers, you're going to think, 'Oh, my God, I'm going too fast.' "

Afterward, Benoit's time was challenged because Kevin Ryan, a marathoner working for a Boston radio station, had run with her. The charge that Ryan had acted as a pacer was dismissed in December at The Athletics Congress convention. But it was ironic that such an allegation would be leveled against someone as fiercely independent as Benoit, and it rankled. "I can't believe it was ever an issue," she said. "If you argue with that, you have to take every single track and field record."

She is a collector of things: records (she holds U.S. marks for 10 kilometers, the half-marathon and 20 kilometers), shells, driftwood, stamps, coins, dolls. She can not bear to throw anything away. "I always think something's got potential," she said. "Ask my mother what I've got under my bed."

Mostly, she collects her thoughts. She is cautious about how many of them she shares and with whom. The gears are always churning. No matter how much she says, you wonder what is left unsaid. "I've got too many things going on inside my head," she said. "People think I'm out to lunch. Spacing out."

She has a reputation as a reluctant interview. For many years, her grandfather wrote a column called Top of the Morning for a Boston newspaper. "I was always told that the less in the paper about you, the better," Benoit's mother said.

"People in Maine are reticent," said Dick Brown, administrator of Athletics West, the club Benoit runs for (she would run for a club located 3,000 miles away). "It's a nice quality. They say what they need to and that's it."

After she won in Boston in 1979, Benoit said she would never run a marathon again. "Everyone wanted another piece of me. If I didn't give it to them, I was terrible. It was a huge maturing process for me."

At age 26, she has reached an uneasy truce with fame. She does what she must to accommodate it, but mostly she does it alone. "I think running is my challenge," she said. "It wouldn't be as large a challenge if I involved other people. I get advice. But it's not like they're monitoring me. I swore up and down I'd never get an agent."

But after the victory in Boston, she hired an attorney, Ed Whittemore, to handle the requests. Whittemore says she since has turned down about $200,000 in endorsements, as well as an opportunity to appear on the Phil Donohue Show. She accepted a one-year deal as a fitness consultant to Dole because the company didn't ask her to do anything before the Olympics and because she uses its pineapple in a salad she makes.

Her marketability (potential long-term deals), her upcoming marriage and her delicate Achilles' tendons are forcing her to consider how long she wants to compete. The pieces are there, but she hasn't quite figured out where they all belong.

"I'll always run," she said. "How long I compete at the rate I'm competing won't be much longer. I may compete three years or five years or 10. I may have a family and come back."

She considered retiring in 1982, when she had surgery on her Achilles' tendons. She would rather quit early than leave as a cripple. She thinks about graduate school in environmental studies, a concern born from her running. Her fiancee, Scott Samuelson, is applying to business school, which could mean a move back to Boston, where she coached the women's distance team at Boston University until last June. Cities make her shudder. But the idea of having her life organized around somebody else for a change is very appealing.

She does volunteer work in the admissions office of her alma mater, Bowdoin, and has taken up cross-country skiing. "People ask me if L.A. doesn't work out, would I hang around for Seoul?" she said. "I tell them my aspirations are more to Calgary (the site of the 1988 Winter Olympics). I'm not being facetious at all. I'd like to switch to cross-country."

People think she is crazy to ski. She tells them running on icy back roads is far more dangerous. But it was a skiing accident in her sophomore year in high school that started her running career. "I always wanted to make it to the level I am in running in skiing," she said. "I started running to get back into shape for skiing. I just loved it."

When she began, she was such an oddity that she walked whenever cars passed. "A few years later," she said, "I felt I was joining a parade."

She was an unspectacular Maine state champion in the mile—her best times were around 5:20—and made it to the finals of the Olympic trials in 1,500 meters. "What she did is put her high school mile back to back for 26 miles in Boston," said Brown, "which is phenomenal."

Her training schedule includes twice daily runs and splitting wood. She plans to run the 3,000 meters at the Olympic Invitational track meet and is committed to at least one road race, a 10-kilometer, this spring.

Severny has no doubt that she can break 2:20. But he says it won't happen this year. At the trials, she will be concerned only with making the team. The heat and smog in Los Angeles will be conducive to a tactical race, not a record. "I don't know how much faster I can get," she said. "Maybe we'll never know. I may not be competing

that hard after the next year."

She is a wisp of a will. You wonder where it comes from. "She grew up with boys," her mother said matter of factly.

"I know I started training because I broke my leg skiing," Benoit said. "We were brought up on skiing because my father was in the 10th Mountain Division of the Army. My father has always been a hard worker. My mother is very dedicated, a dedicated mother. They never quit on us."

She has finished every marathon she ever started. She has never quit in the middle of a training run, never walked in. It is a methodical, compulsive process. "Every once in a while, there's a moment of joy, and that's what I do it for," she said. "This morning, it was below zero and the wind was in my face. I had icicles all over my face and my fingers were curled inside my mittens and I said I better not stop. I turned out of the wind and it was a great run.

"I know I'll be in trouble the first time I give in. I've been entertaining the thought more and more frequently. Then I realize that I've got plans for this year. If I can just hold on a bit longer, that's when I usually start running my best."

The obsessiveness troubles and enlivens her. "I get down on myself," she said. "I spend all this time running. Why don't I do something constructive? I've thought about going to medical school. I don't know if I could get in. But I'd want to do sports medicine. How could I work with all those compulsive athletes who defy doctors' orders and not work with someone who wants to walk or see or live?

"It's funny. I'm attracted to things that don't have any impact on life. People say I've done a great thing for women. I don't think I have. People say I've given people courage. That makes me feel good, but I don't see how I do that.

"I think my running is a selfish thing. But it provides the challenge that allows me to feel good about myself. How can I expect to do well in other activities if I don't feel good about myself?"

So she keeps running in circles. She has eight loops. She tests herself and her fitness against them. "I'll go out on a 2½-hour run and say, 'I could be in Boston. What have I done? I've run one big circle.' It's a compulsive thing. That's where I get hung up."

In the quiet of the winter, she lies on her living room floor wrestling with her puppy Creosote and the contradictions. A pair of dog-eared running shoes sits by the wood-burning stove, the only sign of the athlete.

She thinks marathoning is "nuts." "It still seems crazy," she said. "I ask myself why I'm running in circles. I'm always running in circles in every facet of my life, including my running. I always have too many irons in the fire. When I do, I'm not happy. When I don't, I'm not happy."

She is thinking about writing a book, one of the many ideas that flicker through her head. The title? "That's a good question," she said. "Stark Raving Mad"?

She has been thinking it over and has decided she's not. "I don't think I'm ridiculously hooked," she said. "Now I'm finding time for my runs instead of fitting everything around my running. So I don't think I'm insane."

How would the journalist's granddaughter write about herself? "I'd probably put it in another section of the paper that wasn't the sports section," she said. "If you went into my bedroom of my parents' house, you'd never figure out what I do."

"Above it all?" her brother, said, teasing.

She gave him a look that said he knew better. It's a matter of definition, that's all.

Decker Running Hard For Olympic Gold

OLYMPIC TRACK

By *RAY DIDINGER*

From the Philadelphia Daily News
Copyright © 1984, Philadelphia Newspapers Inc.

It was on the final straightaway in Helsinki, Finland that Mary Theresa Decker became one with her destiny.

It was there in the 1983 World Track Championships, with Zamira Zaitseva at her elbow and America's hopes draped across her shoulders, that Decker finally embraced her promise and carried it home.

All the years of pain, the broken bones, the broken hearts, the broken marriage, none of it mattered anymore. This was Mary Decker, all grown up, doing the one thing in her life that made sense from the beginning.

She was running . . . running against the Soviets' best. She was 10 meters from the tape, eyes closed, teeth clinched, driving to the finish with a stride that was more purpose than poetry.

This time, dammit, Mary—*our* Mary—was going to win.

No boycott, no crutches, no "Sorry, honey, you're too young." No tears, no excuses, no Harlequin novel endings. Just Mary Decker and her will pitted against the rest of the world. We all know that's no contest.

Carl Lewis walked away from the long jump to watch. Dave Laut dropped his shot put. The Finnish crowd was on its feet cheering. Track is a sport known for its moments of theatre but seldom are they this eloquent or universal.

"People talk about the Super Bowl," Lewis said later. "Man, Super Bowl is nothing compared to this."

Zaitseva had done all she could do to unnerve Decker throughout the 1,500 meters. She bumped Decker and stepped on her toes early, then she cut her off on the final turn.

As a teenager, Decker had thrown her baton at a Soviet runner who used similar tactics. This time, Mary kept her cool.

"I was angry," she said, "but I decided the best way—the only way—to get even was to beat her."

Decker closed the gap on Zaitseva, overtaking her in the stretch. Desperate, the Soviet champion threw herself at the line. Zaitseva fell short and sprawled across the track.

Decker coasted to a stop and, finally, almost reluctantly, opened her eyes.

She did not know she had won until she saw the replay on the stadium scoreboard. It was her second gold medal of the championships—she had won the 3,000 meters four days earlier—and it left us all to shake our heads in wonder.

"Until now," said Bob Hersch of Track and Field News, "we never knew how good Mary Decker was." (Hersch had predicted Decker would not even make the U.S. team for Helsinki.)

Those last 10 meters made Mary Decker famous in a way her seven world records (six indoors) and nine American records never could.

She didn't beat a stopwatch, she beat a Russian. Better yet, she beat a Russian who played dirty. She said, "In your faceski sister" and it was like Lake Placid all over again.

Months later, Decker's coach at Athletics West, Dick Brown, told Sports Illustrated: "I continue to be amazed at the number of people, not necessarily track fans, who come up to say, 'I get goosebumps or I get tears in my eyes when I think about it.' "

Recently, several top women gymnasts were discussing the athletes they most admire. Olga Korbut and Nadia Comaneci were 1-2, naturally. But Julianne McNamara never hesitated.

"Mary Decker," the two-time U.S. Olympian said. "I can still see her finish in Helsinki. The determination on her face. What intensity, what a killer.

"Imagine if we were all like that," McNamara said, smiling. "Wow . . ."

★   ★   ★

Mary Decker, now 26, was sitting in the weight room at the University of Oregon track. She was wearing blue slacks and a gray sweater and she looked nothing like a killer.

She looked slender and lovely and, yes, even vulnerable. Of course, the glowering presence of her boyfriend-bodyguard, British discus thrower Richard Slaney (6-foot-7, 290 pounds), more than made up for that.

Decker can't explain what it is that makes her run the way she does. She has heard all the theories—she runs to win because she had a tough childhood, because she needs love, etc.—but she thinks we are reaching for something that's not really there.

Maybe Decker runs to win because that's the only thing she knows. Maybe she runs to win because it beats the hell out of finishing fifth.

"I'm a competitive person," Decker said.

She glanced over at Slaney, who was listening while he wrestled with Decker's Rottweiler pup, Samantha. Slaney rolled his eyes.

"OK," Decker said, getting the message. "Make that *very* competitive.

"I get myself into that frame of mind when I race. You can be best friends with someone off the track but, in the race, only one person can win. That's how I approach it.

"From the time I started running, I won. I got used to it. To me, that was the only place to finish. I wasn't like some kids who would finish second and say, 'I ran a good time.' Good time, heck. I want to win. I'll do anything I have to to win.

"People say the other runners fear me," Decker said. "I don't know if that's true. I can't read their minds. All I know is I'm out there to beat them. But afraid? You can't be afraid to win. If you are, then why bother running?"

"Mary has what Vince Lombardi called 'singleness of purpose' " said Brown, who has coached her the last four years. "She has mental toughness to fight through anything. And I mean literally anything.

"Look back over her career, count up all the injuries (dozens) and operations (six). Consider all she had to go through to come back. It would have been so easy for her to say, "This is crazy. Let's try something else.' But she didn't. She won't quit, ever."

"Maybe (British miler) Steve Ovett is as competitive as Mary," Slaney said. "I can't think of too many others."

That's what attracted everyone to Mary Decker in the first place.

Here was this attractive woman (who else wore gold earrings and make-up to work out?) who loved junk food, stuffed animals and Rod Stewart, who was so typically Cosmo, but who carried a stiletto on the track.

Rick Reilly, a writer for The Los Angeles Times, described Decker as "farm town fresh, yet with a certain Manhattan in her smile, as though she could drink Dom Perignon with a straw and make it look elegant." Yeah, our Mary Decker was all of that, urbane and charming. But deep down, she was something more.

"Mary," miler Steve Scott once said in admiration, "is an animal. Don't get in her way or you'll pay."

Case in point: The Great Baton Toss in Moscow. That was 1974 and little Mary, then 16, was disqualified for hurling her baton at the Russian who elbowed her off the track in a 4x400 relay.

Decker expressed only one regret. "I missed," she said. "Twice."

We liked that, even though we might not have cared to admit it. It was poor sportsmanship and worse politics, but it was undeniably spunky. And Americans are suckers for spunky kids in braces and pigtails. "Mary showed 'em," we said. It was as if our daughter had punched out the school bully. We couldn't tell the teacher we approved, but we really did.

Over the years there were other incidents, like the time Decker shoved a lapped runner aside at the Millrose Games in New York. And the way she never bothered to learn her opponents' names. Critics wondered just where was the line between being competitive and being cruel?

"What you've got to understand about Mary," Tracy Sundlun, one of Decker's former coaches told Newsweek, "is that she judges her worth as a person solely by what she accomplishes on the track.

"It's scary to contemplate, but the competitive nature that we so admire in this woman is actually a huge personality flaw."

Bill Bowerman would agree. Bowerman is the retired Oregon track coach who was hired by Dick Brown awhile back to supervise Decker's training. He lasted two weeks.

"It was not a pleasure," Bowerman told Reilly. "I couldn't adjust to her. She had quite a temperament. I just couldn't put up with the tantrums. I'm not a very patient person.

"But Dick is exactly right for her. If they hadn't come together, she never would have survived."

Brown is a quiet, unassuming man with a manner best described as soothing. He knows track and he knows sports medicine and, in short, he knows what's best for Mary Decker, who self-destructs more often than the Democratic party.

Brown's calm, low-key approach is just what Decker needs, particularly in an Olympic year when the newsmen, the advertisers and the promoters are lining up at the door. Brown's temper is as long as Decker's is short and, between them, they make things work. Usually.

There still are occasional problems, like the time Brown told Daily News photographer Prentice Cole he could shoot a workout and Decker decided she didn't want her picture taken that day. She ran off the track and up the bleachers, screaming at the photographer to get out.

"Some days I just want to be left alone," Decker explained. "Everyone feels that way from time to time and we say it's natural. I feel that way and people say I'm a prima donna. I can't win.

"I'm sensitive to it, but probably not as sensitive as I should be. The older I get, the more things there are. It's everything—appearances, interviews, commercial exploitation. Yet you don't want to snub the people who are genuine.

"It's just hard to sort it all out," she said with a shrug. "It's a tough balance. They say you owe the public something, but don't you owe yourself something, too? This (fame) is the worst part of being Mary Decker."

Brown agrees Decker can be difficult. The same qualities that made her hard to beat in the 1,500 meters at Helsinki also make her hard to deal with on a regular basis. Sometimes tenacity and stubbornness are one and the same.

"To understand Mary, you have to understand what she has gone through to get here," Brown said. "If she were any less competitive than she is, she wouldn't even be running much less preparing for the Olympics.

"I spend half my day telling people why Mary can't do things . . . TV shows, fashion shows, commercials. They say, 'Can't she fly to L.A. for the afternoon? This will only take three hours?' They don't have any idea what's involved in her training.

"I say, 'No, she can't' and they feel we're being unreasonable. They say, 'Who does she think she is?' It's not a question of who Mary thinks she is but what she wants to be and that's an Olympic champion. Like it or not, that takes a special commitment.

"Mary has worked her whole life for this," Dick Brown said. "This is her moment and she's going to call the shots. She used to try to please everybody but that didn't work. Maybe this will."

★   ★   ★

Mary Decker was born in Bunnvale, N.J., the daughter of a tool-and-die maker. The family moved to California in 1967 and settled in Garden Grove, a quiet L.A. suburb.

At 11, Mary was looking for things to do. She saw a notice for a cross-country race sponsored by the local parks department. She liked to run. She figured, "Why not?"

With no training, running in a T-shirt and sneakers, Mary won the race with ease. Don DeNoon, coach of the Long Beach Track Club, was at the finish line asking for her name and address. That's how it all started.

Within a year, Mary was running for the Long Beach club. And running. And running . . .

In one week, she ran five races: the 440, the 880, the mile, two-mile and marathon. The next day, she had an emergency appendectomy that the doctors blamed on "extreme stress."

Everyone blamed DeNoon and Jackie Decker, Mary's mother, but the truth is no one pushed Mary like Mary.

The day after her release from the hospital, she came to practice and jogged with her teammates. She held the surgical stitches together with the palm of her hand.

By the time she was a junior at Orange High School, Decker had shin splints and her ankles ached when she walked. She was taking 12 aspirin a day to numb the pain, but she never missed a workout.

All along, Mary Decker knew what she wanted.

"I wanted to run," Decker says now, looking back. "I liked it even before I knew I was good at it. Then once I started having success, that only made me like it more.

"People were saying I should have been home playing with Barbie dolls. Hey, I was enjoying myself. My parents never pushed me to train. If I missed my ride to practice, I threw a tantrum.

"A lot of girls would hide in the bushes during workouts, then jump out so they'd finish with the team. Or they'd take off for the restroom and miss five or six intervals. Those girls didn't like to train. I did."

It's not so hard to understand. Track was very good to Mary Decker. She was "Little Mary," so cute and lovable even crusty, old sports writers would pat her on the head after an interview.

When she was 14, she upset Niele Sabaite, the Olympic silver medalist, in a U.S.-Soviet dual meet in Minsk. (She appeared on "To Tell the Truth" the next week. At 5-feet, 86 pounds, she stumped the panel.)

When Decker was 15, she broke three world indoor records and toured Africa with the U.S. national team. The premier of Senegal presented her with a bronze statue of a soldier on a horse. (She still has it in her Eugene, Ore., living room.)

The trouble was things weren't going well at home—her father had left and her mom was working as a cocktail waitress to support the three kids—and Mary began using her coaches as a substitute for family.

Track was the one thing she could hold on to as the rest of her world was falling apart. She trusted the sport and its cast the way she would trust mom and dad and it just didn't work. She was eager to please and people were quick to take advantage.

Where a father would have seen the pain in her stride and told her to ease up, the coaches sought to keep her running. And where most teenagers can retreat to their rooms and close the door, Mary always seemed to be center stage.

"Mary never had a chance to be a kid," Nancy Gregorio, an old friend, said. "She had to be a star from the beginning. She was always around older people, flying around the world.

"Her need to be loved stems from her dad leaving her as a kid. She needs to know someone is there who cares for her."

Decker has heard the story a million times and she still isn't sure she accepts it. She cringes at the old Frank Shorter quote about her being "exploited." It all sounds so, well, melodramatic.

"Most of my problems stem from injuries," Decker said, "and who's to say what causes injuries? People say I trained too hard but I've always been like that. To trace it all back to an unhappy childhood is a little much."

Whatever the reason, Decker's career slowed, then came to a crippling halt at age 16.

She developed a condition called compartment syndrome, which meant her calf muscles had outgrown her legs. When she ran, the muscles would press against surrounding tissue and cause cramping and severe pain.

For three years, she traveled from doctor to doctor. She had X-rays, cortisone, dye injections, acupressure and acupuncture. She had her legs in casts for months at a time. Nothing worked. The '76 Olympics came and went without Little Mary.

She probably should have given up at this point, but she did not.

She went to Boulder, Colo., enrolled at the university and took a part-time job at Shorter's running shop. Anything to stay close to the action.

In 1977, Dick Quax, the 1976 Olympic silver medalist in the 5,000 meters, came to train. Quax had compartment syndrome in 1973 but he overcame it through corrective surgery. The doctors cut open the tissue sheaths surrounding the muscle and allowed it to expand. Simple as that.

"You ought to try it," Quax said.

"What do I have to lose?" Decker said.

She was in the hospital five days and, two weeks later, she jogged a half-mile. Pretty soon, she was up to a mile. The pain was gone. There was no stopping her.

Quax became her coach, then her boyfriend. That got complicated. "We had what you'd call a personality conflict," Decker said. In '79, Quax ran one way, Mary the other.

There were two more operations on her legs, not to mention three automobile accidents that set her back. Once she was at a Jackson Browne concert on her crutches and she accidentally was knocked to the floor in the crowd.

"Things seem to happen to me," Decker said. "My mother said I'm my own worst enemy and maybe I am. The thing is I never stay down long. If I'm good at anything, it's coming back."

In 1980, Decker was at her peak. In January, she broke the world outdoor mile record (4:21.7). Two weeks later, she set the world indoor 1,500-meter record at the Millrose Games (4:00.8). One week later, she ran a 4:17.55 mile in the Astrodome, then she became the first woman to run the 880 indoors in less than two minutes (1:59.7).

She was primed for her first Olympics, then President Jimmy Carter interceded. Disheartened, Decker went on a grueling European tour that wound up with her blowing out her Achilles tendon in Brussels. More surgery, followed by 16 months rehabilitation.

In 1982, Decker launched yet another comeback, this time with the paternal Brown providing the direction. She had daily applications of DMSO (an anti-inflammatory drug) and four times a week she had massages to loosen the muscles before she ran.

"If we keep you healthy," Brown said, "no one can beat you."

He was right. Decker broke seven world records that year, three in six weeks. She was the fastest U.S. woman in all six distances from 800 to 10,000 meters. She set a record in the 10,000 meters (31:35.3) at an "all-comers" meet at Eugene. She did it after flying 16 hours from Oslo, Norway.

She wasn't even wearing track shoes that day. She was wearing flats because Brown didn't want her overdoing it. So she went out and set a world record.

"I didn't know," Decker said later. "It felt easy."

As if Little Mary ever knew what easy was. She was married at the time to marathoner Ron Tabb. That lasted 22 months. Heaviest laundry line in Eugene. She claimed her husband couldn't handle her success. He claimed Mary was too wrapped up in her career.

"There were times when I wanted to do things, I wanted her to be a part of it," Tabb told the Denver Post. "Mary felt it would interrupt her career too much. I had a little resentfulness.

"What was good for me wasn't necessarily good for her. I didn't think that was quite fair. She's very selfish with her running . . . I guess we have to be a little more selfish with our careers if we're going to accomplish what we want to."

Both parties escaped with careers intact. Ron ran second in the '83 Boston Marathon and announced: "Maybe now I'll be known again as Ron Tabb instead of Ron Decker."

Mary went on to Helsinki where she enjoyed her finest moment, defeating two-time Olympic champion Tatyana Kazankina in the 3,000 meters, then outgutting Zaitseva in the 1,500 meters.

"Very few people thought I could win at Helsinki," Decker said, smiling at Slaney. "The people close to me knew I could but the so-called experts didn't think so.

"They said, 'Oh, Mary does real well running against other Americans. She doesn't have much competition here. But the Russians and the East Germans . . . that's another story.' Of course, all that did was help motivate me.

"You know how I trained for that meet? I ran with the cross-country team from the college. I knew there were no women around who could push me and I needed the work. I said 'OK, guys. Get physical. Bump me around. Don't hold anything back.' "

Decker did not finish the story. The first day, four men showed up to run and three dropped out, exhausted by Decker's pace. One crawled off the track and threw up in the grass.

"I proved a point in Helsinki," Decker said. "I'm sure when the Russians passed me on that final lap, they thought that was it, that I'd break. But I didn't. If I've learned one thing in this life it's that you can't quit.

"So many people call that meet the turning point of my career. I don't see it that way. I feel like my whole life is like a ladder that I'm climbing and Helsinki was the next rung leading to the Olympics.

"I don't think I'll be satisfied until I have that [Olympic] medal," she said. "It's something I've always wanted to do, always felt capable of doing, it's just the circumstances kept me from competing. I was too young in '72, I was hurt in '76 and '80, well, let's not get into that.

"But it's worked out so that I'll be competing in Los Angeles where I grew up. Maybe that's the way it was meant to be all along. I know it's going to be crazy there. It's already crazy. That's why I'm here [in Oregon]. All that Olympic stuff, day and night. I couldn't take it."

But even in Eugene, Ore., the pressure is building. Surely, Mary Decker knows there are millions of people out there counting on her to win not one but two gold medals in LA?

Her visibility never has been greater. She is in magazine ads for Nike and Timex. She is also the official Kodak Camera Girl of the Summer Games. (The Kodak press release describes her as "slim, trim, prim, full of vim and smiling from rim to rim.")

"It's all part of the package," Decker said, smiling weakly. "Like I said, having cameras and microphones shoved in my face is my least favorite part of the day. When I walk away from all this, that's the one thing I won't miss.

"But I've put up with it for 10 years, a few more weeks won't make much difference. Dick [Brown] does a good job screening requests. And, of course, Richard [Slaney] can be very helpful discouraging trespassers."

(Reilly's profile suggested Slaney "eats photographers for between-meals snacks and practices scowling in the mirror at night." Could be. We weren't asking.)

"But that's all secondary," Mary Decker said. "What counts is what happens out there [pointing toward the track]. And out there is where I'm at my best."

Lightin' 'Em Up Down in the Valley

COLLEGE FOOTBALL

By *RON BORGES*

From the Boston Globe
Copyright © 1984, Boston Globe

The explanation for how it all began is simple, like the answer to so many complex questions. It started when there wasn't much left to try but to lock the doors and move on down the road.

"I dare to take chances," The Gunslinger is saying, "I dare do what others think about.

"They never won around the Valley until I came here. The day I showed up, I made a statement: 'Make room at the top for us.' People laughed. They said Bear Bryant couldn't win at Valley.

"I told 'em, 'I ain't the Bear. I'm Cooley. The Gunslinger. I shoot straight.' When I first explained my offense to (San Diego Charger offensive coordinator) Larrye Weaver, he said, 'Archie, they'll either say you're a genius or they'll laugh you out of football.'

"Ain't nobody laughing at the Valley now."

Archie Cooley's got that right. They don't laugh at Mississippi Valley State's Delta Devils anymore, not since Archie loosed the Awesome Air Force and took off to a 9-1 season and a No. 6 Division 1-AA ranking.

No, they don't laugh when you average 60.9 points and just under 500 yards passing per game, not even if you line up with five wide receivers, no running back and no huddle.

Nope. They may cry, but they don't laugh.

"When you're trying to stop them, you start by saying, 'Our Father who art in Heaven,'" says Alcorn State defensive coordinator Theo Danzy, whose team was the only one to stop them this year, 42-28.

This may all be a passing fancy, but at the moment what Cooley has created is enough fancy passing to do something more than win football games.

He may have kept the school itself alive for another year or two, buying it time to try to erase a deficit that has grown to $1.5 million in a state that doesn't cotton to deficit spending.

"If it's possible that a football team can save a university's hide, then I think this is what happened to us," athletic director Joe Curtis says.

"The legislature has been talking about consolidating us with another black school. Enrollment was down, but now it's on the rise again. Football is bringing in some money."

"We had to do this with hard work and nothing else," Cooley says. "There's nothing here for me but pay day. No fringe benefits.

"We're undermanned, understaffed and underfinanced, but we've outgrown this campus. There's something beautiful happening here that won't let me leave. But, man, emotions won't pay bills.

"If we were in the right situation, there wouldn't be nothing I could ask for that I wouldn't get. But here, I don't even have a secretary. I don't have a credit card. We got a budget of $23,800 and $20,000 goes for equipment. That leaves us $3800 and a WATS line to recruit with."

Now you might think Ol' Archie is poor-mouthing just a bit until you walk to the practice field, where the goal post is on its third coat of rust and the mud in the beanfield is so thick this time of year you check it with a dip stick.

And if you're still skeptical, take a look inside the ballbag. Truth be told, they don't really need a whole bag since they only own five footballs, but take a look anyway.

"You think (Mississippi State coach) Emory Ballard could win here?" Cooley says. "No. But Archie Cooley could win here.

"This school is at the mountaintop. We've been on national television. The New York Times. USA Today. Everybody wants to see the team that scores all them points and doesn't huddle.

"But you still have people right here at home who don't appreciate you. That's the part that hurts."

★   ★   ★

THE COACH

The Valley's been a hurting place from the day it was born 34 years ago on 350 acres of share-croppers' land hard by the Yazoo River. It's all mud flats, cotton fields, yellow brick and underfinanced dreams.

The youngest and one of the smallest predominantly black colleges in America, Valley is one of those schools they set up in the South years ago to keep black students as far away from white students as racial prejudice could stomach.

In the case of Mississippi Valley, it was a long, long way, down Highway 82, about 12 miles past Greenwood ("The Cotton Capital of the World"), out to Itta Bena (a "Home in the Woods" according to the Choctaw dialect). It's a town where there are two bars and no hotels and good reasons for both.

For years, football teams lost and lost big at Valley. Even after Archie Cooley came to town in 1980 after 14 years as an assistant coach at Alcorn A&M and Tennessee State, Valley remained the most popular homecoming opponent in the Southwestern Athletic Conference.

But in his first 5-5 season, something seemed different. Somebody named Cooley wanted to win, and he was willing to pay the price. Full price.

"I give my coaches money out of my pocket to go see kids," Cooley said. "We got no money. But we got a dream, and so do these kids.

"They're from sharecropper families. They just been living day to day. They don't know disappointment because they never had anything.

"Eighty percent of them are the first child in their family who'll ever graduate from college. I tell 'em all success is about work. Not eight hours, not no nine-to-five. It's about work—16, 18 hours a day. It's about getting up in the middle of the night because you got an idea."

Cooley's idea was a monster. He took the best five plays he'd seen from every team he ever opposed and turned them into about a 200-formation, five-receiver offense in which four players often line up in a stack-I formation on one side and the fifth, All-America and sure-fire No. 1 NFL draft choice Jerry Rice, on the other.

Throwing to them is a lanky long-armed junior quarterback from Coila, Miss., named Willie (Satellite) Totten, who has passed for nearly 5,000 yards.

But there is more. Or really less. No huddle. None. Not ever.

"I was out jogging one day with one of my assistants, James Norwood," Cooley says. "He said, 'Coach, how come we huddle? We call the play at the line anyway.'

"I said, 'Coach, because everybody huddles.' "

"Yeah, but why do we?"

"I didn't have no answer for that. So I tried it."

"The first day he told us, I kept thinking, 'How we gonna do this?' We'd come to the line of scrimmage and be looking around. We'd have 12 guys on the field and people running into each other.

"But that night, he told us the philosophy behind it. Defensive teams are used to going to the huddle to regroup. Now they don't have time.

"The way we throw, they have to pass-rush 60 times with no rest. Try it. When we saw how hard it was for our defense to stop, we knew it'd be rough for our opponents."

In some ways, that is Cooley's objective in life—to make it rough for his opponents—because that's how the road has been for him.

Even now, with his creation going wild each Saturday, it is rough because around Itta Bena they don't take to Cooley's Mercedes or the huge satellite dish sitting in his yard.

They like his team, and they love the extra $100,000 it's brought to the school's bank account, but they wonder about a fringe-free, $35,000-a-year salary and a Mercedes in the same yard.

Of course, someone has wondered about Cooley most of his life, which is why it doesn't bother him a lick.

"My father," Cooley says. "That man is why I'm able to ignore the frustrations, the logjams, the people who fought me so dearly.

"That man made me able to withstand Valley. At home you didn't start nothing you didn't finish. And you were disciplined.

"If he told me to get him four sticks, and I brought back five—pow—I'd get a whipping. 'Can't you count?' he'd say. People ask about pressure. Man, that was pressure. I lived it every day."

It was pressure that made Cooley, just as it is pressure that has made his offense. But Cooley learned more from his father than a pressure-cooker lifestyle. He learned about pride and fear.

"We had a little cafe down in Laurel in the '50s," Cooley says. "Back then, if you were black, you couldn't go downtown with shades on because someone might say you were looking at a white girl.

"One day, this white guy came in and ordered coffee. My Momma made it. He said it was too sweet, and he poured it on my Momma's hand. She screamed. Daddy came out of the kitchen and turned him over.

"You didn't do that to a white man then if you didn't want trouble, but he hit that white man over my Momma. Right then he became the greatest man that ever walked to me.

"From that day on, if I knew I was right, I didn't fear no man. If we're all equal, then say what you believe."

And do it.

★　　★　　★

THE SCORES

It only took one week to make an impression.

MVSU 86, Kentucky State 0.

Right then, everyone wanted to know about Mississippi Valley.

But up in Topeka, Kan., they didn't wonder. Washburn College's coach, George Tardiff, figured he'd slap some defense on these black guys from Mississippi when Washburn played them. He even said so in the papers.

"He called us overrated and said he'd show the world how to stop this mess," The Gunslinger says.

Cooley didn't like that.

MVSU 77, Washburn 15.

Tardiff didn't like that.

"He came up after and said, 'Coach, I hope I get a chance to embarrass you the way you did me,' " Cooley says. "I said, 'Hey, man, you should have been embarrassed yesterday when that paper came out. We play football down here.'

"Couple days later, they cancelled next year's game. Well, people been doing Valley like this for years. I don't run amuck. I just put my team on the field.

"Who says how many you're supposed to score? I could have scored 150 against Kentucky State, but we pulled up. But if you're running a 100-yard dash and you got a big lead, you don't pull up at 80 yards, do you?

"I don't give a damn what they say. Maybe the day'll come when they put 'em up on me, but by that time, I'll have offers to go somewhere else. HBO already wants to do a movie.

"I've given Valley five years of my life, and what have they given me? Nothin' but these kids. We're breaking the laws of football. With this offense, I've gone beyond Archie Cooley.

"But if I'm supposed to stay here, I'll stay. If I'm supposed to go, I'll go. Until then, I'll send my team out against yours and take the advantages while I got 'em."

★   ★   ★

THE PLAYERS

Valley's offensive line averages 292 pounds. It is known as The Ton of Fun.

Valley has a defense that will knock your chops off and a fullback named Carl Byrum who rushed for over 1,000 yards as an afterthought.

But no one drives to Itta Bena to see them. They come to see Cooley coach and Totten throw and Rice catch. They're seldom disappointed.

• Against Kentucky State, Rice caught 24 passes for 294 yards, and Totten threw 9 TDs.

• Against Prairie View, Totten passed for 599 yards, completing 45 of 60.

• Against Southern, Totten delivered 553 passing yards. Against Grambling, 554.

• In the regular season's final game, it was 41-3 . . . at the end of the first quarter.

• For the year, Rice has grabbed 106 passes, the second straight year he's caught over 100, and Totten has thrown 55 touchdowns. And the Division 1-AA playoffs are still to come, beginning today with Louisiana Tech.

"We're here to pass," Cooley admits. "We might even stop the bus on the way and throw a little."

But to do that, Cooley knew he needed a Totten and a Rice.

He found them among the cotton fields.

Rice was one of eight sons of a Crawford, Miss., bricklayer, a skinny, 170-pound kid with fast feet who wanted to go to Mississippi State. They didn't share his enthusiasm then. Today he has to beat the agents off with a stick.

"This has turned into something I could never have dreamed of," Rice says. "This has turned into a future. I've had it hard. Hard as it could get. My farher tried to help, but there were so many of us.

"I got a chance now, but I wasn't even a player until the 10th grade. I was skipping a class, and an instructor slipped behind me and scared me. I took off running.

"I ran so fast that he couldn't catch me, so he ran to the football coach and told him he'd just seen the fastest class skipper ever. That's how it started."

From those beginnings, Rice has become the most coveted receiver in college football. Pro scouts all make the trek to Itta Bena. Agents call daily. One offered $40,000. Another a car, any car.

At 6-foot-3, 200 pounds with 4.5 speed and hands the size of plywood sheets, Rice knows there is more to come. Soon he will be a millionaire leaving the Valley behind, something Cooley would like to do himself.

And next year, Totten, if his numbers don't disappear along with Rice, could be in the same position, just as he was in Rice's position four years ago.

"Nobody wanted me," Totten says. "I was a skinny guy who never did anything in high school but hand off."

But Cooley went looking for a punt returner one night and spied someone throwing without effort on the sideline. He saw potential.

"You try to find the diamonds in the rough and polish 'em up," Cooley says.

Three years of buffing and Valley took off. But where does it go from here? Who knows? Cooley knows.

"People want to see winners," Cooley says. "It doesn't matter what color they are. They hear about what we're doing and they want to see it.

"Money's short, but ain't nobody going to close down a winner."

Maree Rejoices in U.S. Citizenship

TRACK

By *PHIL HERSH*

From the Chicago Tribune
Copyright © 1984, Chicago Tribune

He walked out of the old courtroom into the noontime of a glorious day, a day unashamed to recite the poetry of spring.

The brilliant sunshine fairly shouted of hope and renewal as it flooded every angle of Sydney Maree's face. There were no shadows now, no places where the light could not reach. The darkness was gone from without and within.

He had stepped out from a life in the gray areas, of walking fearfully in no man's land. He was standing firmly on the lawn in a spot so American the grass might as well have been red, white and blue. Behind him was Independence Hall, next to him Congress Hall, all around him the legal beginnings of the country which had just lawfully admitted Maree to its citizenry.

So was a horde of media, attracted to this coming-in party for 40 men and women from 24 countries because one of them was special. Sydney Maree is a middle-distance runner of world-class stature—had ESPN ever covered a naturalization ceremony before?—whose world had once been very confining.

When the last of the microphones and minicams retreated, a woman walked up to shake his hand. "Congratulations," she said. "I am South African."

They are both South Africans, but the tourist's white skin provided her with freedoms that were denied Maree because of his black skin. He accepted the congratulations that owed, ironically, to having rejected a homeland that officially wants no part of *his kind*.

He knows the uselessness of yelling "Don't you know me? I'm your native son" at ears as tin as the shack in which he had lived. He knows South Africa's rulers listen to whites and hopes the tourist will return with tales of how things are in America, which honored Maree even as it was making him a citizen.

He got more than a naturalization certificate. The shoe company which pays him handsomely to foot its billing presented a framed copy of the document signed 208 years ago in Independence Hall. With those papers in hand, Maree was declared independent of the injustice of apartheid.

"We hold these truths to be self-evident, that all men are created equal . . ."

On the track, where the truth is told in cold numbers, Sydney Maree was better than his countrymen of all races. But the track, too, was a cruel deception. At home, he ran into the barriers of institutional discrimination against blacks.

Abroad, he ran into the reaction against that discrimination. International meets and the Olympics were closed to him because of a ban against South Africa.

He was allowed to go to the United States seven years ago, an unwitting pawn in a government effort to improve South Africa's image by showing off its black star. The visit led him to Villanova, where Maree became a five-time NCAA champion. The visit led him away from South Africa.

"I realized after six months that my place is in this country," Maree said. "I went back and saw conditions in South Africa I knew I could not survive."

There was a straight but long path between that awareness and the realization of a dream for the 27-year-old Maree Tuesday morning in Congress Hall. In the building where George Washington was sworn in for his second term as president, Maree vowed "to absolutely and entirely renounce and abjure any allegiance and fidelity to any foreign prince, potentate, state or sovereignty, of whom or which you have heretofore been a subject or citizen."

He was being asked to renounce a state that subjected him to second-class citizenry. It was not hard.

"I have never seen him in any doubt about the decision," said his wife, Lisa.

". . . That they are endowed by their Creator with certain inalienable rights . . ."

His voice resounded through the room where the U.S. House of Representatives once sat. Maree was delivering the response on behalf of the new citizens.

"Some of us have endured hardship, deprivation and persecution in our former homelands, not for things we did or were guilty of, but because of who we were or what we believed in.

"Now we can reflect on those bitter memories with mixed feelings of sorrow and joy: sorrow, that such needless suffering will continue for others less fortunate than ourselves; joy, that as American citizens we need never tolerate such injustices or indignities again without cause."

In South Africa, Maree was twice thrown into a police wagon for being without the identity card required of blacks. During a recent return to see his mother, an attempt to eat in an airport restaurant was rebuffed with a "your people go on the other side."

"It built me and broke me," he said. "Most of all, it built me. I can now understand defeat and disappointment."

He was frustrated so often, unable to run against men the clock said he could run with. By 1981, the U.S. opened a door by giving him a "Re-Entry Permit" with the designation "stateless." It allowed Maree to set a world record in the 1,500 meters that was not recognized as an American record. It allowed him into every meet but the Olympics.

"*. . . That among those are Life, Liberty, and the Pursuit of Happiness.*"

The rights of a U.S. citizen include voting, holding a passport and representing the country in the Olympic Games. Maree, the second fastest 1,500-meter runner ever, will be favored to make the American team at the June trials in Los Angeles.

"This is the most important day in my life," Maree said. "This day means to me freedom, dignity and opportunity in life. I am now standing at the starting line in Los Angeles."

He had felt this way once before, on the starting line at the 1981 World Cup, his first international meet. Maree looked at the "USA" on his jersey and saw the fans waving the Stars and Stripes for him, and he cried over being accepted as an American.

"I would like to add," Maree said at the end of his ceremonial speech, "on behalf of all newly naturalized citizens, how tremendously proud we all feel to finally be able to greet you as "Our Fellow Americans.' "

There was no need to answer the thanks. America had already told Sydney Maree, "You are welcome."

The Other Side of College Basketball

COLLEGE BASKETBALL

By *JERRY IZENBERG*

From the Newark Star-Ledger
Copyright © 1984, The Star-Ledger, Newark, N.J.

Earlier in the season, they were down by 40 or so against Jersey City State with about five minutes to play when the gym door opened and out popped Darryl Parroway. When they saw him, his five teammates, who were about to bring the ball up the court, froze as one and shook their clenched fists in salute. On the sidelines, the entire bench—all one of it, which at that moment was named Tyrone Whitehead—leaped into the air.

It was the world's smallest standing ovation.

It was also the world's most genuine.

You can throw away your "Road to the NCAA Round of Four" hymnals today. Forget about the Big East's quest to crown The Beast of the East, Bobby Knight, Pat Ewing, the entire ACC and the rest of what makes college basketball the money game these days.

This is one about the other side of college basketball, where the coach and his assistant aren't even budgeted into the program as full-timers, where the administration operates on the old-fashioned theory that its degree means something (and does it ever) so it will throw you out of school if you flunk and sit you down if you are marginal, where there are no athletic scholarships and where a class, a lab or an after-school job takes proper precedence over basketball.

The basketball team at the Newark branch of Rutgers University has played 23 and lost 23 this season, and if they don't get it tonight against Ramapo College (which logic says they won't) they are going to finish at 0-24. They began the season with 14 players. Academic attrition and personal economic necessity have pared the squad to seven ever since mid-January.

Three of them never played high school basketball and one of them never played any sports at all. Parroway is a fencer and an excellent one and several times this year he has raced from fencing meets to wherever the Family happens to be playing that evening, which explains the story about his last-minute appearance against Jersey City.

"Yes, we did stop the game and cheer for him that time," a 6-foot sophomore named Denton Bryan explained the other night before the Family went out and lost by 38 to Bloomfield College. Denton is carrying a dual major in engineering and computer science. "You have to understand we don't have some giant banging down the middle of the floor and slam-dunking it home. So we can't thrill to that. But here was Darryl sacrificing just to be with us. That meant something to each of us. That was our own private slam-dunk of the evening."

This is a commuter school where the academics are real and so is the economic need. It has produced Pulitzer Prize winners and authors and scientists and lawyers and there were times when it produced dandy basketball, too. It has always been the place that made quality education available to the sons and daughters of blue-collar North Jersey.

Paul Reid, the assistant coach, once played there, too. "You can't believe how much these kids want to play until you see what they go through to do it. It's really their team. As for recruiting, well, we have to sell the Rutgers degree and the super quality education. Kids who overlook that owe themselves a visit here. I really believe that would be enough but with the whole staff part time, it's tough when a high school senior asks to see the coaches and they aren't there."

Three times this year fouls have reduced them to fewer than five men on the court at the finish. Against New Jersey Institute of Technology they led by two at the half and they were down by one with only four minutes to play. Then they started fouling out.

"We lost by seven. When we were down to three players on the court, we played what I called the 0-0-3 zone and we actually outscored them, 6-4. When they went into a stall our kids were furious," says Matt Shoban, the head coach.

He is a studious-looking fellow who has coached more basketball than his appearance would indicate. He was out at an NAIA school in Montana and coached boys and girls high school ball near San Francisco among other places. Three years ago he answered a newspaper ad placed by the school for an assistant coach.

He does not delude himself and he tries to do as much teaching as coaching during a game. Sometimes either he or Reid will put on a uniform to enable the club to have a full-court practice scrimmage. "We want kids with good grades who want to play and who understand what a Rutgers degree can mean to a grad school dean or a potential employer. You get the same education here as you do down in New Brunswick."

So there they stand . . . seven against the world . . . playing because they want to play and, for the moment, counting their victories in sequences rather than entire games. A few teams have run it up on them deliberately. One coach, when fouls had cut them down to just four players, ordered his team into a full-court press against them.

"That's all right," Denton Bryan was saying the other night. "They'll be on the schedule again the next two years. Chances go around at this level. We'll remember who they were."

On Monday night, the seven of them huddled around Shoban and Reid. There was Bryan and Derek Moses (5-9) . . . Dexter Cotton (6-0) and Parroway (5-10) . . . Joe Rosado (5-9) and Whitehead (6-3 and the tallest but who never played any sport before this). And there was Bob McGrady.

He is a 5-7 frosh, who played as sixth man for a fine high school team and he is the team's most experienced ballplayer. They put their hands in the circle just like North Carolina does and they came out cheering the way Georgetown does.

Naturally, they played like neither but who has the nerve to tell them? As Denton Bryan said:

"People look at the record and think we are just out there messing around. We aren't. We play to win. There isn't a quitter in this family."

Twice McGrady came out with cramps and went back in. Joe Rosado twisted an ankle, came out in pain and went back in when McGrady was hurting. When they stole the ball near the finish and scored on a fast break to cut the deficit below 40, you'd have thought they had just won the NCAA title.

"You have to love them," Reid said.

Indeed, you do.

Leap Frog

by Eric Gay of the Dallas Times Herald. Texas Rangers shortstop Jim Anderson was playing a different kind of game when he used Milwaukee shortstop Robin Yount's head during a double-play leap in a 1984 American League game. Copyright © 1984, Dallas Times Herald.

PRIZE-WINNING WRITERS IN BEST SPORTS STORIES 1985

William Gildea (American Summer: A Baseball Odyssey) is a member of the *Washington Post* sports department. The 1960 Georgetown University graduate attended graduate school at Columbia University in 1961 and then worked for two years for the *Baltimore Sun* before taking a job with the Post. Gildea has worked as a sports columnist and feature writer and also spent six years as an assignment editor for the Post's style section. The 1978-79 Nieman Fellow is making his third appearance in *Best Sports Stories*, his first as a winner.

David Halberstam (The Man Who Said No), a historian, biographer and writer specializing in politics and international affairs, became a contributing editor to *Parade* magazine in 1983. The Harvard graduate began his journalism career with the *Daily Times Leader* in West Point, Miss., from 1955 to 1956 and then spent five years with the *Nashville Tennessean*. Halberstam worked as a foreign correspondent for the *New York Times* in the Congo, Vietnam and Eastern Europe from 1960 to 1967 and became a contributing editor to *Harper's* magazine in 1967. Halberstam received a Pulitzer Prize for his reporting during the Vietnam War. His books include *The Noblest Roman, The Making of a Quagmire, One Very Hot Day, The Unfinished Odyssey of Robert Kennedy, Ho, The Best and the Brightest, The Powers That Be* and *The Breaks of the Game*. This is his first appearance in *Best Sports Stories*.

Richard Hoffer (She Throws Pair of 10s, Takes All-Around) has been writing features and covering boxing and a variety of other sports for the *Los Angeles Times* for the last six years. The Miami (Ohio) University graduate previously wrote for the *Massillon (Ohio) Evening Independent, Riverside (Calif.) Press-Enterprise* and the *Cincinnati Post*. Hoffer, who also holds a master's degree from Stanford University, is making his third consecutive appearance in *Best Sports Stories*.

Steve Jacobson (A Son's Death, a Father's Life) has been covering a wide range of sports for *Newsday* since 1960. Jacobson, whose columns include everything from the Olympics to high school sports, is a graduate of Indiana University and lives on Long Island with his wife Anita, and two children, Mathew and Neila. Jacobson, who has a book to his credit, *The Best Things Money Could Buy,* is making his second winning contribution to *Best Sports Stories*. This is his fifth appearance in the anthology.

OTHER WRITERS IN BEST SPORTS STORIES 1985

Ira Berkow (Emotional Pain Dooms Ex-Football Star) is a sports feature writer and columnist for the *New York Times*. The former sports editor and columnist of *Newspaper Enterprise Association* holds degrees from Miami (Ohio) University and Northwestern. Berkow has written six books, including *Maxwell Street* and *Beyond the Dream,* a collection of his sports columns. He has appeared in *Best Sports Stories* several times.

Joel Bierig (Life at Camp Meyer) covers baseball, college basketball and other seasonal sports for the *Chicago Sun-Times.* Before joining the Sun-Times, the newspaper he grew up reading, in 1983, Bierig worked for the *Minneapolis Star and Tribune, Louisville Courier-Journal, Memphis Commercial Appeal* and the *Shreveport Journal.* Bierig is a 1975 University of Missouri graduate.

Hal Bodley (Starting Over) became executive baseball editor of *USA Today* in 1982. Before moving to his present position, Bodley served as columnist and sports editor for the *Wilmington (Del.) News-Journal* newspapers for 11 years. He joined that publication in 1960 as a sportswriter and worked his way up as night sports editor and assistant sports editor before taking over the department. The University of Delaware graduate wrote a syndicated sports column for the Gannett News Service from 1977 to 1982 and his column, *Once Over Lightly,* won numerous national and regional awards. Bodley, a former weekly correspondent and columnist for *The Sporting News,* where his Rose story appeared, still contributes on a special-assignment basis to the publication. Bodley was selected Delaware Sportswriter of the Year 12 times and in 1981 was chosen the top sportswriter among the 88 Gannett daily newspapers. Bodley, an instrument-rated pilot, also has worked on radio and television projects and served two years as the national president of the Associated Press Sports Editors. Bodley has been listed in *Who's Who in the East* and *Who's Who in America* since 1975.

Ron Borges (Lightin' 'Em Up Down in the Valley) began covering sports 11 years ago when he went to work for a small Massachusetts weekly newspaper. From there he went to California and stints on the *Sacramento Union* and the *Oakland Tribune.* Borges left Oakland in 1982 for the *Baltimore News American,* where he covered the Baltimore Orioles for a season. He now covers a wide assortment of sporting events and personalities for the *Boston Globe.*

Thomas Boswell (Gibson's Two Homers Win Series for Tigers) is a reporter for the *Washington Post.* The 1969 Amherst College graduate, who ranks as one of the most respected baseball writers in the country, contributes to such publications as *Golf Digest, Esquire* and *Playboy.* Boswell has written two baseball books, *How Life Imitates the World Series* and *Time Begins on Opening Day.* Boswell, a three-time winner in *Best Sports Stories,* is making his eighth appearance in the anthology. He also is a former winner of the American Society of Newspaper Editors first prize for sportswriting.

Rick Bozich (A City in Flames Mars World Series) has been a sports columnist for the *Louisville Times* since 1981. The Indiana University graduate, who grew up in Gary, Ind., joined the Louisville publication in 1978. Bozich is making his second appearance in *Best Sports Stories.*

John Ed Bradley (Woody: The Private Wars of an Old Soldier) covers sporting events for the *Washington Post.* Before arriving in Washington, Bradley attended Louisiana State University, where he earned four letters as a center for the LSU football team. Bradley, who was captain of the 1979 squad, is making his first appearance in *Best Sports Stories.*

Gene Collier (Life in the Bushes) is a sports columnist for the *Pittsburgh Press.* The 1975 Penn State graduate began his career with the *Pittstown Mercury* and moved to the *Camden Courier-Post, Philadelphia Journal* and *Pittsburgh Post-*

Gazette before taking his current position with the Press in 1984. Collier is making his first appearance in *Best Sports Stories.*

Ken Denlinger (For Colleges, the Need Is Integrity) has been a sports columnist for the *Washington Post* since 1975. Denlinger, a 1964 graduate of Penn State University, worked two years for the *Pittsburgh Press* before joining the Post. Denlinger has co-authored two books, *Athletes for Sale* and *Redskin Country/From Baugh to the Super Bowl.* Denlinger lives with his wife and two children in Olney, Md., and is included in *Who's Who in America.*

Ray Didinger (Decker Running Hard for Olympic Gold) is a sports columnist for the *Philadelphia Daily News.* The 1968 Temple University graduate began his career as a news reporter for the *Delaware County Daily Times* before joining the *Philadelphia Bulletin* as a sportswriter. He joined the Daily News sports staff in 1980. The 38-year-old Didinger, who has won five Keystone Press Association awards and two Associated Press Sports Editors awards, is making his fifth appearance in *Best Sports Stories.*

John Feinstein (Georgetown's Pressure Cooks, 84-75) grew up in New York City and received a degree in history from Duke University in 1977. After serving as a summer intern at the *Washington Post,* he was hired as a metro staff reporter and served three years before moving to the sports department. In his first four years as a sportswriter, Feinstein covered pro soccer and Maryland football, basketball and baseball. He currently is the Post's national college basketball writer and he covers tennis during the summer. Feinstein, who is making his second appearance in *Best Sports Stories,* has contributed to such publications as *Sports Illustrated, The Sporting News, Inside Sports, the Washington Post Sunday Magazine* and *Outlook.*

Randy Harvey (Decker's Fall Stirs the Great Debate) covers pro basketball and other special assignments for the *Los Angeles Times.* Harvey, born, raised and educated in Texas, worked at the *Tyler Morning Telegraph, Austin American-Statesman* and the *Dallas Times Herald* before moving to the *Chicago Sun-Times* in 1976. He went to the *New York Daily News* in 1980 and moved to Los Angeles in September of 1981. Harvey, who holds a journalism degree from the University of Texas at Austin, is making his third appearance in *Best Sports Stories.*

Phil Hersh (Maree Rejoices in U.S. Citizenship) handles special assignments for the *Chicago Tribune.* The 1968 Yale graduate arrived in Chicago after a stint with the *Baltimore Evening Sun.* When the *Chicago Daily News* folded, Hersh went to work for the *Chicago Sun-Times* before moving over to the Tribune. Hersh, who as been honored several times as the top sportswriter in Illinois, is making his third appearance in *Best Sports Stories.*

Mickey Herskowitz (J.C. Snead: Bad Guy or Good Ol' Boy?) is a Houston-based author and television commentator. He has written 18 books, including collaborations with Howard Cosell, Dan Rather, Leon Jaworski and Gene Tierney. Herskowitz is a frequent contributor to *Golf Digest,* profiling such subjects as Lee Trevino, Ben Crenshaw, Lanny Wadkins and J.C. Snead. Herskowitz is making his first appearance in *Best Sports Stories.*

Hal Higdon (Jim Fixx: How He Lived, Why He Died) is a senior writer for *The Runner* magazine, which is based in the midwest. Higdon has written on every facet of running and fitness and is one of the most prolific of today's writers on the subjects. He has written more than 25 books on a wide range of topics. Higdon, once a leading runner himself, is among the forces behind the growth of the fitness movement in the United States. He is making his first appearance in *Best Sports Stories.*

Stan Hochman (Slaughter Learns Bias Exists Off the Field) has been writing about sports for the *Philadelphia Daily News,* first as a baseball writer, then sports editor and now columnist, since 1959. Before going to Philadelphia, Hochman worked for newspapers in Georgia, Texas and California. The Brooklyn native, who holds a master's degree from New York University, is not the only member of the Hochman family with a flair for journalism. His wife, Gloria, is an award-winning medical writer and his daughter, Anndee, is a reporter for the *Washington Post.*

Jerry Izenberg (The Other Side of College Basketball) is a syndicated columnist based in Newark, N.J. Among the newspapers that carry his columns on a regular basis are the *Newark Star-Ledger,* in which the above story appeared, and the *New York Post.* Izenberg is the author of seven books and more than 500 magazine articles. He also wrote and directed *A Man Named Lombardi,* an Emmy-winning television show.

Tom Jackson (Sacked, Sorry and Silent) has been a sports columnist for the *Washington Times* and a contributing writer for *Inside Sports* magazine since March 1983. Before going to the nation's capital, he was executive sports editor of the late *Tampa Times,* which won an assortment of state and national design and content awards in contests sponsored by the *Associated Press* from 1979-82. In 1984, Jackson placed fourth in a national feature-writing competition sponsored by the AP. His work also has appeared in the NFL's *Pro!* magazine. Jackson, a graduate of the University of Florida, is making his second appearance in *Best Sports Stories.*

Bruce Keidan (Drugs Scar Scurry, Mar Baseball) is sports editor of the *Pittsburgh Post-Gazette.* He came to Pittsburgh after 11 years with the *Philadelphia Inquirer.* Keidan also spent some time with the *Seattle Times* and the *Associated Press* before making the move to Pennsylvania. He is making his first appearance in *Best Sports Stories.*

Jane Leavy (Lives Overshadowed by a Day in the Sun and Marathoner Benoit: The Reign in Maine) is a style-section reporter for the *Washington Post.* Before joining the Post's sports department staff in 1979, Leavy worked at *Women Sports* magazine and free-lanced for such publications as the *New York Times, Village Voice, Ms.* and the *Daily News* magazine. After joining the Post, Leavy covered baseball, tennis and many off-beat sports. She began work in the summer of 1983 on the Post's Olympic coverage and followed on through the 1984 Games in Los Angeles. Leavy is a graduate of Barnard College in New York and did graduate work at the Columbia University School of Journalism.

Frank Lidz (Come See the Dinka Dunker Do and Oh, That Old College Spirit) is a staff writer for *Sports Illustrated.* Lidz, a graduate of Antioch College, effectively mixes the off-beat with sports and approaches life in much the same manner. Lidz has been a disc jockey, a soda jerk, an improvisational actor, a South American wanderer, a Boston cabbie and a bus driver near Baltimore. Lidz is making his first appearance in *Best Sports Stories.*

Mike Littwin (Matter of Grit: Hazzard Era Begins at UCLA and Ceremony Is Much More Than a Show) is a sports columnist and feature writer for the *Los Angeles Times.* Before moving to Los Angeles to cover the Dodgers in 1978, the University of Virginia graduate worked for the *Newport News Times-Herald* and the *Virginian-Pilot* in Norfolk, Va. Littwin's biography of Dodger pitcher Fernando Valenzuela, *Fernando,* was published in 1981. He is making his fourth appearance in *Best Sports Stories.*

Jon Masson (Tackling the Odds) is a sportswriter and columnist for the *Colorado Springs Sun.* Masson, a graduate of Drake University, has worked at the Sun since September 1982 after stints as a general assignment reporter for the *Des*

Moines Register and the *Indianapolis Star.* Masson is making his first appearance in *Best Sports Stories.*

Roy McHugh (Larry Holmes: At Home in Easton) is a former sports editor and columnist for the *Pittsburgh Press.* The 68-year-old McHugh retired in 1983, but continues to contribute to the Press on a periodic basis. A graduate of Coe College in Cedar Rapids, Ia., McHugh began his newspaper career with the *Cedar Rapids Gazette* in 1940. After rejoining the Gazette following service in World War II, McHugh moved to the Press in 1947 before taking the sports editor's job with the *Evansville (Ind.) Courier and Press.* McHugh returned to Pittsburgh in 1969 as sports editor and added the column to his duties three years later.

Leigh Montville (This Valley Guy's in the Fast Lane) has been a sportswriter with the *Boston Globe* for the past 17 years, the last 11 as a sports columnist. He also writes a general column for the *Boston Globe Sunday Magazine,* which last year won a National Headliners Award in the local-interest category. Montville's previous experience came on the sports desk of the *New Haven Journal-Courier.* Montville, a 1984 *Best Sports Stories* winner in the reporting category, is making his fifth appearance in the anthology.

Gordon Morris (32nd Place: A Triumph of the Olympic Spirit) is a writer for the *Los Angeles Times* Special Events Department. Morris has contributed stories to more than 30 publications, including the *Detroit News, Autoweek* and *Westways.* In 1983, he won the top magazine writer award in the competition sponsored by the 400-member American Auto Racing Writers and Broadcasters Association. Morris is making his first appearance in *Best Sports Stories.*

Gary Nuhn (Jaeger's Losses Show Something Had To Give) covers golf and college sports for *Dayton Newspapers Inc.* and is a frequent contributor to *Golf* magazine. Nuhn, a Geneva, N.Y., native and Ohio State University graduate, has earned 22 national writing awards. He is making his third appearance in *Best Sports Stories.*

Ron Rapoport (Cubs Lore No Longer So Poor) has been a sports columnist for the *Chicago Sun-Times* since 1977. He was the 1984 winner of the National Headliner Award for "consistently outstanding sports columns." Before moving to Chicago, Rapoport worked for the *Los Angeles Times, Associated Press* and *Sport* magazine. He has been named top sports columnist in Chicago twice and is making his fifth consecutive appearance in *Best Sports Stories.* Rapoport has a degree from Stanford University and did his graduate work at the Columbia University School of Journalism.

Rick Reilly (To Louganis, Diving's the Easiest Part) has been a sports columnist and feature writer for the *Los Angeles Times* since 1983. The 1981 University of Colorado graduate began his career with the *Boulder Daily Camera* and jumped to the *Denver Post* before moving to Los Angeles. Reilly won two national awards at the Associated Press Sports Editors convention in 1984 and won Best Feature award at the Associated Press Editors convention the same year. He is making his first appearance in *Best Sports Stories.*

Dave Remnick (Bird: A Flawless Gem in Solitaire Setting) is a sportswriter for the *Washington Post.* His beats include the United States Football League, boxing and the National Basketball Association. Remnick has contributed to such publications as the *New Republic* and *Partisan Review.* He is making his first appearance in *Best Sports Stories.*

John Schulian (Only the Good Die Young) took his nationally syndicated sports column to the *Philadelphia Daily News* in 1984 after spending six years with the *Chicago Sun-Times.* Schulian is a two-time winner of both the *Best Sports*

Stories commentary award and the Associated Press Editor's column-writing competition. He also has received a National Headliner Award, an Emmy and two nominations for a Pulitzer Prize. Schulian's prose has appeared in a variety of magazines, including *Playboy, Sports Illustrated* and *Gentleman's Quarterly.* His 1983 book, *Writers, Fighters and Other Sweet Scientists,* brought him favorable comparison with Red Smith and A.J. Liebling.

Michael Shapiro (Opponents: Faceless, Necessary Losers) is a free-lance writer now living in Tokyo, Japan. He has contributed to such publications as the *New York Times,* in which his above story appeared, *Sports Illustrated* and *Sport* magazine. Shapiro, who owns a master's degree in journalism from the University of Missouri, began his career as a staff writer for the *Courier-News* in Bridgewater, N.J., and later worked for the *Chicago Tribune's Suburban Trib.* He also served as associate editor of *Collector-Investor* magazine. Shapiro is making his first appearance in *Best Sports Stories.*

Art Spander (Pincay: Monkey Off His Back) has been the lead sports columnist for the *San Francisco Examiner* since 1979. After graduating from UCLA in 1960 with a degree in political science, Spander went to work for *United Press International* in Los Angeles. A later stint at the *Santa Monica Evening Outlook* was followed by a 14-year hitch with the *San Francisco Chronicle,* where he covered golf, pro basketball, football and baseball. Spander was voted California Sportswriter of the Year in 1980, won the top prize in the 1982 San Francisco Press Club competition and has been honored many times by the Golf Writers Association of America. Spander, who has appeared in 14 of the last 15 editions of *Best Sports Stories,* including a first-place in reporting in 1971, formerly wrote a wine column for *San Francisco Magazine* and is a current weekly columnist for *The Sporting News.*

Thomas Stinson (For Cremins, It's Been Wild Ride From Bronx) has worked for the *Atlanta Journal and Constitution* since 1980, covering the National Basketball Association, Georgia Tech sports and the Atlantic Coast Conference. Before coming to Atlanta, Stinson spent time at the *Washington Star* and the *Naples (Fla.) Daily News.* The 1975 Ohio Wesleyan University graduate grew up just outside of Pittsburgh. He is making his first appearance in *Best Sports Stories.*

Jim Terhune (Schnellenberger: He'll Leave Mark on U of L) is a sportswriter for the *Louisville Times.* The 1962 Hanover College graduate has written about a wide range of topics, including college football, college and pro basketball and golf. Terhune, who was born in LaPorte, Ind., and grew up in South Bend, is making his first appearance in *Best Sports Stories.*

Gary Van Sickle (The World Is Watching Carl Lewis and Now Crenshaw Stands Second to None) has been a sports reporter with the *Milwaukee Journal* since 1976. Van Sickle, a University of Wisconsin graduate, has covered golf, the Summer Olympics, Big Ten football, basketball and pro football since coming to Milwaukee. He was voted Wisconsin Sportswriter of the Year in 1983. Van Sickle is making his second appearance in *Best Sports Stories.*

Michael Wilbon (Cubs: One Race Won, Another Still Waiting) has been a sportswriter at the *Washington Post* since graduating from Northwestern University in 1980. He had worked as an intern at the Post in 1979. Wilbon primarily has covered college football and basketball at a national and local level, but other assignments have taken him to professional tennis matches, the World Series, the World University Games and the 1984 Summer Olympics in Los Angeles. The 26-year-old Chicago native, who is an avid tennis player and old-movie buff, will move to a major league baseball beat in 1985. He is making his second appearance in *Best Sports Stories.*

Vic Ziegel (Sweating and Starving for a Pound of Flesh) is a free-lance writer out of New York. The former *New York Post* sportswriter and columnist has written for numerous publications, including *Inside Sports, Reader's Digest, Sport, Look*, the *New York Times* and the *Washington Post*. The above story appeared in *Rolling Stone*. Ziegel co-authored the 1978 best-seller *The Non-Runners Book* with Lewis Grossberger and was co-creator of the CBS television series, *Ball Four*, in 1976. Ziegel has been a frequent contributor to *Best Sports Stories*.

PRIZE-WINNING PHOTOGRAPHERS IN BEST SPORTS STORIES 1985

Jayne Kamin (Victory Hug) is a staff photographer for the *Los Angeles Times*. The 26-year-old Kamin graduated from the University of Miami with a Communications degree in 1979 and joined the Times staff in February 1980. While going to school in Miami, she worked as a stringer for the *Associated Press*. Kamin won the best feature category of the Los Angeles Press Photographers competition in 1981.

Adrian Keating (We've Got It) had taught English in Connecticut public schools for seven years when he decided it was time for a career change. He began free-lancing for several New England publications in 1977, including the *Associated Press* and *United Press International* in Hartford, Conn. In May of 1983, he began working part time for the *Bristol Press*, where he now is a full-time staff photographer.

Robert Langer (The Agony of Defeat) is a staff photographer for the *Chicago Tribune*. Langer began his newspaper career as a copyboy for the Tribune in 1959 and worked his way up to the paper's photo lab. He remained there until 1965 when he became a full-time photographer for the *Chicago Sun-Times*. During his 17 years at the Sun-Times, Langer won more than 100 photography awards. He returned to the Tribune in 1983 as a sports photographer and was assigned to the 1984 Summer Olympics in Los Angeles, where he shot the pictures that captured the top prize for color photography in *Best Sports Stories 1985*.

OTHER PHOTOGRAPHERS IN BEST SPORTS STORIES 1985

Eric Lars Bakke (Tongue Out of Cheek) works for the *Denver Post* as chief photographer, a position he has held since 1982. He was a staff photographer for the *Topeka (Kan.) Capital-Journal* before joining the Post in 1981. The 33-year-old Bakke, who graduated magna cum laude from the University of Northern Colorado with a journalism degree, was raised in Colorado and is a former member of the Winter Park Ski School and the Junior Ski Patrol.

Bruce Bisping (Programmed Goal) has worked as a staff photographer at the *Minneapolis Star and Tribune* since 1975, the year he graduated from the University of Missouri with a photojournalism degree. Before going to Minneapolis, Bisping interned at the *Cleveland Press* and the *Virginian-Pilot and Ledger-*

Star in Norfolk, Va. The 30-year-old photographer has won numerous state and national awards, including the National Press Photographers Association Newspaper Photographer of the Year award in 1976. Bisping, who was elected director of Region Five of the NPPA in 1982, also won third place in the national Newspaper Photographer of the Year competition in 1975 and has judged photojournalism competitions in eight states.

Mike Brown (Moment of Glory) doubles as photographer and assistant sports editor of the *Plattsburgh Press-Republican* in Plattsburgh, N.Y. Brown, who graduated from St. Michael's College in Winooski Park, Vt., in 1977, began combining his photographic and writing talents for the Plattsburgh publication the same year. That lasted until 1980, when Brown became sports editor of the *Oneonta (N.Y.) Daily Star.* While in Oneonta, Brown covered such events as the 1980 Winter Olympics in Lake Placid, the baseball Hall of Fame ceremonies in Cooperstown and the soccer Hall of Fame ceremonies in Oneonta. In 1982, Brown started his own weekly sports publication, *The Sporting Eye,* but gave that up and returned to Plattsburgh in 1984.

Mary Butkus (Punchy) is a free-lance photographer who works out of St. Louis. Her primary efforts are as a stringer for *United Press International,* for which this picture was shot. The Southern Illinois University-Edwardsville graduate, who has been producing pictures for UPI for five years, is the only woman in the St. Louis area who covers sports on a regular basis.

Louis DeLuca (Close Quarters) is a staff photographer for the *Dallas Times Herald.* DeLuca began his career with the *Shreveport (La.) Journal,* moved to the *Chicago Sun-Times* in 1983 and to Dallas a year later. The 28-year-old DeLuca was named 1982 Photographer of the Year in Louisiana, Texas and New Mexico and he has won more than 25 awards in his young career. DeLuca captured first prize in the black and white action category in *Best Sports Stories 1984.*

Jim Forbes (Final Instructions) has been taking pictures for the *St. Louis Post-Dispatch* for the last 10 years. He worked for two years in the photo department of the *Topeka Capital-Journal* while working toward his degree in photojournalism at Kansas University. After graduating in 1973, he worked briefly in Parsons, Kan., and then worked at the *Miami News* for two years before moving to St. Louis. The 35-year-old Forbes has photographed more than 20 covers for *The Sporting News.* He has received numerous awards from the National Press Photographers Association, the *Associated Press* and *United Press International,* and he has won five plaques in the Pro Football Hall of Fame contest since 1977, including two first-place awards.

Eric Gay (Leap Frog) is a photographer for the *Dallas Times Herald* and a student at North Texas State University. He previously worked for the *Denton Record Chronicle* and held internships at the *Times Herald* and the *St. Petersburg Times and Evening Independent.* Gay won the 1982 sweepstakes award in the Texas APME contest and has been honored in other photojournalism competitions.

Richard Gentile (Study in Concentration) is a free-lance sports photographer in the Washington D.C.-Baltimore area. His work has been published in many of the leading sports publications, including *The Sporting News* and *Basketball Digest.* Much of Gentile's work is in association with the National Football League as a regular member of the photography team that covers the Washington Redskins.

Art Phillips (Touchdown!) is a photographer for the St. Louis bureau of *United Press International.* He received a degree in business management from Southern Illinois University at Edwardsville, Ill., and began working part time for *UPI Newspictures* in 1961. He became a full-time employee in 1965. Phillips and wife Beverly live in St. Louis with their two children, Sherry and Gary.

Mary Schroeder (Homeward Bound) is a sports photographer for the *Detroit Free Press.* She came to Detroit in 1979 after graduation from Ohio University. The 27-year-old Schroeder was born and raised in Manitowoc, Wis.

Dale Young (Look Out Below) is a staff photographer for the *Detroit News.* After graduation from Iowa State University in 1979 with a major in journalism and a minor in landscape architecture, Young spent three years working for the *Associated Press* in New York, Chicago and Detroit. He was born in Seattle, Wash.

The Panel of Judges for Best Sports Stories 1985

Brian Brooks is the *St. Louis Post-Dispatch* Distinguished Professor of Journalism at the University of Missouri and managing editor of the *Columbia Missourian*. The former reporter and editor at the *Memphis Press-Scimitar* is co-author of *News Reporting and Writing* and *The Art of Editing*, best-selling textbooks in their fields.

George Kennedy is an associate professor of journalism at the University of Missouri and city editor of the *Columbia Missourian*. Before moving to Columbia, Kennedy spent 7½ years as a reporter and editor with the *Miami Herald* and two summers as a writing coach for the *San Jose Mercury*. He is co-author of *News Reporting and Writing* and *The Writing Book*, two college and professional textbooks.

Ken Kobre is an associate professor and director of the photojournalism sequence at the University of Missouri. The former *St. Petersburg Times* and *Boston Phoenix* staff photographer is the author of two leading books on photography and director of the national Pictures of the Year competition.

Daryl Moen is a professor at the University of Missouri and chairman of the School of Journalism's editorial department. He is the former managing editor of the *Columbia Missourian* and two other dailies. Moen also is co-author of *News Reporting and Writing* and *The Writing Book* and author of *Newspaper Layout and Design*.

George Pica is an assistant professor at the University of Missouri and director of the J. C. Penney-Missouri Awards Program. He is a former prize-winning editor of the feature and magazine sections of the *Eugene (Ore.) Register-Guard* and assistant managing editor of the *Seattle Post-Intelligencer*. Pica is a regular judge for other national writing competitions.